19722868

Managing Projects and Programs

The Harvard Business Review Book Series

Managing Projects and Programs

With a Preface by
Norman R. Augustine
Chairman and Chief Executive Officer
Martin Marietta Corporation

A Harvard Business Review Book

Library of Congress Cataloging-in-Publication Data

Managing projects and programs/with a preface by Norman R.
  Augustine.
    p.   cm.—(The Harvard business review book series)
    Includes bibliographies and index.
    ISBN 0-87584-213-5
    1. Industrial project management.   I. Series.
  HD69.P75M364 1989   89-11032
  658.4′04—dc20   CIP

Harvard Business School Press
Boston, Massachusetts

Note: Some articles included in this book were written before researchers, writers, and editors began to take into consideration the role of women in management. These articles have been included because their insights far outweigh their anachronistic qualities. Nevertheless, the assumption that a manager is necessarily male is regrettable. The editor and the publisher hope outdated gender assumptions will not undermine the value of those essays.

All of the articles included in this collection are available as individual reprints. For information and ordering contact Operations Department, Harvard Business School Publishing Division, Boston, MA 02163, telephone (617) 495-6192 or 6117, Fax (617) 495-6985.

The paper used in this publication meets the requirements of the American National Standard for Permanence of Paper for Printed Library Materials Z39.49-1984.

Contents

Part II Organizing

Part III Leading

Preface

Norman R. Augustine

Worst-case forecasts are always too optimistic.

Readers who possess a copy of my book *Augustine's Laws*—a very select, small group, as it happens—may think they recognize the statement above as one of that collection of contrapuntal rules about business. Instead, the adage is but one of many nuggets offered for the real-world manager in the illuminating discussions of program and project management in this collection of *Harvard Business Review* articles. The perspective on forecasts suggested by the quotation is, however, consonant with Augustine's thirty-second law: "Ninety percent of the time things turn out to be worse than you expected. The other ten percent, you had no right to expect so much."

That is not to say business is for pessimists, but merely that realists tend to survive to the chapters beyond eleven.

It has been wisely observed that two of the most difficult things about business are getting into it and getting out of it. The role of program and project management is to do the former, or, more accurately, to *stay* in it. The program manager is the captain of the ship—admittedly not the commander of the whole flotilla, but merely the person who determines whether or not the individual elements of the flotilla go aground. He or she is also the coach, cheerleader, chaplain, quarterback, and policeman. And the best of them are, alas, extraordinary firemen.

Although there is no established convention for dealing with such matters, program management might be defined as the art of bringing to fruition some significant end-item of value to a user. Project management, on the other hand, usually describes a similar function related to a major *component* of a program.

Few schools teach anything called, or even vaguely resembling, program management. This is in itself provocative, given the field's importance to the success or failure of most current business enterprises. Practitioners of program management tend more often than not to be people who performed their postgraduate work at that institution fondly known as the School of Hard Knocks, which awards scar tissue in lieu of sheepskins. Such is the case of many of the authors of this collection of articles, which takes the reader on a tour through program and project management from start to finish or, as the article titles note, from "How to Plan. . ." to "Knowing When to Pull the Plug."

As Bismarck said, "Fools you are. . .to say you learn by your experience. . . . I prefer to profit by others' mistakes and avoid the price of my own." And that is exactly the opportunity afforded within these pages, heavily spiced as well with the opportunity to learn from the *successes* of others. The underlying character of program management, and of this collection, can be gleaned from a sampling of terms found in the titles of the various chapters: "Pitfalls," "Risky Projects," "Audits," "False Economies," "Critical Path" and, yes, "Pulling the Plug." Clearly this is not a profession for the timid, although such additional examples as "Team Work," "New Product," and "Growth" show there is ample room for hope.

With cautionary realism, one author, Jasper H. Arnold, notes:

> When undertaking a large expansion program, management usually acknowledges that it might face some short-term reversals or minor problems, but it generally is convinced that nothing serious will happen and that the project will succeed. This optimism is unjustified. In fact, most projects—more than 50% by my estimate—encounter big setbacks. . . .
>
> The sky has fallen on many industries—textile manufacturing, chemical production, cement manufacturing, commercial real estate development, and home computer manufacturing—just when managers thought they had found the pot of gold at the end of the rainbow.

Faced with baleful circumstances, a program manager possesses no magic formula that assures success, but most such individuals do seem to have certain traits in common. There are the obvious characteristics such as a willingness to work hard, very hard; to take prudent risks; to enforce discipline, including self-discipline; and to make the tough decisions. The latter is of particular importance. Very often most everyone knows what must be done—the difficult thing is doing it.

But there are also a large number of more subtle characteristics that seem to distinguish the effective program manager from his or her less successful counterpart. Somewhere near the top of that list is the ability to plan an undertaking so as to ensure some degree of reserves: reserves in dollars, time, product performance, or whatever. This is necessary because even the best-managed projects will, somewhere along the line, encounter problems. If provision has not been made in advance to work one's way past these unforeseen roadblocks, the program manager will almost assuredly find a great deal in common with the pilot who plans flights with no fuel reserves. The leader of any complex undertaking is more than likely to find it necessary, figuratively speaking, to "bring up the reserves" at some point (or points) in time.

Having a clear goal, understood by everyone, is also critical to the success of a project, as is a means of *measuring* progress toward that goal. This is where, incidentally, most software projects get into trouble. Such projects seem to fit the description "Everything was going great—right up to the start."

As will be noted, however, *people* are the sine qua non—especially when molded into a team. There is very little room for soloists in the business of managing programs. Team players are the essence of success. Perhaps the most gratifying aspect of this collection of articles, as viewed from today's world of corporate raiders, greenmailers, and arbitrageurs, is that no article (in fact, not even a mention) appears here on the subject of hostile takeovers, breakups, or other forms of corporate terrorism. This is a book on internal growth, management, and achievement: in short, *value-added*. Along with discussions of strategy, organization, leadership, and even formulas for achieving specific ends, the point comes through in piece after piece that *people,* through decisions and actions, are what make anything work.

It is people, rather than analytical tools, who make decisions.

The issue is not which buttons to push on a calculator, but rather the appropriate interpretations.

There's no preaching in this collection. This is its central theme: how to gear up for internal growth—the most essential gears being *individuals and groups of individuals.*

This book was written by a cross-section of people from industry, the financial world, and academia, each with worthwhile experiences and judgments to relate and the genuine ability to do so in a conversational, persuasive, verbally disciplined manner that does not run on as this sentence is doing.

Most of the articles are from the 1980s, but a few go back as far as the 1960s and one even to 1959 for discussions of important concepts such as PERT, the Critical Path Method, and how to set up dedicated organizations under project managers to run major technological undertakings. This timelessness might be viewed as a tribute to the power of fundamentals. In this regard, the reader will also be reminded of the universality of certain business situations, in which the same basic problems seem to plague computer producers and bubble gum manufacturers alike—and the fact that the more things change, the more they don't.

One article discusses the fact that the United States today faces an enormous problem in how to ensure undisputed—or even disputed—technological leadership. Among the main impediments to leadership may be our management processes. Somehow, the management of technology has too often been the tunnel at the end of the light. Project management must be part of the answer and not part of the problem. The success of American technological advancement and its management during the next decade will very likely shape our economic destiny and may determine whether we continue to prosper or enter into a period of demise.

> The role to be played by project management in these years ahead will be challenging, exciting, and crucial. Truly it will be the acid test of the project manager and the project concept, but it will be much more than that. It will be a momentous trial of free enterprise, business administration, and progressive industrial management as we know them today.

The above quotation is borrowed from "The Project Manager" by Paul O. Gaddis—written just thirty years ago.

Today, America finds itself rather suddenly embedded in a global marketplace with boundaries that no longer coincide with geopolitical boundaries and with new participants who play by a heretofore unprecedented set of rules. The new rules may not be at all illegal or even unethical by the standards of this new market, but merely different—including the formation of tight bonds among such institutions as government, academia, and industry. Collegialism in this new marketplace threatens to supplant adversarialism, which may have served America's legal system well over the years, but has far less to recommend it within the modern business environment. It would seem likely that if America is to succeed in the new world of international competition, its program managers and the executives to whom they report will have to find means of similarly harnessing such diverse assets on our own behalf. All of which is to suggest that the already incredibly difficult job of program manager is likely, in the next century, to demand substantially broadened skills, such as dealing in multinational undertakings and understanding technologies that did not even exist a few years earlier.

This book springs from the fundamental notion that it is not enough to do things right. The right things must be done throughout the life of a project. A great deal of sound advice appears along the way:

Desperate measures taken to stop the hemorrhage of funds during development, such as cutting back on contingency programming, can cripple a project for life.

Rarely anywhere does a new project, especially a high-tech undertaking, come on line on time, on budget, and up to scratch.

Starting new projects is fraught with risk. Costs may escalate and operational capabilities may decline as a project develops and goes on stream. Inadequate early cost estimates and improper budgeting increase risks and often lead to enormous overruns.

When an overrun becomes serious, the only sensible recourse is to rework the project from the ground up and, if necessary, either abandon or rebudget. Minor cost cutting to buy time is counterproductive.

When a new project overruns its budget, managers should seek causes before remedies.

. . .we learn more from mistakes than from successes. That's not to say we should make mistakes easily. But if we do make mistakes, we ought to make them creatively.

If your company is like most, you spend thousands of hours planning an investment, millions of dollars implementing it—and nothing evaluating and learning from it.

Such is the nature of the advice offered on program management, a profession of unending challenge and excitement with enormous opportunities for real, tangible accomplishment. Unlike the life of a pilot, which has been described as long periods of utter boredom interspersed with moments of sheer terror, the life of a project manager might more aptly be said to be one of long periods of sheer terror interspersed with rare moments of utter boredom. It is a life filled with risk, hard work, and career exposure. Truly, in most kinds of business, this *is* where the rubber meets the road.

But when all is said and done, the rewards are commensurate. It is usually the program manager, not the CEO or the CFO or the corporate auditor or even the general counsel, who can point to a completed, definitive, and tangible project and say, "I did this."

Program management may be the most rewarding job in business and most who have had the privilege of serving in this capacity consider themselves very lucky indeed. Lucky, at least, in the sense of a sign posted on a ranch in Wyoming which proclaimed:

NOTICE:
LOST DOG
Left ear missing
Large scar on right side
Tip of tail gone
Recently castrated
Answers to the name,
"Lucky"

Such is the lot of the program manager.

PART
I

Evaluating

1
Today's Options
for Tomorrow's Growth

W. Carl Kester

Since the rise in the use of discounted cash flow techniques, most managers face an increasingly difficult choice in evaluating complex investment decisions. Should they pursue risky projects that offer a below-target rate of return but could create valuable strategic opportunities later? Or should they stick with a less risky and more immediately profitable bet?

Whether it's a diversified company trying to keep pace in a fast-growing market or a smokestack company struggling to regain its competitive edge, the choice must be made. Take the case of a large, technology-based company. Despite a cut in spending plans to avoid outside financing, the capital appropriations committee decided to consider a special project that would require a plant for the large-scale manufacture of a new, proprietary material that had been successfully produced in a pilot plant.

On an ordinary net present value basis, high construction costs, low projected cash flows, and a high sensitivity to cyclical fluctuation combined to make the project unattractive. Opponents argued it would hurt reported earnings, diminish near-term cash flows, and depress an already low stock price.

Proponents pointed out the project's long-term strategic benefits. Wide acceptance of the material would produce a virtual cascade of new commercial development and capacity expansion projects. The project's value came not so much from cash flows directly attributable to the new plant as from opportunities for growth. In the end, the proponents prevailed by not falling back on the corporate culture. They recalled a similar project the company had pursued just before World War II—one on which much of its post-war success was built.

The committee finally approved the project but, because of uncertainty and the lack of stronger analytic support, it deferred final appropriation for one year. Ultimately, the new material succeeded. Production efficiencies were achieved, user acceptance developed, and new applications proliferated. But the initial delay proved costly. A competitor's substitute product gained an early foothold in the new material's primary market, forcing the first company to spend more money than originally planned.

How could the project's proponents have made their argument more convincing so that funds would have been committed at once? More to the point, what if a manager doesn't have history to back up his argument? What analytic framework can be used to give a hard edge to the "soft" strategic side of the investment argument?

Based on my research into the investment and capital budgeting decisions of companies (see Appendix A), I've concluded that one answer is to think of future investment opportunities as analogous to ordinary call options on securities.[1] Most managers are familiar with call options since they trade actively on public exchanges and such options are often an important part of a compensation package.

Securities options give the owner the *right* (as distinct from an obligation) to buy a security at a fixed, predetermined price (called the exercise price) on or before some fixed date (the maturity date). By way of analogy, a discretionary opportunity to invest capital in productive assets like plant, equipment, and brand names at some future point in time is like a call option on real assets, or a "growth option." The cost of the investment represents the option's exercise price. The value of the option (its underlying "security") is the present value of expected cash flows plus the value of any new growth opportunities expected through ownership and employment of the assets. The time to maturity is the amount of time available before the opportunity disappears.

Like call options on securities, growth options represent real value to those companies fortunate enough to possess them. Any investment project whose implementation can be deferred, that can be modified by the company, or that creates new investment opportunities can be analyzed using this framework. This would include opportunities to:

Expand capacity, make new product introductions, or acquire other companies.

Increase budgets for advertising, basic research, and commercial development programs (insofar as these budgets represent investment in assets like brand names or technical expertise).

Make outlays for maintenance and replacement projects (since these too are discretionary projects that can be forgone if management decides to shrink or leave a business).

Just as securities traders would price a bond-warrant unit to reflect both of its sources of value—that is, the cash from the bond and the option value from the attached warrant—so too should a company analyze an investment in such a way as to delineate all its sources of value.

The importance of growth options can be recognized by looking at the difference between the total market value of a company's equity and the capitalized value of its current earnings stream (see Exhibit I). The difference is an estimate of the value of its growth options. As the last column indicates, valuable growth options constitute well over half the market value of many companies' equity.

While only large, publicly traded companies are represented in this exhibit, small, privately held organizations share similar characteristics. In fact, growth options probably dominate the equity value of small, high-growth companies marketing innovative products. The plethora of companies making initial public offerings at high price-earnings multiples attests to this fact. Genentech went public with annual revenues of $9 million and an operating cash flow of only 6¢ per share. At the initial public offering of $35 (a level quickly surpassed in the immediate aftermarket), the market value of its equity was $262 million—almost entirely based on options for future growth, not on the attractions of its current cash flow.

Strategic Capital Budgeting

While some strategically important investments allow for straightforward evaluation using ordinary discounted cash flow (DCF) techniques (for example, a cost-reduction project for a company whose competitive advantage rests exclusively on being the low-cost producer), others seem to defy such analysis. This is true because they are but the first link in a long chain of subsequent investment decisions. Future events often make it desirable to modify an initial project by expanding it or introducing a new production technology

Exhibit I. Growth Option Value as a Component of Selected Companies' Total Equity Value

	Market value of equity* $ millions	Anticipated earnings* $ millions	Capitalized value of earnings using various discounted rates** $ millions			Estimated value of growth options† $ millions	Percent of market value represented by growth options
			15%	20%	25%		
Electronics							
Motorola	$ 5,250	$ 210	$ 1,400	$ 1,050	$ 840	$ 3,850– 4,410	73–84%
Genrad	550	17	113	85	68	437– 482	79–88
RCA	2,200	240	1,600	1,200	960	600– 1,240	27–56
Computers and peripheral							
Apple Computer	2,000	99	660	495	396	1,340– 1,604	67–80
Digital Equipment	5,690	285	1,900	1,425	1,140	3,790– 4,550	67–80
IBM	72,890	5,465	36,433	27,325	21,860	36,457–51,030	50–70
Chemicals							
Celanese	1,010	78	520	390	312	490– 698	49–69
Monsanto	4,260	410	2,733	2,050	1,640	1,527– 2,620	36–62

Union Carbide	4,350	280	1,867	1,400	1,120	2,483– 3,230	57–74

Tires and rubber

Firestone	1,090	88	587	440	352	503– 738	46–68
Goodyear	2,520	300	2,000	1,500	1,200	520– 1,320	21–52
Uniroyal	400	47	313	235	188	87– 212	22–53

Food processing

Carnation	1,790	205	1,367	1,025	820	423– 970	24–54
Consolidated Foods	1,190	171	1,140	855	684	50– 506	4–43
General Foods	2,280	317	2,113	1,585	1,268	167– 1,012	7–44

* Source: *Value Line Investment Survey.* August 12, 1983.

** Anticipated earnings are treated as a perpetuity.

† Ranges of growth option value are determined by subtracting the high and low values of capitalized earnings from the market value of the equity.

at some later date. Other spin-off opportunities such as the conversion of by-products to usable goods or the development of complementary products to fill out a line may also arise.

Precisely how and when subsequent investment decisions will be made depend on future events. But the array—and attractiveness—of future investment opportunities at the company's disposal depends critically on the assets put in place in the present.

Realizing the importance of strategic investments and the difficulty of using quantitative techniques to analyze them, companies have developed a number of other methods of evaluation. Unfortunately, none has proved totally successful in practice. (For a rundown of the current methodology for analyzing investments, see Appendix B.)

In fact, existing cures for quantitative shortcomings may be worse than the disease. What is needed in their place is an approach that overcomes both the restrictiveness of ordinary net present value (NPV) analysis and the lack of analytic discipline that characterizes qualitative evaluation.

Take the opening case example. Proponents of production of the new material understood the value of the opportunity but could not convince skeptics without recalling a precedent. Lacking that precedent, their unstructured application of intuition and judgment would not have overcome formal, quantitative arguments.

The proponents should have organized their arguments around the concept of growth options. They could have argued more effectively that:

Discounted cash flow analysis understates the value of the project.

The risk associated with the project was one of the best reasons to preserve, not reject, it.

In an environment of high and rising interest rates, the capital budget should have been weighted in favor of such projects.

The options approach might have spared the company its subsequent mistake in delaying the capital commitment. In particular, it would have enabled the committee to recognize those conditions under which it should implement the project quickly and those under which it would be safe to defer.

How Valuable Are Growth Options?

The value of a call option on an asset depends on the value of the asset itself and the cost of exercising the option. If, for example,

IBM's stock traded at $120, a call option, giving its owner the right to purchase a share of IBM at $100, would be worth at least $20 and probably more.

The same logic applies to growth options. The opportunity to undertake a project is worth at least the present value of the project's cash inflow less the present value of its outflow. But the *opportunity* to invest can be worth even more than the project's NPV. How much more depends on:

THE LENGTH OF TIME THE PROJECT CAN BE DEFERRED.   Time is valuable when deciding whether to exercise an option. The ability to defer the decision gives the decision maker time to examine the course of future events and the chance to avoid costly errors if unfavorable developments occur. It also provides an interval during which a positive turn of events can make a project dramatically more profitable. The longer the interval, the more likely it is that this will happen; hence, the longer a project can be deferred the more valuable a growth option will be.

Even a project with a negative NPV can be a valuable "out-of-the-money" growth option if the company can put off the investment decision for a while. A company might maintain such out-of-the-money options even if they require ongoing spending for engineering, product development, market research, and so on, provided there is a realistic chance that future events will make the project more valuable.

PROJECT RISK.   Paradoxically, risk is a *positive* factor in the determination of a growth option's worth. If two investment opportunities have identical NPVs and can be deferred for the same amount of time, the riskier of the two projects will be a more valuable growth option. This is because of an asymmetry between potential upside gains and downside losses when an option matures. As Exhibit II illustrates, large gains are possible if a project's NPV increases. However, losses can be cut by simply choosing not to exercise the option whenever the project's NPV is negative. This ability means that high risk increases the chance of eventually realizing a large gain without equally increasing the chance of incurring a large loss.

THE LEVEL OF INTEREST RATES.   High interest rates generally translate into higher discount rates and lower present values of future cash flows for any given project. Clearly, that should depress the value of an option to undertake a project.

But higher discount rates also imply a lower present value of the future capital necessary to exercise an option. Such a countervailing effect helps to buoy the option's value as interest rates rise. This can give certain kinds of projects—specifically, those that create new growth options—a crucial comparative advantage in the capital budgeting process.

HOW EXCLUSIVE THE OWNER'S RIGHT IS TO EXERCISE THE OPTION. Unlike call options on securities, there are two types of growth options: *proprietary* and *shared*. Proprietary options provide highly valuable, exclusive rights of exercise. These result from patents or the company's unique knowledge of a market or a technology that competitors cannot duplicate.

Shared growth options are less valuable "collective" opportunities of the industry, like the chance to enter a market unprotected by high barriers or to build a new plant to service a particular geographic market. Projects to cut costs are also shared options since competitors usually can and will respond with cost reductions of their own, thus minimizing the benefits to any one company.

Shared growth options are less attractive than proprietary ones because counter investments by the competition can erode or even preempt profits. Only if a company is in a sufficiently strong competitive position to ward off assaults and grab the lion's share of a project's value can a shared growth option be valuable.

Implications for Capital Budgeting

Thinking of investments as growth options challenges conventional wisdom about capital budgeting. For example, a company may be justified in accepting projects with a negative NPV. Some projects, such as the one in the opening example, may initially drain cash flows. But they may also create options for future growth. If the growth option's value more than offsets that lost from the project's cash flows, then it is worthwhile.

Suppose a company found the present value of construction and future operating costs for a genetic engineering lab to total $5 million. As a basic research lab, it would not, of course, generate

positive cash flows, only opportunities for future commercial development of new discoveries. Still, the project would be justifiable
if, in management's judgment, these growth options were worth $5
million or more.

If new growth options are involved, high-risk projects might be
preferable to low-risk ones. In light of the beneficial impact of risk
on growth option value, companies should hold options on projects
whose value swings widely rather than only slightly over time. Projects that create new growth options in risky environments should
have an advantage in the capital budgeting process. As an executive
of a major consumer products company noted:

"If you know everything there is to know about a [new] product,
it's not going to be a good business. *There have to be some major
uncertainties to be resolved.* This is the only way to get a product
with a major profit opportunity." [Emphasis added.]

When capital is scarce and interest rates rise, projects that create
new growth options may be less adversely affected than those that
generate only cash. This makes them relatively more attractive in
the capital budgeting process. Normally, companies tilt their preferences toward projects that generate cash when capital is tight.
But one large technology-based company discovered a different kind
of comparative advantage during a capital squeeze in the late 1970s.
A member of the capital appropriation committee described the
problem:

> Allocating capital would be easy if you could do it just "by the
> numbers," but you must consider "directional" factors as well.
> The idea of a hurdle-rate [to evaluate projects] becomes even less
> important in periods of tight capital because directional factors
> take precedence. When capital is tight, we take a longer-haul view
> and pick up the savings and cost-reduction projects later.

These "directional" factors are valuable growth options that the
company looks for in new or growing markets.

Deciding when to exercise a growth option depends on a comparative analysis of the advantages and disadvantages of going
ahead with a project as soon as possible. Because this *option* to
invest is worth more than the NPV of the underlying project, a
company should wait until the last possible moment before committing funds. That preserves the option's premium while protecting

the company from costly and avoidable mistakes. A decision to commit funds to a project any earlier than necessary sacrifices this value.

Experience shows that companies often commit investment funds at a very early date despite their ability to defer a final decision. Companies that do so must believe that the cost of deferring the decision exceeds the value sacrificed from early exercise. For instance, a competitor may preempt the move or take action that raises the cost of the project, as happened to the company in the opening example. In general, a company will find it pays to exercise its growth options earlier than necessary when: competitors have access to the same option; the project's net present value is high; the level of risk and interest rates are low; and industry rivalry is intense.

Exhibit III shows how a company should time the exercise of its growth options based on the extent of industry rivalry and on the exclusiveness of a company's right to exercise the options. The upper right and lower left quadrants offer straightforward directions for companies. The other two present intermediate cases with less obvious results. A company may wish to exercise even proprietary growth options early, for example, if the industry is intensely competitive and a timely commitment is likely to discourage attack.

A company generally tries to obtain a dominant competitive position in order to achieve and protect high returns on investment. But by giving a company the right to *time* the investment more selectively, the growth option provides an important, though often overlooked, motive for dominating the market. One executive stated:

> What you're really trying to do with capital is create a strong competitive position. . . . We say [to our division managers] "Do what you have to do to retain a leadership position in the short run." Of course, over the long run, you can stay a leader only if you have the best cost position, so we must pay attention to that. But get the strongest leadership position, and *that* is what is going to pay off.

The advantage of being number one in an industry is the opportunity to initiate changes in technology and pricing. If one initiates change, one is in a much better position to take advantage of it because one can, in effect, control the timing and anticipate the outcome.

*Exhibit II. The Asymmetry Between Upside Gains and Downside Losses in Option Ownership**

Exhibit III. Timing the Commitment of Capital

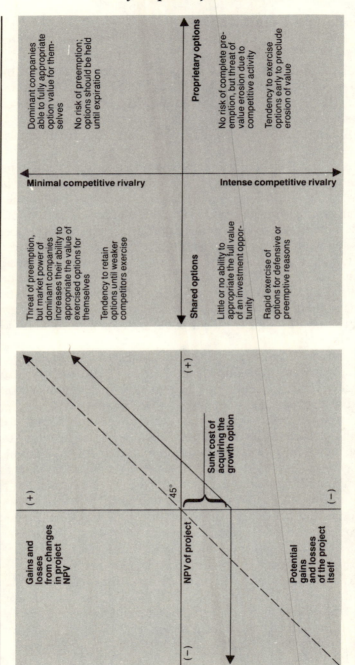

Exhibit II labels:

Gains and losses from changes in project NPV

(+)

45°

NPV of project

(+)

Sunk cost of acquiring the growth option

(−)

Potential gains and losses of the project itself

*As NPV of project declines below zero, the value of the growth option stops falling and goes flat.

Exhibit III labels:

Minimal competitive rivalry

Intense competitive rivalry

Proprietary options

Shared options

Dominant companies able to fully appropriate option value for themselves

No risk of preemption; options should be held until expiration

No risk of complete preemption, but threat of value erosion due to competitive activity

Tendency to exercise options early to preclude erosion of value

Threat of preemption, but market power of dominant companies increases their ability to appropriate the value of exercised options for themselves

Tendency to retain options until weaker competitors exercise

Little or no ability to appropriate the full value of an investment opportunity

Rapid exercise of options for defensive or preemptive reasons

Using the Framework

Given the determinants of a growth option's value and the many different characteristics it can display, no single formula can embody its value reliably. Consequently, the first assessment of a project expected to generate new growth options might best be qualitative, although rooted in established principles of option valuation.

As a first step, the company should classify projects more accurately according to their growth option characteristics. Classification along traditional functional lines such as replacement, cost reduction, capacity expansion, and new product introduction provides little guidance. A more appropriate classification begins by distinguishing between projects whose future benefits are realized primarily through cash flows (simple options) and those whose future benefits include opportunities for further discretionary investment (compound options). Simple growth options—like routine cost reduction and maintenance and replacement projects—create value only through the cash flows stemming from the underlying assets.

Compound growth options—like research and development projects, a major expansion in an existing market, entry into a new market, and acquisitions—lead to new investment opportunities and affect the value of existing growth options.

A simple growth option requires only that the company evaluate cash flows according to net present value or rate or return methods. The complexity of compound options, their role in shaping a company's strategy, and even their impact on the survival of the organization all demand a broader analysis. A company must consider these projects as part of a larger cluster of projects or as a stream of investment decisions that extends over time. Given the company's strategy, executives should question whether a particular option will bring the right investment opportunities in the right markets—within a time frame suitable to their company's needs.

The company must separate projects that require an immediate decision from those on which it can defer final action. For growth options with a shorter time frame, executives need to focus only on the value gained or lost from acceptance. However, deferrable projects should be analyzed according to the relative costs and benefits of deferral.

Finally, the company must ask whether it can capture the option's benefits for itself or whether they will be available to other competitors as well.

To illustrate, let's look at a generic chemical investment and alter it to fit different circumstances. A chemical company wants to build a facility for producing a toxic chemical next to a user's plant. The chemical is a commodity, the facility is to be owned and operated by the company, and the user is scheduled to purchase a fixed percentage of the plant's capacity output under a take-or-pay contract. If the company doesn't construct the facility immediately, however, the offer expires and the user will build and manage a plant on its own.

The chemical company's opportunity is a *simple, expiring, proprietary* growth option. The company should evaluate it by calculating the net present value of cash flows. The project's stand-alone cash value in the present is the only measure of the project's worth needed, since that is the value to be gained or lost.

Suppose this offer does not expire within a year and the potential exists for a relaxation of regulations controlling production of the toxic chemical. Under these circumstances, the company now realizes the new facility can be built at a much lower cost in the future. At the same time, the company discovers that the user has approached other chemical companies with the same offer. The company classifies the project as a *simple, deferrable, shared* growth option. Again, the company needs to evaluate only cash flows but must study the impact of deferral on cash since it shares the option with competitors. The company should channel project evaluation into a comparison of potential costs and benefits from either immediate exercise or deferral.

Finally, suppose that the toxic chemical is actually a new compound developed by the company. As a substitute for existing chemicals, it offers users significant cost savings. If the facility can produce the new compound in volume and the company can prove the cost savings, it can expect demand to grow rapidly, and realize new opportunities to build additional production facilities. On the negative side, the compound is difficult to produce, and government regulations could change radically. Moreover, the user continues to consider proposals from producers of a conventionally used chemical.

This last growth option is *shared, compound,* and *deferrable.* Even if cash flow analysis indicates that the company should reject or defer the project, top management may accept it immediately if preemption by competitors could seriously erode the worth of future growth options.

A New Perspective

The key advantage of the growth-option perspective is that it integrates capital budgeting with long-range planning. Within the framework, capital budgeting is simply the execution of a company's long-range plan.

Because investment decisions today can create the basis for investment decisions tomorrow, capital allocations made in any year are vital steps in the ultimate achievement of strategic objectives. By the same token, a long-range plan necessarily implies the cultivation of particular investment opportunities and can have a direct, dollars-and-cents impact on a company's stock price in the near term as well. The two activities are different but related means to the same end: maximizing the value of the company's equity.

To explicitly link capital budgeting and long-range planning, a company should place them both under the supervision of a single executive or an executive committee. Top management will impose a strategic perspective on what might otherwise be an uncoordinated aggregation of isolated capital expenditures.

Operating with a growth option perspective allows responsible executives to focus on the single, overriding objective of enhancing the value of the company's equity. The capital budgeting process will not be confused by linking the seemingly divergent and mutually exclusive aims of investing for future growth and maintaining a high stock price in the present. Once headquarters understands that some of the strategic benefits of investments are valuable options on future growth, it becomes clear that such investments add to the value of the company's equity, just as do projects that yield immediate cash flow. The only difference: value comes initially in the form of growth options rather than cash flows.

Such recognition will mark a critical shift in executive attention. A company should not spend time and effort trading off growth with ROI or market share with profitability. Rather, the company's focus should be on the kind of value the investment will create, its durability, and the auxiliary decisions required to protect or enhance it over time.

An executive of a *Fortune* 500 company once claimed that, "You simply can't put a dollar sign on a technological future that may have a tremendous payoff." The executive may be right. But that does not mean future investment opportunities have no value for the company's shareholders. Moreover, it certainly does not mean a company should abandon or distort the one approach available to put a dollar sign on the future—the discounting of expected cash flows using appropriate discount rates.

To be consistent with the objective of maximizing equity value, executives must broaden their perspective on the process of resource allocation so that they can integrate "strategic" factors logically and systematically into the capital budgeting process.

By thinking of discretionary investment opportunities as options on real assets, executives will address other relevant questions that have received little attention so far. How, for example, are growth options created, and which will be most valuable? How permanent and how liquid are growth options as components of company value? Does it matter whether a company owns a growth option exclusively as a collective option of the industry? What influence do industry structure and competitive interaction have on growth option value? What auxiliary financial decisions are required to permit the future conversion of growth options to real assets?

The answers to questions such as these will vary from one situation to another. Thus, the growth-option framework reaffirms the potentially valuable role that executive judgment and experience can play in the resource allocation process. But regardless of the specific situation, the growth option framework establishes a common basis for the analysis needed to answer fundamental questions and provides a coherent structure for organizing the application of executive judgment.

Appendix A

Research Methodology

Clinical data and impetus for this article came from my involvement in field research on financial goals and resource allocation conducted in 1979–1980 by Professors Gordon Donaldson and Jay Lorsch at the Harvard Graduate School of Business Administration. Twelve *Fortune* 500 -size companies with varying degrees of product

2
Pitfalls in Evaluating Risky Projects

James E. Hodder and
Henry E. Riggs

In recent years, the leaders of American companies have been barraged with attacks on their investment policies. Critics accuse American executives of shortsightedness and point out that managers in Japan and Europe often fix their vision on more distant horizons. Here, it is claimed, managers pay too much attention to quarterly earnings reports and not enough to such basic elements of industrial strength as research and development. Some analysts see the root of this problem in the tendency of American companies to rely on discounted cash flow techniques in weighing long-term investments.[1] These critics argue that DCF techniques have inherent weaknesses that make them inappropriate for evaluating projects whose payoffs will come years down the road.

We disagree with the contention that DCF techniques are inappropriate for evaluating long-term or strategic investment proposals. We do believe, however, that companies often misapply or misinterpret DCF techniques. Misuse is particularly serious in evaluating long-term capital investments, such as ambitious R&D projects, that appear to involve high risk.

Misapplication of DCF techniques can certainly contribute to an unwarranted aversion to making long-term investments. However, the problem lies not in the technique but in its misuse. Money has a time value in every economy, and cash is the life-blood of every business. To evaluate cash flows (costs or revenues) generated in different periods requires a procedure for making comparisons. For evaluating and ranking investment proposals, whether they have short or long lives, and involve capital equipment, R&D, or marketing expenditures, we need techniques that recognize that cash flows occur at different times. Discounting provides a rational and conceptually sound procedure for making such evaluations.

Unfortunately DCF techniques, like computers, can yield impressive-looking but misleading outputs when the inputs are flawed. Managers with biased assumptions may end up with biased conclusions. The fault, however, lies not with the technique but with the analyst. The path to improved capital budgeting requires education in the proper use of rational techniques rather than their rejection out of hand.

In our view, DCF techniques provide valuable information to *assist* management in making sound investment decisions. We emphasize the word assist because it is people, rather than analytical tools, who make decisions. Managers may have many objectives and face many constraints in their decision making. Nevertheless, they need information on the relative financial merits of different options. Properly employed, DCF techniques provide such information. The alternative is to ignore the time value of money and implicitly assume that, for example, a dollar earned ten years from now will have the same value as a dollar today.

DCF procedures, as commonly applied, are subject to three serious pitfalls:

Improper treatment of inflation effects, particularly in long-lived projects.

Excessive risk adjustments, particularly when risk declines in later phases of a project.

Failure to acknowledge how management can reduce project risk by diversification and other responses to future events.

Awareness of these pitfalls should help managers avoid uncritical use of DCF techniques that may lead to poor decisions.

An R&D Project, for Example

Although the comments here apply to a variety of investment proposals, we shall illustrate these three major pitfalls with the analysis of an R&D project. (Exhibit I lists examples of other investment projects that are frequently misevaluated for the reasons described in this article.) Because of their risk characteristics, R&D projects present some especially thorny problems. The pronounced uncertainties in these projects affect the analysis of risk in many

Exhibit I. Long-Term Risky Investments Frequently Misevaluated

1	A consumer goods company considers test marketing the first of a proposed new family of products.
2	A paper company studies investment in a new processing technique that could revolutionize paper making.
3	A drug company looks at increasing its investment in biomedical research and the pilot plant that will be required if the research is successful.
4	A real estate developer analyzes the first-stage investment in improvements at a greenfield site for industrial-commercial facilities.
5	A financial services firm considers investment in a telecommunications facility that could radically alter the future distribution of its services.
6	A natural resources company evaluates a mineral-rights lease of a site that will require extensive development.

ways. As a result, R&D projects with acceptable—even exciting—risk/return profiles may fail to meet the payoff criteria that management has established.

Let's look at a typical (hypothetical) project that would be rejected on the basis of the incomplete DCF analysis common in industry today. Then we'll show how a more complete and careful analysis reveals the project to be not only acceptable but highly desirable.

Our project has three distinct phases, as shown in Exhibit II. If the research (Phase 1) is successful, the project moves to market development (Phase 2), after which the resulting product may enjoy a long and profitable period of production and sales. The research and market development phases are periods of investment; returns are forthcoming only during the third period (Phase 3) when the product is sold.

It is important to differentiate between these phases, since each has decidedly different risk characteristics. Market development (Phase 2) will not be undertaken unless the research (Phase 1) is successful; thus, considerable uncertainty disappears before Phase 2

Exhibit II.   Project Description

Phase 1	Research or product development
	$18 million annual research cost for 2 years
	60% probability of success
Phase 2	Market development
	Undertaken only if product development succeeds
	$10 million annual expenditure for 2 years on the development of marketing and the establishment of marketing and distribution channels (net of any revenues earned in test marketing)
Phase 3	Sales
	Proceeds only if Phase 1 and Phase 2 verify opportunity
	Production is subcontracted
	The results of Phase 2 (available at the end of year 4) identify the product's market potential as shown below:

Product demand	Product life	Annual net cash inflow	Probability
High	20 years	$24 million	.3
Medium	10 years	$12 million	.5
Low	Abandon project	None	.2

Note:

For simplicity, we assume that production is subcontracted in Phase 3 and that all cash flows are after tax and occur at year end. This assumption permits us to ignore some potentially complex tax issues involving depreciation and financing strategies. While a radical departure from reality, this assumption allows us to focus on issues of cash flow timing and risk that appear to be less widely understood.

proceeds. Similarly, the sales period (Phase 3) follows only after successful results from research and market development. The information from Phase 2 will refine market projections, and Phase 3 cash flows are relatively low risk. In sum, uncertainty about the project diminishes progressively as we acquire more information.

According to the probabilities shown in Exhibit II, the project viewed as a whole (rather than by phases) has the expected-value cash flows shown in Exhibit III and an expected internal rate of return (IRR) slightly over 10%. This appears distinctly unattractive, even ridiculous, when compared with customary rates of return (hurdle rates) of 20% or more for high-risk projects. Given this analysis and results, most managers would almost certainly reject the project unless other strategic reasons dictated the investment.

Many (if not most) U.S. companies, unfortunately, would probably analyze the project in this way, concluding that it is indeed risky and has an expected IRR below normal hurdle rates. The interpretation of these "facts" is far from obvious, however, and requires a deeper understanding of DCF calculation procedures. The issue is not which buttons to push on a calculator, but rather the appropriate interpretation of the inputs and consequent output since the DCF procedure is no more than a processing technique. The analysis appears sophisticated with its use of probabilities and discounting, but it is incomplete and seriously misleading.

Adjusting for Inflation

The most obvious shortcoming of the analysis is that it ignores how inflation will affect the various cash flows. At one extreme,

Exhibit III.   *Expected Cash Flows for the Project in $ millions*

Years	Expected value calculations	
1		− 18
2		− 18
3	.6(− 10)	= − 6
4	.6(− 10)	= − 6
5–14	.6(.3 × 24 + .5 × 12)	= 7.92
15–24	.6(.3 × 24)	= 4.32
Expected IRR = 10.1%.		

they may not be affected at all. On the other hand, the cash flows may adjust directly and completely with inflation, that is, an 8% inflation rate next year will raise cash flows in that and following years by 8%. Most likely, inflation will affect different components of the cash flows in different ways and, when aggregated, the cash flows will adjust partially with inflation. Meaningful interpretation of the calculated IRR requires knowledge of this inflation adjustment pattern.

If complete adjustment were anticipated, the calculated IRR would represent an expected real return. However, comparing such real returns with nominal hurdle rates—including inflation—or nominal investment yields (for example, from government bonds) is not appropriate.[2] Historically, real yields on low-risk investments have averaged less than 5%, and the real yield on short-term U.S. Treasury securities has equalled close to zero. For higher risk investments, a frequent standard of comparison is the return (including dividends) on the Standard & Poor's "500" stock index. Over a 53-year period (1926–1978) the real rate of return on the S&P "500" averaged 8.5%. While we cannot be certain that history will repeat itself, long-run averages do provide one standard for comparison. Since listed securities represent an alternative investment, projects of comparable risk reasonably should have expected returns at least as great.

Returning to our hypothetical project, if cash flows adjust fully with inflation, the project offers a real return greater than the historic 8.5% of the S&P "500."

Many types of cash flows, of course, do not adjust fully with inflation, and some do not adjust at all. For example, depreciation tax shields, many lease payments, fixed-rate borrowing (like debentures), and multiyear fixed-price purchase or sales contracts do not change with the inflation rate. Consequently, a proper analysis requires an understanding of the inflation adjustment patterns for different cash flow segments.

While American managers' awareness of the impact of inflation on project evaluation has risen in the last decade, even today many of them have at best a cursory understanding of it. Failure to incorporate inflation assumptions in DCF analyses can be particularly troublesome in decentralized companies. Corporate financial officers commonly specify companywide or divisional hurdle rates based on a current (nominal) cost of capital. Furthermore, analysts at the plant or division level often estimate future cash flows (particularly cost savings) based on current experience. Unless those analysts consciously include anticipated inflation, they will under-estimate future cash flows and, unfortunately, many good projects may be rejected.

Parenthetically, the converse is unlikely to occur: it is hard to conceive of an analyst using inflated cash flows with real discount or hurdle rates. Also, projects that go forward usually undergo several reviews that are likely to result in some tempering, or low-ering, of overly optimistic cash flow assumptions. By contrast, re-jected projects are seldom given subsequent reviews that might reveal unrealistically low inflation assumptions.

The mismatch of inflation assumptions regarding cash flows and hurdle rates is generally most pronounced for projects with payoffs years down the road. So long as the inflation rate is positive (even if declining), the gap between projected real cash flows and their nominal equivalents grows with time. For example, suppose that inflation rates for the next three years are expected to be 8, 6, and 4% respectively. Consider an item that sells for $1 now. If its price will increase at the rate of inflation, its nominal price should be $1.08 next year, $1(1.08)(1.06) = $1.14 in two years, and $1(1.08)(1.06)(1.04) = $1.19 in three years. These inflated prices, rather than the current $1 price, should be incorporated into the DCF analysis if discounting is to occur at nominal rather than real interest rates.

The error that arises from the failure to include inflation in cash flow estimates compounds with time as long as inflation is positive. Under these circumstances, distant cash flows, such as those char-acteristic of research and development investments, have present values that are more seriously understated. It is difficult to know how widespread such errors have been during recent years, but almost surely they explain in part the shift toward shorter lived projects and myopic investment decisions in many businesses.

Avoiding Excessive Risk Adjustments

A second flaw in the original DCF calculations for our hypothetical R&D project is the use of a single discount rate (IRR) for a project in which risk declines dramatically over time. As a result, the project appears less attractive than it really is. If we make appropriate adjustments for the differing risks in different stages of the project, the investment becomes much more attractive.

A typical discount rate (k) used in DCF analyses may be viewed as composed of three parts: a risk-free time value of money (RF), a premium for expected inflation (Eπ), and a risk premium (Δ) that increases with project risk. This relationship can be represented as:

$$1 + k = (1 + RF)(1 + E\pi)(1 + \Delta)$$

For example, a risk-free rate of 3% with 10% expected inflation and a 6% risk premium would imply $1 + k = (1.03)(1.10)(1.06) = 1.20$, or a nominal discount rate of approximately 20%.

Since inflation, as well as project risk and even the risk-free rate (RF), can vary over time, we should permit k to have different values at different times. The subscript t indicates the relevant time period; thus k_t is a function of the RF_t, $E\pi_t$, and Δ_t values for that period. To focus on situations where project risk is expected to change significantly through time, we will use real (deflated) cash flows and real discount rates with RF constant. It is, of course, very important to adjust for expected inflation properly. Without losing sight of that point, let's shift the focus of discussion to risk adjustments by assuming that the inflation adjustments have been executed properly.

Denoting the real (risky) discount rate for period t as r_t, we have:

$$1 + r_t = (1 + RF)(1 + \Delta_t)$$

This differs from k_t simply by the removal of the inflation factor $(1 + E\pi_t)$. Then by definition, the NPV of a project with expected real cash flows (CF_t) occurring in two periods is:

$$NPV = \frac{CF_1}{1 + r_1} + \frac{CF_2}{(1 + r_1)(1 + r_2)}$$

$$= \frac{CF_1}{(1 + RF)(1 + \Delta_1)}$$

$$+ \frac{CF_2}{(1 + RF)^2(1 + \Delta_1)(1 + \Delta_2)}$$

This brings us to a key point. If $\Delta_1 = \Delta_2 = \Delta$, this formula collapses into the familiar form with a single discount rate:

$$NPV = \frac{CF_1}{(1 + RF)(1 + \Delta)} + \frac{CF_2}{(1 + RF)^2(1 + \Delta)^2}$$

$$= \frac{CF_1}{1 + r} + \frac{CF_2}{(1 + r)^2}$$

In practice, virtually all DCF calculations are performed using a constant discount rate such as r. Indeed, financial calculators are programmed that way. Under what conditions, however, can we assume that $\Delta_1 = \Delta_2$ (even approximately)?

This assumption is reasonable if we anticipate that errors in predicting real cash flows result from a random walk process—that is, predictions one period into the future always entail the same uncertainty. Thus if we were at time 1, each dollar of real cash flow in period 2 would look just as risky as each dollar of CF_1 looks now. However, predicting two periods into the future is more risky; thus CF_2 viewed from the present deserves a larger risk adjustment. Consequently, CF_2 is multiplied by $1/(1 + \Delta)^2$ as opposed to simply $1/(1 + \Delta)$ for CF_1. In more general terms, the risk adjustment factor for a cash flow t period in the future is $1/(1 + \Delta)^t$. The risk adjustment grows geometrically with time.

Using a single risk-adjusted discount rate, therefore, implies an important and somewhat special assumption about the risks associated with future cash flow estimates: such risks increase geometrically with chronological distance from the present. On the infrequent occasions when this assumption is mentioned, it is usually justified on the grounds that the accuracy of our foresight decreases with time. While that argument has merit, consider what can happen when an investment proposal does not fit this pattern.

Recall our R&D project. If the cash flows of Exhibit II are in real terms, the project has an expected real IRR of 10%; but there is a 40% chance of investing $36 million (real, after tax, but undiscounted) during the first two years and receiving nothing. Many decision makers would demand a much higher return than 10% (real or otherwise) to undertake such an investment. If the project proceeds to Phase 3, the cash flows in that phase are considered relatively low risk. The large risk adjustments that were appropriate for early phases are no longer appropriate once we reach Phase 3.

To highlight this point, let's suppose that Phase 3 could be sold if the project successfully proceeds through the first two phases. Given its low risk, potential investors might evaluate Phase 3 with a low discount rate such as 5% (real). Suppose market research reveals a high demand for the product during Phase 3: 20-year life with annual net cash inflows of $24 million. Discounting these flows at 5%, we reach a value at the beginning of Phase 3 (end of year 4) of $299 million. Thus if strong demand develops for the product, it's possible the rights to produce and market it could be sold for

Exhibit IV.   Anticipated Phase 3 Values If Sold in $ millions

Demand	Probability	Value of Phase 3 Year 4
High	.3	299
Medium	.5	93
Low	.2	0
Expected value =		136

a considerable sum. This value depends, however, on the marketing results from Phase 2. Thus we need to check what happens if less favorable demand conditions are revealed in Phase 2. Performing similar calculations for the other possible market conditions, we obtain the values in Exhibit IV.

Even though there is a 20% chance of low demand, the overall expected value of selling Phase 3 is $136 million. Suppose we now recalculate the project's expected IRR assuming such an outright sale of Phase 3 for its expected value: $136 million. Using the 60% probability of Phase 1 success, we calculate the expected cash flows to be those in Exhibit V. Those net expected cash flows are equivalent to an expected IRR of approximately 28%. In other words, the prospect that Phase 3 could be sold as just discussed leads us to revise the overall expected IRR for investing in the project from 10 up to 28%. Since these calculations are in real terms, the project now appears quite attractive.

Pushing this analysis one step further, let's assume the project could also be sold at the end of Phase 1 if the research is successful.

Exhibit V.   Expected Cash Flow with Phase 3 Sale in $ millions

Year	Outflow	Inflow	Net
1	− 18		− 18
2	− 18		− 18
3	− 10 × .6		− 6
4	− 10 × .6	136 × .6	75.6

That is, the new owner after purchasing the project would pay an estimated $10 million per year of Phase 2 costs and receive the Phase 3 value (depending on marketing research results) as shown in Exhibit IV. The purchaser would now encounter the expected cash flows indicated in Exhibit VI.

Clearly this proposition is riskier than just buying Phase 3, since the marketing research results of Phase 2 are not yet known. Suppose a potential purchaser evaluated the cash flows in Exhibit VI using a 20% discount rate (well over twice the historic real return on the S&P "500"). The implied purchase price (present value at the beginning of Phase 2) is slightly over $79 million. But what is the implied return to the first owner—the initial developer of the product who undertakes the risky proposition of investing $18 million for each of two years in research—if a successful project could be sold at the end of two years for $79 million? The expected real return (including the 40% chance of Phase 1 failure) is over 63%—a far cry from our initial estimate.

This analysis illustrates a pitfall in evaluating projects with risk patterns that differ significantly from the simple random walk assumption. In our example, uncertainty is greatest during the first two years. But it is unreasonable to penalize more than 20 years of subsequent cash flows for that risk. To dramatize this point, we have assumed that the project can be sold in its latter phases. Indeed, the project acquires a dramatically high value if Phase 1 succeeds—a point missed by the initial IRR calculation, which implicitly discounted all cash flows at the same rate.

The difficulty with using a single risk-adjusted discount rate (or IRR) is that the analysis blends time discount and risk adjustment factors. Unless project risk follows a simple random walk pattern, this blending is inappropriate. Although this problem is discussed in the academic literature,[3] it is generally ignored in practice. For projects with dramatically different risk phases, the result can be a serious misestimation of project value.

Exhibit VI. Expected Cash Flows for Purchaser of Phase 2 in $ millions

Year	Outflow	Inflow	Net
3	− 10		− 10
4	− 10	136	126

A more appropriate procedure for evaluating such projects is to separate timing and risk adjustments using the concept of certainty equivalent value (CEV). The CEV of a cash flow in a given year is simply its risk-adjusted value in that year. If we converted all future cash flows to CEVs, we could then discount the CEVs to the present using a single risk-free discount rate. With the timing and risk adjustments thus separated, we avoid the possibility of compounding risk adjustments unintentionally.

As a practical matter, attempting to convert each year's cash flow into a CEV can be cumbersome since the CEV for period t may depend on probabilities for cash flows in the previous period $(t - 1)$, which in turn depend on probabilities from $t - 2$, and so on. In our example, the cash flows in Phase 3 depend on results from Phases 1 and 2. Indeed, we have assumed that management would abandon the project altogether if the research is unsuccessful or market tests indicate low demand.

Although it is important to consider interactions among cash flows in different periods, the analysis of all possible management responses or other contingencies would be extraordinarily complex and unwieldy. Thus we need reasonable approximations. Managers and analysts must exercise judgment regarding which risks and possible actions should be included in the analysis. We recommend that high-risk projects be evaluated as a sequence of distinct risk phases (of perhaps several years each).

In our example, we did not attempt to calculate CEVs for each year in Phase 3. Rather, we estimated a value for the whole phase conditional on the demand level. Similarly, our calculated $79 million value for the project if Phase 1 succeeded is a CEV (at the beginning of year three) for Phases 2 and 3 combined. In both cases, these CEVs are estimates of the project's potential selling price—its market value at the end of years two and four, respectively. While the project might be worth more to the company if it retained all phases, the market CEVs represent opportunity costs for retaining Phases 2 and 3 that are useful (and conservative) yardsticks for evaluating the entire project.

Estimating market values for different phases is obviously an imprecise process. Using a single risk-adjusted rate for an entire phase (rather than separate rates or CEVs for each cash flow) produces only an approximation, unless risks within that phase have a random walk pattern. The approximation is reasonable, however, if the discount rate is low and/or the phase covers a fairly short period of time (as in Phases 1 and 2 above). If a phase is both long and risky, analysts should divide it into subphases.

To restate our argument, we recommend segmenting projects into risk phases, then valuing sequentially each phase, working backward from the last. This procedure can be used to determine either an expected IRR on the initial phase (as already illustrated) or an NPV for the project. In general, we prefer calculating NPVs since this avoids technical problems with IRR, including scale ambiguities. Although slightly more complex than a standard expected NPV or IRR calculation, our approach is not difficult per se. It simply entails a short sequence of expected NPV calculations using different interest rates to value different risk phases. When a project's risk pattern differs substantially from the simple random walk assumption, such differences should be recognized and the evaluation procedure modified accordingly. As we have shown, evaluation based on inappropriate analysis can be very misleading.

Considering the Eye of the Beholder

A third major problem in project evaluations is correctly assessing project risk and how managers can influence its nature and level. Here it is important to consider the perspective of the analyst. Risk that seems excessive to an R&D or project manager may appear reasonable to a corporate executive or a shareholder who can diversify the risk by spreading it across other investments. Also, managers can influence the level of risk by future actions that affect the ultimate payoff of a project investment.

Frequently, the major uncertainty in R&D investments is whether the research phase will produce a viable product. From the perspective of financial market theories such as the Capital Asset Pricing Model (CAPM), risks associated with the research phase are apt to be largely diversifiable. Consequently, a public shareholder with a well-diversified securities portfolio will probably voice little or no concern about these risks. Success or failure in the lab is probably correlated weakly (if at all) with broad economic forces or other systematic nondiversifiable factors that affect returns in the stock market as a whole.

The CAPM and related theories stress that a project's total risk normally contains both diversifiable and nondiversifiable components. To the extent shareholders can easily diversify their holdings in the financial markets, they can reduce *their* portion of the project's diversifiable risk to a very small level. Under these circumstances, the shareholders need worry only about the systematic portion of project risk. Thus a financial market approach suggests that the typical R&D project is much less risky from the perspective of a well-diversified public shareholder than it may appear to the individual performing the DCF analysis.

In contrast, managers, creditors, and even suppliers may focus on total risk (including both diversifiable and systematic components) at the company level. These groups have interests that are not easily diversified in the sense that the CAPM assumes. Thus they are concerned about total cash flow variability but at the company (not project) level. Even at the company level, however, the R&D budget may be spread across many projects. A multi-industry company of even moderate size is probably sufficiently diversified to allow large reductions in cash flow variability per dollar of R&D investment. Once again, the risk of a particular project appears lower from a portfolio perspective than from the perspective of an analyst looking only at the project itself.

Most managers are aware of portfolio effects and the arguments regarding shareholder welfare based on financial market models such as the CAPM. Nevertheless, it is understandable that they view a project with over a 50% chance of no payoff (as in our example) as highly risky. Under such circumstances, it is easy to ignore portfolio effects and worry too much about the risk of that particular investment opportunity. This excessive risk aversion is frequently manifested in a too-high discount or hurdle rate, thus compounding the pitfalls already discussed.

Analysts may also use conservative estimates: overestimates of development time or costs and underestimates of both the magnitude and duration of subsequent payoffs. Although the tendency toward excessive conservatism is both inevitable and difficult to overcome, management needs to be aware of its existence and sensitive to its consequences. As we said earlier, projects that have been rejected are seldom reevaluated. It is all too easy for a good project to be lost.

While excessive risk adjustments are certainly not unique to R&D proposals, the problem may be more severe here because R&D projects involve large and obvious uncertainties. The key is that these risks are likely to be highly diversifiable. Failure to recognize this fact represents a systematic bias against R&D projects.

Managers can also affect the level of risk by influencing the distribution of project payoffs. In our example, there is a 30% chance that Phase 3 will be worth $299 million. There is not a symmetric chance of losing $299 million—because the company will abandon the project if faced with low product demand. The result is an *expected* value for Phase 3 ($136 million) which is $43 million above the *most likely* estimate of $93 million. Unfortunately, many project evaluations consider only the most likely cash flow estimates and ignore the asymmetry or skewness of the payoffs. This practice understates the project's true value in situations in which future management actions can improve profits or limit losses.

This problem is more significant for R&D projects than for other investments because the company has greater flexibility to expand production for highly successful products and to abandon apparently unprofitable efforts. Such managerial actions can result in greater returns than estimated originally (larger revenues over a longer period) as well as reduced downside risk.

In our example, suppose progress can be monitored throughout Phase 1, and management has the option to abandon the project at the end of the first year if certain goals are not met. If the probability of research failure is equally divided between years one and two (20% each), the expected IRR from an initial investment in Period 1 research increases from 63% to 83%, with no change in our other assumptions (Exhibit VII shows the relevant cash flows). Clearly management's ability to skew a payoff distribution in the company's favor can have an important influence on a project's desirability.

DCF Analysis in Perspective

How much the misuse of DCF techniques has contributed to the competitive troubles of American companies is a matter of conjecture. It is clear, though, that incomplete analysis can severely pen-

Exhibit VII. *Expected Cash Flows If the Project Can Be Abandoned During Phase 1 in $ millions*

Year	Expected outflow	Expected inflow	Expected net cash flow
1	−18		−18
2	−18 × .8	79 × .6	33

alize investments whose payoffs are both uncertain and far in the future. Given these perils, one might argue that DCF procedures should be avoided or should be accorded little weight in long-term investment decisions. We strongly disagree. It is foolish to ignore or to indict useful analytical tools simply because they might be used incorrectly or incompletely. Rather, analysts and decision makers should recognize potential problems and be careful to ensure that evaluations are performed correctly. Managers cannot treat a DCF evaluation like a black box, looking only at the output. They need to break open the box, examine the assumptions inside, and determine how those assumptions affect the analysis of a project's long-term profitability.

DCF procedures can help evaluate the implications of altered price, cost, or timing assumptions, but managers must first specify the correct assumptions. These procedures can also be used to examine the effects of different capacity expansion or R&D strategies under many scenarios. However, again managers must specify the strategies or scenarios to be examined. In short, discounting is only one step in evaluating alternative investment opportunities. This fact has frequently been lost in the arguments (pro and con) about the use of discounting procedures.

Blaming DCF procedures for shortsightedness, biased perceptions, excessive risk aversion, or other alleged management weaknesses does not address the underlying problems of American industry. However, understanding the pitfalls in the casual use of DCF techniques can both improve the analysis of capital investment projects and place these techniques in a more appropriate perspective.

It is important to remember that managers make decisions. DCF techniques can assist in that process, but they are only tools. Correctly used, these techniques provide a logical and consistent framework for comparing cash flows occurring at different times—an important aspect of virtually every investment project.

Appendix

Calculating Inflation's Effects

To correctly allow for inflation in a DCF analysis, some analysts include it in the cash flows and use nominal discount rates. If inflation rates are expected to vary, different discount rates can be used for different years in a net present value (NPV) calculation. Such a procedure, however, entails cumbersome calculations. Furthermore, consistency on a companywide basis requires specifying the annual series of discount and inflation rates to be used by analysts. The simple approach is to use a single "average" inflation rate with a single nominal discount rate, but this is not ideal. Although in many cases the distortion associated with this approximation is not serious, the pattern of cash flows and projected inflation affects the size of the distortion.

A preferable procedure is to use deflated cash flows with real discount rates. In this approach, analysts estimate the cash flow in each period, including the increase from inflation applicable to each of its segments (for example, zero for depreciation tax shields). Analysts then deflate the cash flow to present (for example, 1985) dollars using the projected inflation between now and that period. If the cash flow is expected to adjust fully with inflation, the deflation adjustment will exactly cancel the included inflation. If not, the real value of that future cash flow will be altered by the extent to which it does not fully adjust with inflation. The series of deflated (real) cash flows can then be discounted using real discount rates. Since the real time value of money appears to be considerably more stable than its nominal counterpart, this second procedure is superior to using a single nominal discount rate.

Notes

1. See, for example, Robert H. Hayes and David A. Garvin, "Managing as if Tomorrow Mattered," HBR May–June 1982, p. 71.

2. James C. Van Horne, "A Note on Biases in Capital Budgeting Introduced by Inflation," *Journal of Financial and Quantitative Analysis,* January 1971, p. 653.

3. See, for example, Alexander A. Robichek and Stewart C. Myers, "Conceptual Problems in the Use of Risk-Adjusted Discount Rates," *Journal of Finance,* December 1966, p. 727.

3

Preapproval Audits of Capital Projects

**Robert J. Lambrix and
Surendra S. Singhvi**

For several decades U.S. business has been using the postcompletion audit as a control tool in capital budgeting. A company will generally undertake such an audit of a large project in order to remind the estimators of their continued responsibility and to form the basis for corrective action if the estimates are faulty.

Nevertheless, after-the-fact is obviously not always satisfactory since by that time the mistakes, if any, are already incorporated into the project and the money is spent. For several years Armco Inc. has used, in addition to the postcompletion audit, a preapproval audit to improve its capital resource allocation procedure. Most large organizations probably have an informal procedure; Armco's is formal.

The audit is an objective review of the main assumptions underlying the justification for a proposal. It is undertaken before it goes to top management for approval. Persons who have no interest in the fate of the project, and who would receive no advantage or penalty because of its acceptance or rejection, carry out the audit. A team appointed for the purpose reports its findings to top management; it makes no decision or even recommendations, since that responsibility belongs to headquarters.

The audit is appropriate only for major projects because of the time and expense and for larger organizations that have decentralized operations detached from close head office supervision. Profit centers in companies tend to be aggressive in expanding their assets, and top management in these organizations may be distant from their affairs.

Profit center management often has several months to prepare a proposal, while headquarters often has only a few days to review it. It is very difficult for top management to challenge or validate all the key assumptions in such a short time, especially when proposals from several profit centers are waiting. Moreover, the quality of the data justifying a project is often deficient.

$50 Million Proposal

Armco started the procedure in 1978 when a division submitted a request for $50 million to buy continuous-casting equipment. The cost-saving project was to yield an estimated discounted cash flow return of 22.6% over its 20-year life.

Considering the size of the proposal, top management decided to appoint an audit team of five persons to analyze it. Representing research, marketing, strategy, operations, and finance, they had had no part in the project-justification effort. Being corporate staff members, they had Armco's interests foremost in their minds. Within two weeks the team submitted its report to the Armco executive committee. The *Memorandum* summarizes the findings. The audit team disagreed with the division's project request about one major element: the capacity utilization assumption. The request cited a 98% capacity utilization over the next 20 years, whereas the division's experience had averaged 74%. The audit team decided to use an 85% capacity utilization assumption, which generated a DCF return of 17.4%. After making minor changes in other assumptions, such as the cost of pollution-control equipment, the team further revised the DCF return to 14.2%.

Following a review of the audit, top management delayed acceptance of the project by two months. During that time the division gathered further supporting documentation, which turned out to be extremely useful later during the postcompletion audit. Headquarters eventually approved the project.

The evaluation of the continuous-caster project became the model for the company's preapproval audit system. Top management found the tool very valuable in making investment decisions. Division presidents realized that they had to do a better job of supporting their assumptions on capital projects. From 1978 until the time of writing, the organization has performed 20 preapproval audits on large projects with these results:

Memorandum

TO: Executive Committee members

FROM: Preapproval Audit Team

SUBJECT: Continuous-Caster Program request
           Summary of findings

The audit team viewed this project as a cost reduction justification and has established the 85% capacity projection as the most realistic condition.

The revised DCF rate of return declined from 23% to 14%.

The team's analysis of the program request follows.

1. The program request shows five levels of cost-saving projections:

Level	Projection	ROI
1	100% of capacity and 100% of sales	32%
2	98% of capacity and 90% of sales	23%
3	85% of capacity and 90% of sales	17%
4	90% of capacity and 90% of sales	16%
5	75% of capacity and 80% of sales	12%

The first two levels of projection, indicating an ROI of 32% and 23%, are based on cost savings on significant additional sales. However, we selected the 85%-of-capacity-level projection for our audit, which justifies the proposed expenditure on a cost-saving basis. Comparable capacity-use data for the last five years and the current year are:

	Year						
	1973	1974	1975	1976	1977	1978 (est.)	Average
Percentage of capacity used	86%	92%	56%	60%	70%	81%	74%

The team members recognize that the historical average of 74% of capacity use is low in light of current operations. An average of 85% seems realistic. Division personnel agree that the 85%-of-capacity-level projection represents a cost-saving justification and probably a realistic analysis.

2. The sales support section does not provide any rationale for a 54% increase in sales between 1981 and 1985. Since the project is primarily justified by a cost saving, a sales justification is unnecessary. If more than a cost saving is to be considered, the request should include a much more detailed sales justification.

3. The projected operating and yield savings of $11 million each year, beginning in 1983, is the important factor in the project's financial justification. During subsequent discussions, the division personnel and the audit team discovered an error due to the use of total shipment other than castable shipment. The revised amount is $9.8 million each year instead of $11 million.

4. We agree that the proposed $50 million expenditure would eliminate any need for a fume exhaust system expenditure. The request assumes that 90% of products will be cast, whereas today only 50% are cast. If the division is unable to cast a large percentage of products, the slab mill will operate at higher levels than projected in the request. As a result, the division might require the fume exhaust system expenditure at some later date.

5. The amount of the projected capital expenditure includes cost escalation from the program request date to the engineering completion date but does not provide for any inflation during the construction period, which is estimated to add $6.4 million to the cost. This treatment of inflation is consistent with past practice. The request has penalized its return by showing $1.5 million of start-up expense in the first year. We believe, and the division management agrees, that such expenses should be spread equally over three years.

Preapproval audit team: Strategy manager
Research manager   Operations manager
Marketing services manager   Finance manager (chairman)

Rejected	5
Approved with modification	5
Approved partially	2
Approved as submitted	8

Whether the five rejected projects would have been turned down in the absence of audits is difficult to say, but we strongly believe that they influenced the thinking of top management. The approval of five other projects after modification is testimony to the impact of the audits on division managers.

Audit Guidelines

As use of the preapproval audit technique grew, the Armco organization developed guidelines for it. They have been especially helpful for first-time team members. Here they are, somewhat altered for publication.

1. The audit should begin no later than five weeks prior to the date of the top management meeting at which approval of the project is to be considered. This span will allow a maximum of three weeks to complete the audit and submit the results. Adherence to this schedule is essential not only for completion of a thorough audit but also for proper evaluation of the results.

2. A preapproval audit should not begin unless a final program request document has been completed and approved by the division president. Deviation from this practice and the timetable requirements should be permitted only when the size, complexity, and/ or strategic importance of the project indicate that a preapproval audit performed concurrently with the development of the program request would be more advantageous.

3. When the preapproval audit team is appointed, a deadline for the report should be established to conform with the previously mentioned timetable. The report deadline and the timetable should be spelled out in the appointment letter sent to each team member.

4. The preapproval audit team should consist of three to five members (including the team chairman), though larger teams may be appointed for audits of projects that are unusual in scope or circumstance. The core team would normally consist of members of the marketing, technology (engineering and/or research), and finance

functional areas. Members of other functional areas, such as strategy, operations, economic research, and industrial engineering, should be included when the project warrants. Members of top management should not serve on the team.

5. In the selection process particular attention should be paid to candidates' experience in their functional areas, particularly experience in review and analysis techniques. Team members should have the authority within their functional areas or departments to use the resources of those departments when necessary for successful completion of the audit. Members need not serve full-time, but their departments should expect to make them available for special projects.

6. The person selected for participation on a preapproval audit team should be analytical, independent, objective, and broad-minded and should have good judgment. Knowledge of the project's product or processes is helpful but not a necessary condition for selection. It is recommended, however, that the individual who is appointed chairman of the team have participated in a preapproval audit and have attained at least the professional level of manager.

7. The audit process is a review of the validity and reasonableness of the assumptions and factors that are essential to the proposed project's success. The key areas common to most investment projects are:

Capital investment—Cost estimate, process feasibility, and capacity.

Market—Size of the served market rather than of the aggregate market, positioning in the market, sales volume and price, competitors' activities, and consistency of program projections with other forecasts.

Financials—Conformity with the company's policies and standards and reasonableness of cost and margin projections.

Strategy—Market penetration strategies and fit with division and corporate strategic plans.

Risk and sensitivity analysis—Appropriateness of application and interpretation of results.

8. These areas and others determined by the preapproval audit team should be reviewed for the reasonableness of the assumptions and data used as a basis for projections. Documentation of existing

business and supporting materials for forecasts should come under scrutiny. The audit team should check whether all claims and justifications for the project are fully documented and readily measurable. Doing so will ensure that the project can be post-audited should it be approved and undertaken.

9. The division where the project originates should provide the information and documentation necessary to support the assumptions and data contained in the program request. The preapproval audit team should use outside sources of information where possible to ascertain the reasonableness of the originating division's supporting data and to identify any omission of material factors that could affect the performance of the project. If the division's personnel take an inactive role in completion of the audit, they will further the independence and objectivity of the preapproval audit process.

10. If material disagreements about the substance of the program request develop between the originating unit and the audit team, the two parties can try to resolve the dispute during the audit process. The originating unit is under no obligation, however, to make any changes the team suggests.

11. On completion of the preapproval audit, the team chairman should coordinate and prepare an audit report detailing the findings. The format of the report should be coordinated where possible with the program request. The report length can be held to two or three pages in most circumstances, with supporting documentation placed in an appendix.

12. The primary objective of the report is to validate the reasonableness of the key assumptions and data used in the project justification. Therefore, the report should have no explicit recommendation to accept or reject the proposed project. That is the role of top management.

13. The report should highlight serious disagreements over justification of the project, whether resolved or not, between the originating unit and the audit team. Immaterial issues not affecting the investment decision—if, for example, the format is not in compliance with the request approval manual—can be relegated to an appendix.

14. The chairman may sign the final audit report on behalf of the entire team. If its members disagree strongly about a material aspect of the program request, the minority may attach its own report to the document.

15. Before the report is distributed, the chairman should review it with the head of the originating unit. It is the chairman's responsibility to get the report into the hands of top management at least a week before its meeting to consider the project for approval.

Check and Balance

Inevitably, friction has occasionally developed when differences arise between partisans of a particular proposal and members of the audit team. But difficulties are smoothed over because of the respect that the preapproval audit procedure has built up and the backing that top management has given it.

As might be expected, the proposers of a project take great pains in preparing their case. Often they call on expertise within the company for data and informal opinion on the feasibility of their project; they know the project will be scrutinized formally later anyway.

For their part, the members of the audit team have the resources of the organization on call to help them in their evaluation. They may ask the economic research function for market growth data or the treasury function for information on interest rates. Outside Armco, the team may get help from such resources as consultants, trade associations, and government agencies.

So the preapproval audit system serves effectively at Armco as a check and balance. It makes capital budgeting more orderly and more effective because it obliges profit center staff to furnish thorough analysis and documentation on behalf of proposals and gives top management an independent evaluation that aids decision making.

4

Assessing Capital Risk: You Can't Be Too Conservative

Jasper H. Arnold III

In the summer of 1981, the top officers of the Cloud Tool Company, a large oil-field equipment manufacturer, were nervous about borrowing $15 million from their bank to finance a large plant expansion. They had chosen this investment over several smaller ones because it would enable the company to hold onto, or even raise, its share of the rapidly growing, and continually profitable, energy market. To ensure that the company was not assuming too much risk, the financial staff did a worst case forecast. The forecast showed that—even under adverse circumstances—the company had enough cash to repay the debt.

By late 1982, management nervousness had turned to fear. The oil business had fallen into a severe recession, the company had reported large losses, and cash generation had dropped. A principal payment on the bank loan was due at the end of the year, and the finance VP had projected that the company would not have enough cash on hand. A default would mean that the bank could foreclose on the pledged assets or force an involuntary bankruptcy. Only then did the managers realize that their worst case scenario had been much too optimistic. If they had opted for a more modest expansion, the existence of their company probably would not be in jeopardy.

Many managers don't realize that when they finance a large expansion project with debt, they may be assuming far too much risk. High profit potential, personal commitment to the project, or faith in the industry can hamper executives' vision of the future. They want it to be rosy, so they avoid acknowledging that a crisis could occur. But if the project incurs large losses, the company's financial resources and flexibility can waste away. At the extreme, the company can fail. A critical part of capital budgeting should be a realistic—worst case analysis.

When a company gets into trouble, lending banks do a staying power analysis. It is a conservative way to assess the company resources available to repay loans under distressed circumstances. To see how well their company could withstand financial setbacks, managers can also use this method before embarking on a capital expansion program. Then if they want to bet the company, at least they know that's what they're doing.

As a banker at a large New York bank and now at a regional bank in Texas, I have been involved in the financing of many capital expenditure programs. I have also turned down requests. In every case, I have heard management justify the investment and have seen the supporting analysis. Over time, I have seen the outcomes of their decisions. These experiences have taught me that:

Most large capital expenditure programs encounter large problems. These problems can be financially destructive if the company has invested on too grand a scale.

Without a realistic worst case scenario, managers often don't appreciate the amount of risk their companies assume.

Staying power analysis helps managers both evaluate worst case performance and decide on a project's size.

When undertaking a large expansion program, management usually acknowledges that it might face some short-term reversals or minor problems, but it generally is convinced that nothing serious will happen and that the project will succeed. This optimism is unjustified. In fact, most projects—more than 50% by my estimate—encounter big setbacks. A Rand Corporation study found that the first construction-cost estimate of process plants involving new technology was usually less than half of the final cost, and many projects experience even worse performance. Research using PIMS data revealed that more than 80% of the new projects studied failed to achieve their market-share targets.[1]

My experience and discussions with other bankers and executives show that in at least one out of five projects, managers regret their investments because of large or persistent losses. An aircraft manufacturer, for example, undertook production of a new commercial jetliner. Its major subcontractor went bankrupt, and there was insufficient demand for the jetliner. The company suffered large losses and eventually had to terminate production. I have seen examples like this in the defense contracting, chemical, and microcomputer industries as well.

When Worst Cases Look Too Good

Today's complex and treacherous business environment raises the chance that a company will encounter trouble. My experience in the last decade with companies in the energy industry motivated me, in large part, to write this article. What occurred there vividly illustrates the business environment's instability and the difficulties this creates in capital budgeting.

After the Arab oil embargo of 1973, the oil business enjoyed the strongest boom in its history. It lasted until the end of 1981 when the posted price of OPEC crude peaked at $34 per barrel. Companies made tremendous investments aimed at finding more oil and gas, and they financed many of these investments with debt. Some companies did implement smaller capital expenditure programs, but many leaned toward large, ambitious projects because of the tantalizing profits and the seemingly permanent nature of the boom.

In early 1982, the bubble burst. Because of the worldwide glut of oil and natural gas, OPEC had to cut prices. The oil companies reduced their exploration activity, and a cataclysmic decline in profits ensued. A large number of companies went bankrupt, and many still teeter on the brink with cash flows barely above the level required to service debt.

The severely troubled energy companies share a common experience: management made capital expenditures that were far too large for the company's size, and it financed them with debt. When earnings are strong, companies may be able to service a large amount of debt, but when business activity and cash flow drop, principal and interest payments can be so large that the company cannot operate for long without defaulting on a loan. Under these circumstances, companies have little time to cut expenses or sell assets to generate cash, and lenders are usually unwilling to advance additional funds to companies they already view as too highly leveraged.

Cloud Tool Company's story is fairly typical. Its top management ignored a business tenet: the bigger the project, the more money it will lose if it gets in trouble. To make large capital expenditures, a business must be able to sustain large losses, either through earnings from other products or, if the company is undiversified, through a large equity base that can absorb the losses and still comfort the lenders by protecting their loans.

Unfortunately, the oil industry's experience is not unusual. The sky has fallen on many industries—textile manufacturing, chemical production, cement manufacturing, commercial real estate development, and home computer manufacturing—just when managers thought they had found the pot of gold at the end of the rainbow. Unstable energy cartels, rapid technological change, deregulation of protected industries, aggressive foreign competition, industry recessions, and legions of professional managers who are well schooled in exploiting their companies' strengths and attacking their competitors' weaknesses contribute to this uncertainty.

Most companies support large capital expenditure programs with a worst case analysis that examines the project's loss potential. But the worst case forecast is almost always too optimistic. When problems occur, the financial results are usually much worse than the predictions. When managers look at the downside, they generally describe a mildly pessimistic future rather than the worst possible future.

A worst case analysis conventionally entails preparing a pessimistic cash flow forecast to determine if operations can generate enough cash to repay debt according to its contractual terms. But this approach has some problems. First, a very pessimistic analysis often reveals that the company cannot service the debt at all, especially if the project is large for the company's size. This unhappy result tends to bias the forecaster toward only mild pessimism when divining the future. Second, cash flow from operations is not necessarily the only source of cash for debt repayment during hard times; lenders will sometimes make additional loans or defer payments on existing debt. Finally, this approach does not indicate the costs of such lender assistance because it is not conducted from a lender's standpoint.

Staying power analysis is a better way to do a worst case forecast. When a borrower gets into financial trouble, bankers employ this technique to see how much additional money they can advance to cover cash deficits or if it would be prudent to defer principal payments until the company's health improves. Management can use staying power analysis to determine if the company can avoid a default on loans or other obligations and thereby avoid an involuntary bankruptcy, a lawsuit for payment, or a foreclosure on pledged assets. The technique can also help managers decide on the appropriate size of an important capital expenditure.

LENDER'S PERSPECTIVE

To conduct a staying power analysis, a manager must understand the lender's viewpoint. A cardinal rule of credit is to have two sources of repayment. The primary source of repayment is always the business's operating cash flow. If the most likely forecast shows that this source is inadequate, the lender will usually not make the loan. The secondary source of repayment is the liquidation value of assets; it comes into play when the company gets into trouble and can only generate a very low—or negative—cash flow.

If a company actually begins to show losses, however, and can't service debt from internal sources, lenders do not like to liquidate assets. Liquidation values are uncertain, and a forced bankruptcy or foreclosure is expensive and time-consuming and may tarnish the lender's competitive image. Lenders would rather work with management to keep the company alive so that repayment can ultimately come from cash generation. Such accommodations, however, are by no means automatic and may be costly. Lenders must have confidence in management's ability and must believe that the company has a good chance of returning to profitability. They must believe that the liquidation value of the assets representing their collateral is, or soon will be, equal to or greater than their outstanding loans. If asset coverage is inadequate, lenders are prone to move immediately against the assets before more losses further reduce their value.

The borrowing base is the maximum loan value that lenders ascribe to the company's assets. It is critical to staying power analysis. Here are some fairly representative borrowing-base values of assets normally considered acceptable collateral: accounts receivable are worth 80% of carrying value; inventory is worth 50% of carrying value; and land, buildings, and equipment are worth 90% of "orderly liquidation value" (the amount that could be realized in a piecemeal sale of the assets after a diligent search for interested buyers and an effort at negotiating a favorable price).

Accounts receivable must be fairly current and owed by financially sound companies. The type of inventory affects the amount of credit it will support. Commodity raw materials, such as petrochemical resins or steel scrap, have a readily determined market value and can be assigned a fairly high advance rate—usually 60% to 75% of cost. Finished goods such as consumer durables, where style is not a factor, or standard steel shapes may be similarly treated. Specialty raw materials or finished goods with a narrow market will have only a 25% to 50% advance rate. Work-in-process inventory rarely has any borrowing value.

Lenders frequently use outside appraisers to value fixed assets. In times of distress, lenders will usually advance 80% to 90% of orderly liquidation value. For analysis purposes, these values should be very low for special-purpose equipment or for large, special-purpose manufacturing plants that would have a limited resale value if an industry got into serious trouble or if a new manufacturing technology failed. Twenty-five to thirty cents on the cost dollar is not unreasonable. Your banker will confirm that such assets have sold for less.

Analyze Staying Power

To illustrate how staying power analysis works, I will use the example of Acme Fabrication Company, an industrial product manufacturer. It reported 1985 sales of $35.1 million and net profits of $1.9 million. In early 1986, management was considering making a large addition to its plant that it hoped would dramatically raise sales. If it made the addition immediately, the cost of the fixed assets would be $12 million. The company could arrange financing in the form of a five-year bank term loan to be repaid in equal annual installments of principal.

Management also had the option of making the investment in phases: $6.5 million in 1986 and then, if things went as expected, another $6.8 million in 1987. Note that for the same amount of capacity the phased expansion was more expensive than the immediate, large investment: $13.3 million versus $12 million. This was because of inflation over two years and the cost economies in constructing and equipping the large-scale project. Another unattractive feature of the phased approach was the prospect of lower sales and earnings over the life of the project relative to the results of the large-scale option because by spending the money in increments the company could not achieve certain production and marketing economies.

The same bank would provide all existing and new debt, and the loans would initially be unsecured. The company had a $6.5 million line of credit at this bank and $3.9 million was outstanding in the form of notes payable.

Both options were analyzed from a strategic standpoint and were found acceptable. The company also used discounted cash flow hurdles, and both alternatives met the minimum standard.

DESCRIBE A HOSTILE ENVIRONMENT. Begin the staying power analysis by forecasting the financial performance that would result from the most hostile environment that might *reasonably* occur. I emphasize the word "reasonably" because one can paint such a bleak picture that survival is impossible. While not a pleasant task, describing a disaster scenario is fairly simple. For Acme, the chief risks were a steep industry recession and rising steel costs. Since the industry's cyclical swings did not always coincide with the ups and downs of steel prices, management thought that the company might have to contend with rising steel costs during an industry-wide recession.

The forecaster then translates the description of the hostile operating environment into financial results. Nearly every risk predictably shows up in a company's financial statements. The impact of the hostile environment on Acme's statements appears in Exhibit I.

ESTIMATE EROSION POTENTIAL. Quantifying the duration of the bad period and the dollar magnitudes is the hardest part. With experience or good strategic risk analysis, management can usually estimate the range of outcomes for each affected financial statement account. When making these estimates, focus on each account's erosion potential: the most deterioration that might occur in the hostile operating environment. For some financial statement variables, thinking in absolute terms is convenient: "Accounts receivable collection period could conceivably rise to 120 days in a severe recession." For others, using percentages is handier: "Sales could fall by 30% over two years."

Historical results are a good source of information for estimating erosion potential, but a tranquil past often gives false comfort. In dynamic and evolving markets, the future may present obstacles never encountered before. Managers, therefore, should err on the

Exhibit I.   Impact of Hostile Environment on Acme's Financial Statements

Risks	Impact on financial statements
Steep industry recession	Declining prices due to falling unit sales volume and lower selling prices
	Slow inventory turnover due to excess or hard-to-move stock
	Slow accounts receivable collection period due to the effects of the recession on customers
Rising raw materials costs	Rise in cost of goods sold because of higher steel costs and higher per unit manufacturing costs due to lower production volume

conservative side and estimate results much worse than those seen in the past. If the worst historical sales performance has been a 25% drop over two years, management might run the forecast based on a 35% drop. In studying historical data, managers should go 10 or 15 years back if possible. They can also gain insights from studying the results of other companies in the industry.

The executives may have trouble admitting that some worst case scenarios are possible, but history shows that they do often happen. Therefore, if the purpose of the expansion is to turn out a new product, assume that unit sales volume is 60% to 85% of the levels your most likely projections assume. The exact discount will depend on the amount of market research and testing done, the competition's ability to retaliate or otherwise preclude you from achieving the anticipated market share, and other factors that might affect the risk of buyer acceptance.

If the purpose of the expansion is to employ new production technology, do what bankers do: run your projections assuming that the project never works and that the company must repay its debt from the base business's cash flows. If you ran a successful pilot plant or implemented other risk-reducing measures, assume large cost overruns and a long delay in reaching commercial production levels.

DON'T IGNORE WORKING CAPITAL. Managers without a financial orientation often ignore or drastically underestimate the total amount of money a project ultimately requires. They think in terms of fixed assets—land, building, and equipment—and do not think enough about the additional investment in net working capital. In Acme's case, the large-scale option required a $12 million fixed-asset investment but, as we will see shortly, the amount needed the first year to get the project under way was much more—$19.3 million. The company needed the additional $7.3 million because the new plant caused sales to rise, which led to higher accounts receivable and meant that more inventory had to be carried. A "spontaneous" rise in accounts payable and accrued liabilities automatically supplied part of the financing to support this, but an external source had to fund the balance. For most companies this source is debt, which increases leverage and, therefore, risk.

INCLUDE COST-CUTTING EFFORTS. The forecaster must also anticipate what cash conservation programs the company would implement when financially distressed. Management would probably make these decisions:

Cut selling, general, and administrative (SG&A) expenses.

Sell marketable securities.

Reduce inventory levels.

Cut the dividend.

Reduce capital expenditures.

Sell unnecessary assets.

Delay paying vendors.

The company can only go so far with some of these actions. In preparing financial forecasts, managers often assume that sales drive many balance sheet and income statement accounts. For example, if sales drop 10%, they assume a 10% decline in accounts receivable, inventory, selling, and general and administrative expenses. But when companies get into trouble this is usually not the case, especially at the onset of financial difficulty. Unsure how severe the situation will get or how long it will last, executives hesitate to reduce inventories or to cut SG&A expenses. And the company's financial condition has to deteriorate dramatically before management will consider firing people.

The same is true about cutting the dividend. Management wants to protect sensitive stockholders and show the stock market that all is well. Capital expenditures may not be easy to reduce either. Equipment-purchase or construction contracts may have been signed months before the problems arose, or the manufacturing process may ruin the equipment so that it must be frequently replaced. So it's best to assume that any big cuts will be delayed and slow to take effect. Moreover, SG&A expenses and capital spending cannot be cut beyond a certain point, and the sales force may be unable to get rid of excessive inventories if the bottom falls out of the market.

One more reality of hard times needs mentioning. I have seen many forecasts in which managers try to reflect a worst case scenario and assume a drop in sales but hold gross margins about in line with historical levels. In most industry recessions, what actually happens is this: declining sales volume stimulates price cutting, and as excess production capacity rises, price cutting becomes rampant as companies try to generate orders that at least cover out-of-pocket costs; as production is reduced to reflect the drop in sales, unit costs rise as fixed costs are spread over fewer units. The impact of this on gross profits is magnified because the falling sales prices and the rising unit costs squeeze the margin on each unit sold, and the company sells fewer units. To make matters worse, the company's customers usually take longer to pay because either they have the power of a buyer's market or they are also hurt by the recession and try to conserve cash.

Acme created its forecasts from these types of assumptions. Based on current backlog and market strength, management thought it reasonable to expect a good year in 1986 followed by a steep, two-year recession with drastically falling sales, shrinking profit margins, and a slowdown in inventory and receivables turnover. The company made the assumption that payables would be stretched and marketable securities sold to generate cash, but that it would delay big cuts in SG&A expenses and capital expenditures until 1988.

Exhibit II shows the staying power analysis for the large-scale project. The top part is the forecast income statement. A $1.5 million loss occurs in 1987 followed by a severe loss of $4.4 million in 1988; thereafter the company returns to profitability.

Exhibit II. **Acme's Staying Power Analysis for a Large Project**
in millions of dollars*

		Actual	Projected				
		1985	1986	1987	1988	1989	1990
Income statement	Income and expenses						
	Net sales	$35.1	$61.1	$53.0	$43.0	$53.0	$56.0
	Cost of goods sold	24.6	44.5	43.4	39.4	40.9	42.4
	Gross profit	10.5	16.6	9.6	3.6	12.1	13.6
	Selling, general, and administrative expense	5.5	9.6	9.6	9.1	7.6	7.6
	Interest expense	1.5	2.9	2.8	2.6	2.4	2.0
	Profit before tax	3.5	4.1	−2.8	−8.1	2.1	4.0
	Income taxes	1.6	1.9	−1.3	−3.7	1.0	1.8
	Net income	**1.9**	**2.3**	**−1.5**	**−4.4**	**1.1**	**2.2**
Balance sheet	Assets						
	Cash and marketable securities	$ .4	$ .4	$ .3	$ .3	$ .3	$ .3
	Accounts receivable	5.8	10.0	9.1	7.7	9.0	9.2
	Inventory	8.8	15.3	15.0	14.5	14.0	14.5
	Current assets	**15.0**	**25.7**	**24.4**	**22.5**	**23.3**	**24.0**
	Net fixed assets	17.5	26.1	23.7	20.8	17.9	15.0
	Total assets	**32.5**	**51.8**	**48.1**	**43.3**	**41.2**	**39.0**

Liabilities and stockholders' equity	Accounts payable and accrued liabilities	4.7	8.2	8.4	8.2	8.5	8.9
	Current maturities of long-term debt	1.0	3.4	3.4	3.4	3.4	3.4
	Notes payable (existing)	3.9	3.9	3.9	3.9	3.9	3.9
	Additional short-term debt	—	2.5	3.6	6.7	6.6	5.3
	Current liabilities	**9.6**	**18.0**	**19.3**	**22.2**	**22.4**	**21.5**
	Long-term debt	9.0	17.6	14.2	10.8	7.4	4.0
	Stockholders' equity	13.9	16.2	14.6	10.2	11.4	13.6
	Total liabilities and stockholders' equity	**32.5**	**51.8**	**48.1**	**43.3**	**41.2**	**39.0**
Sources and uses of cash	**Sources**						
	Net income		$ 2.3	$ −1.5	$ −4.4	$ 1.1	$ 2.2
	Depreciation		3.4	3.4	3.4	3.4	3.4
	Total sources		**5.7**	**1.9**	**−1.0**	**4.5**	**5.6**
	Uses						
	Capital expenditures		12.0	1.0	.5	.5	.5
	Long-term debt repayment		1.0	3.4	3.4	3.4	3.4
	Change in net working capital†		7.3	−1.5	−1.7	.5	.4
	Total uses		**20.3**	**2.9**	**2.2**	**4.4**	**4.3**

Cash flow before external financing (S-U)	-14.6	-1.0	-3.2	.1	1.3
+ New long-term debt or stock	12.0	—	—	—	—
+ Increase (decrease) in additional short-term debt and notes payable (existing)	2.5	1.0	3.2	-.1	-1.3
Change in cash and marketable securities	-.1	0	0	0	0
Borrowing base‡	$28.7	$26.7	$23.8	$23.2	$22.1
- Required indebtedness§	27.4	25.1	24.8	21.3	16.6
Excess (deficient) borrowing base	1.3	1.6	-1.0	1.9	5.5

Borrowing base analysis

* Columns may not add up to total because of rounding.

† Except cash and marketable securities, notes payable (existing), additional short-term debt, and current maturities of long-term debt.

‡ Calculated using year-end balance sheet values: 80% of accounts receivable plus 50% of inventory plus 50% of net fixed assets.

§ The total required borrowings at year end: current maturities of long-term debt plus notes payable (existing) plus additional short-term debt plus long-term debt.

Four Questions

Acme's management must now assess the impact of this worst case scenario on the company's solvency. Does the company have enough staying power to get through the bad years of 1987 and 1988 without a creditor-initiated legal action? Four questions must be answered.

DO WE NEED EXTERNAL FINANCING TO GET THROUGH THE BAD PERIOD? The best outcome, of course, would be to generate enough cash from internal sources to service debt and cover the losses during the downturn. Some companies with floundering projects may be able to do this if: (1) the company is not highly leveraged; (2) the project, while large in absolute dollar terms, is small relative to the company's size; or (3) the project's cash flows are inversely correlated with the cash flows of the base business so that if the project goes bad, the base business can still generate enough cash. Under such circumstances, the company does not have to seek external financing or request deferrals of principal payments. This position indicates a high degree of staying power and suggests that the project does not create excessive risk.

The additional short-term debt line on the balance sheet (as shown in Exhibit II) tells the story. It is the forecasting "plug number" that makes the balance sheet balance. The number rises when the company operates at a cash flow deficit and must obtain external debt financing. It falls when the company generates surplus cash and repays the debt. In Acme's case, the figure takes a big jump to $2.5 million in 1986, a profitable year, because the company must boost its current assets to support the new sales the plant expansion generates. The company obtains this amount by drawing under its line of credit, which would then be fully used.

Then in 1987 and 1988, the problem years, the company needs $4.2 million more in short-term borrowings because of the losses and the repayment of long-term debt. Thus if the worst case scenario came to pass, Acme would have to get the bank's assistance.

DO LENDERS HAVE TO SUPPLY ANY "NET NEW MONEY"? Banks and other lenders are more willing to work with a troubled borrower if they do not have to raise their risk exposure. Provided that the company has minimal collateral coverage—one dollar of borrowing base for each dollar loaned—they view their existing loans as spilled milk that they hope eventually to recover from cash flow after the borrower has returned to profitability. Under such circumstances, lenders will usually advance funds to make payments on other debts owed to them or, more likely, defer the payments.

But if a forecast shows that, in spite of attempts to conserve cash, the company must still seek net new financing, then the risks may appear too high. Banks and other lenders do not see themselves as suppliers of money to finance losses; equity capital does that. Nor do they like to advance money to a severely troubled company so that it can repay other lenders.

While bankers will occasionally advance limited amounts of new funds, forecasters are foolish to presume that the bank will be willing to raise its loss exposure. The conservative forecaster should not expect to get net new money unless the company has a legally binding revolving credit commitment and the forecast shows that no restrictive covenants would be broken that would permit the bank to cancel the commitment. Draws should be assumed under a nonlegally binding line of credit only during the first year of a problem period because these credits are renewable at yearly intervals at the bank's option. The draws should be covered at least one-to-one by the borrowing base since the bank, which is only morally bound under a line of credit, could refuse the draw requests unless the company has collateral coverage.

Acme borrows from one bank, so even though additional short-term debt rises in 1987 and 1988, the decline in required indebtedness (shown at the bottom of Exhibit II) means that the short-term bank loans merely furnish the cash to repay the bank's long-term debt on time. Thus the bank does not have to supply any net new money. In reality, the bank would probably defer the principal payments on the long-term debt. Its willingness to support Acme will depend on Acme's having minimal collateral coverage.

CAN THE COMPANY STAY IN COMPLIANCE WITH ITS BORROWING BASE? At the bottom of Exhibit II is the borrowing base analysis, which shows how much debt Acme's assets will support. The analysis shows that the company lacks the staying power to survive. It would need to incur maximum borrowings (required indebtedness) in 1988 of $24.8 million, but it can only support debt of $23.8 million. Thus if Acme implements the large-scale expansion and encounters very hard times, it could not count on lender support when debts and other obligations come due. Acme could face an involuntary bankruptcy or other legal action. It should, therefore, reject this expansion option as too risky.

WHAT ARE THE COSTS OF LENDER ASSISTANCE? Lender assistance may take several forms depending on the situation: loans under existing credit commitments, deferrals of principal payments, or advances of new money outside existing commitments. At the least, the costs of this assistance will include tougher loan terms:

A pledge of collateral if loans are unsecured or additional collateral if they are already secured.

Guarantees of repayment by subsidiaries.

The owners' personal guarantees if the company is privately held.

New covenants that tightly control or eliminate various cash drains: dividend payments, capital expenditures, and outside investments.

An interest rate increase.

In addition to these changes in loan terms, as a lender's risk of loss grows, it will usually pressure management or the board of directors to reduce expenses (that is, cut head count) and sell assets to generate cash, seek a buyer for the company, or replace management.

The following guidelines will help managers gauge the costs of lender assistance:

Demands for more stringent loan terms start if company losses persist past three or four quarters, especially if the company violates a restrictive covenant in a loan agreement. But a high borrowing base coverage will postpone or minimize these demands.

Regardless of borrowing base coverage, if losses continue more than two years, lender demands will be heard, and unless coverage is high, the lender will apply some pressure.

If principal deferrals are necessary, expect the full range of demands and expect pressure to be brought to bear. If the borrowing base coverage is low or losses are large, the resulting pressure can be intense.

When the company's committed credit facilities are fully used and it still needs new money, the lender may exert intense pressures and deny the loan requests. Such denials will usually lead to a default on one or more obligations.

Acme did a staying power analysis on phase one of the $6.5 million small-scale expansion. Additional short-term debt would be necessary in 1987 and 1988. Even though earnings were considerably less than in the large-scale option, since less debt had to be repaid, the company had an adequate borrowing base to survive the recession. The total borrowing requirement was $18.6 million in 1988; it was narrowly covered by a borrowing base of $19.5 million. Acme would need additional short-term debt in 1987 and 1988 to repay existing long-term bank debt, that is, a principal deferral. In exchange for this assistance, management should expect intense demands and pressures since the losses would be long lasting and the borrowing base coverage would be low.

The Decision

The type of lender assistance, if any, needed during the problem years plus the borrowing base coverage tell whether a capital-spending program would leave the company with enough staying power to avoid creditors calling a default and demanding payment during hard times. Exhibit III shows how to determine if a company has enough staying power.

Going ahead with a project that has insufficient staying power means risking the entire company. Even if the analysis reveals sufficient staying power, management still needs to consider:

The likelihood of the worst case scenario becoming a reality.

The costs of any needed lender assistance.

Management's attitude toward outside interference.

The strategic necessity of the investment.

The potential profitability of the investment.

Since Acme's survival would not be at risk, management might well accept the small-scale option with the intention of embarking on phase two in a year if things go as planned.

A short aside: a company with publicly held bonds usually has less staying power than a company that relies on bank debt and privately placed bonds. If we change the Acme example and assume that the long-term debt was in the form of public bonds, then Acme's bank would have to loan the additional short-term debt that results in the analysis of the small-scale option because arranging principal deferrals on publicly held debt is extremely difficult. Thus Acme's

Exhibit III.   Assessing Staying Power

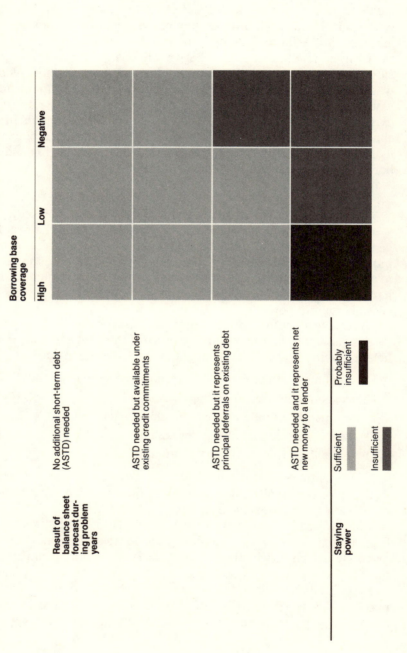

bank would be called on to supply substantial net new money, and it would probably refuse because of the low borrowing base coverage. The conclusion of the analysis would change: the $6.5 million small-scale project is also too risky.

In the late summer of 1981, an oil-field supply company I handled made a large loan request. As part of my due diligence work, I made a telephone survey of executives at some 20 companies involved in various aspects of the energy business to obtain their forecast of drilling activity. The people I called were high-ranking officials at major oil companies, drilling contractors, and large oil-field equipment manufacturers. Virtually every one said that drilling would remain strong for two to five years. I made these calls less than six months before the boom ended.

This incident illustrates how wrong bright and experienced business people can be about their companies' and industries' future. No matter how convinced managers may be of a capital expenditure program's profit potential or strategic necessity, they should take a hard look at the project's downside to make sure the company does not assume an imprudent amount of risk. Staying power analysis is a good way to do this.

Note

1. David Davis, "New Projects: Beware of False Economies," HBR March–April 1985, p. 95.

PART

II

Organizing

1
How to Set Up
a Project Organization

C. J. Middleton

Lockheed Aircraft Corporation uses project management at its Puget Sound shipbuilding facility for new ship contracts and conversion contracts. Functional departments do the work, but project managers see to it that assigned projects are completed on schedule, within budget, and in conformance with specifications.

Avco Corporation assigns project managers at its Research and Advanced Development Division to two types of activities: space systems and ballistic missile reentry systems. Project managers maintain total program control, assisted by a staff of technical, administration, and functional department personnel.

General Dynamics Corporation established a project organization at the Fort Worth Division for accomplishing the F-111A and F-111B aircraft programs. At the same time management beefed up the B-58 bomber project organization. Why? To ensure proper managerial attention and support in providing spare parts and services for B-58's already delivered or to be delivered to the customer.

Three companies—The Boeing Company, Douglas Aircraft Company, and Lockheed—set up extensive project organizations for their competition for the C5A transport aircraft program. Large numbers of employees were hired, transferred, or borrowed from other jobs to devote full time to the competition effort. When Lockheed won the award, the other companies disbanded their project organizations.

These examples show that companies are finding it advantageous to establish project organizations for handling such special assignments as developing a new product, building a factory, and investigating departures from their traditional business.

This article explains the aims of management in setting up project units, the varieties of forms they have taken, the problems of dividing assignments with functional segments of companies, and the techniques of forming the work force. It also discusses the costs of project organizations and the possible temporary or lasting effects of these organizations on companies.

Criteria for Use

Typically, a project organization is responsible for completing an assigned objective on schedule, within cost and profit goals, and to established standards. The objective is usually one requiring special management attention and emphasis for a long period of time. Projects lasting only a few weeks or months, however, can be accomplished with a minimum of disruption by teams or task forces. A team or task force borrows employees from existing company organizations, but jobs are not held open elsewhere in a company for project organization personnel.

Generally, the project approach can be effectively applied to a one-time undertaking that is:

- Definable in terms of a specific goal.
- Infrequent, unique, or unfamiliar to the present organization.
- Complex with respect to interdependence of detail task accomplishment.
- Critical to the company because of the threat of loss or serious penalty.[1]

The one-time undertaking often involves a new product, where the emphasis is on research, development, testing, and production. Although such an effort is mainly developmental, the project manager cannot ignore the ultimate marketability of his product any more than a product manager can ignore the development of products which he is marketing.

IMPORTANT ROLE

The traditional functional form of organization is based on the premise that there will be a continuous flow of products or services, with substantial similarity in the performed tasks. Functional organizations often cannot accomplish unusually complex or markedly different projects because of these conditions:

No one in a functional organization besides the company or division manager is entirely responsible for project costs and profits. Functional department executives are concerned only with doing specialized work within budget.

Functional departments often are jealous of their prerogatives, and fight to promote and preserve their specialties rather than work toward a unified project objective.

The total perspective of a project is lost among functional departments. They can be guilty of "tunnel vision"—that is, a concern for only their own portions of the task without regard for the impact of their actions on the company and on the project.

More and faster decision making is required on a new project, and it is slowed by passing interdepartmental problems to the top through all levels of functional departments. This process often delays important project decisions or prevents them from being made.

Functional departments performing repetitive tasks often lack the flexibility and responsiveness necessary to cope with new and rapidly changing project requirements.

The project organization can provide the arrangement, emphasis, and control necessary to counteract any weaknesses, functional or otherwise, that could impair successful completion of the project.

WIDE RESPONSIBILITY

To be able to wield total control, a project organization must be responsible for:

1. *Product Definition*—Define or direct the definition of products to be developed in terms of hardware, software, and services, including standards for performance, quality, reliability, and maintainability.
2. *Task and Funds Control*—Assign tasks and allocate funds to all groups performing the tasks and/or procuring hardware and services for the project.
3. *Make-or-Buy Decisions*—Coordinate analyses of company capabilities, capacities, and efficiencies, and make final decisions on whether the company supplies or buys hardware and services for the project. Participate in selection of major sources.

4. *Scheduling*—Develop master project schedules and coordinate schedule requirements with affected company organizations, associate subcontractors, and customers.

5. *Project Status*—Establish status-reporting systems and continuously monitor project expenditures, schedules, task completions, cost to complete, and deliveries.

6. *Identification and Solution of Problem*—Identify problems significant to project success and initiate action to solve them.

7. *Project Change Control*—Approve and exercise control over all project changes, including design changes.

8. *Associate or Subcontract Control*—Have control of major subcontractors involved in team arrangements on major tasks.

9. *Customer and Public Relations*—Serve as the outside contact for the project.

10. *Market Potentials*—Maintain awareness of customer attitudes, customer desires, and any other factors which could affect the project. Develop plans for logical follow-up action, potential or new applications, or new versions of the project hardware or services.

All of the above controls are required for a product design-development effort. Not all of them are needed for other types of projects, but all essential controls must be in the hands of the project organization if it is wholly accountable for results.

Organization Table

The size of an organization needed to exercise project control can vary from one person to several thousand employees organized by departments, sections, and groups. In all cases, however, management must appoint one person as the project head.

KINDS OF PROJECT UNITS

The organization structure and the elements needed for project control are governed by the desires of top management and by company and project circumstances:

An *individual* project organization consists of only one person—the project manager. He exercises project control through the functional departments performing all the work on the project. No activities or personnel (except clerical support) report directly to him.

In a *staff* project organization, the project manager is provided a staff to exercise control through activities such as scheduling, task and funds supervision, and change control, and to carry out any functions unique to the project, like testing or site activation. Functional departments still perform the primary tasks of engineering, procurement, and manufacturing.

An *intermix* project organization is established when some of the primary functions are removed from functional departments and are assigned to report directly to the project manager, along with staff functions.

Under an *aggregate* organization, all departments and activities required to accomplish a project report directly to the project manager.

A project organization can change radically in form during its lifetime. For example:

One aerospace company formed an individual project organization, supported by a team of representatives borrowed from functional departments, during the proposal stage. After the company received the contract award, it created an intermix organization which included engineering and manufacturing for the development phase. After starting the production phase, the company reduced the group to a staff-type for production and all follow-on contracts.

A project organization can also be the beginning of an organization cycle. The project may become a long-term or permanent effort that eventually becomes a program or branch organization. The latter in turn may become separated from the parent organization and be established as a full-fledged product division, functionally organized. Then management may create a series of new project organizations within the new product division, starting the cycle over again.

SUPERVISORY LIMITS

Large unit size, particularly in the cases of intermix or aggregate groups, may cause the manager to lose personal control over the project, forcing him to rely more on formal organization and procedures. With a staff of 100 or more, he must create a formal structure with written outlines of responsibility. Except in the case of the aggregate project unit, the project manager must rely on support and services from functional organizations. His degree of authority and his relationship to functional departments therefore are critical and must be spelled out to ensure successful use of the concept.

The extent of delegated authority has been established by different companies in different ways. For instance:

1. Project managers in Company A are authorized to direct any department or division to take whatever action is necessary to maintain good program performance, ensure the timely delivery of reliable, qualified products to customers, and encourage follow-on business. Each department performing work on a project appoints a representative who is responsible to the project manager for work done in the department. The project manager is head of an individual project organization and can prescribe to functional departments only what is required on the project and when. How the task is performed remains under the departments' supervision.

2. The project organization exercises overall management of the XXX weapons system for the president of Company B. It translates customer requirements into task definition and assigns the tasks to functional organizations. While no line authority extends from the project manager into the functional departments, he monitors their performance. The functional departments appoint sections or individuals to discharge their responsibilities under XXX project management control. When a new function must be created in order to fulfill unique project requirements, the function is established in the project management unit only if it is not feasible to do it within an existing functional department. This project manager is head of a staff project organization and exercises more authority than the project manager of Company A.

3. A project of major scope is placed in a division of Company C under the direction of a project manager, who reports to the president. The project manager brings together and directs all of the division's functions and resources required for successful completion of the project. The division's functional departments transfer their functions and personnel to the project when it can be done logically, practically, and economically. Those operations that cannot continue in a divided condition remain in the division's functional departments, although the departments still furnish the required services. This is an example of the intermix project organization, and the project manager here has more authority than the project manager from Company B.

Some companies have found that a project manager can adequately control a project—even though none of the organizations working on the project reports directly to him—if he controls the money, sets the schedules, and defines the performance criteria. When the project is on schedule, within cost and profit objectives, and advancing well, everyone is satisfied. If problems arise, the project manager can identify the functional persons who are responsible and make sure they take corrective action—if higher management backs him.

FUNCTIONAL RESPONSE.   Other companies have found that the need for departments reporting directly to the project manager depends on the effectiveness, responsiveness, and attitude of the functional organizations. For example:

> The engineering department in a West Coast aerospace company had a reputation for its expeditious and efficient product designs that met performance specifications. Company management decided that little could be gained by forming an engineering department within the project organization. So the company located the engineering groups near the project manager to shorten lines of communication on product definition, change control, and customer technical coordination. The project manager experienced no difficulty in maintaining project control.

In many companies the project manager's authority is defined in an organization description, but in practice it may be something else. Then he exercises only the limited authority he can acquire by his own devices. Sometimes the project organization has been created at the request of the customer. Functional unit supervisors often dislike the project concept, partly because it superimposes the project manager and his organization on a functional structure that has existed for many years. Most of the managerial know-how and experience is in functional departments, and their supervisors often have difficulty in adjusting to becoming service organizations for the project and relinquishing some of the authority they previously enjoyed.

There are no definite ground rules for determining the extent of project management authority. It must be decided by each company after consideration of project requirements and organizational and managerial strengths. Whatever approach is used, top management can avoid problems by:

1. Delineating the extent of the project manager's authority over the project and in his dealings with functional organizations.
2. Supporting the project manager to enable him to exercise his authority.

Otherwise, the program will be impeded as project managers and functional group managers engage in muscle-flexing and infighting to see who really runs the show.

TASK ALLOCATION

Dividing functions between project and functional organizations when a staff or intermix project group is being formed poses a number of problems. An important factor to be considered is whether leaving the functional unit intact is necessary to maintain company capability. Obviously, some operations, such as machine shops, laboratories, electronic data processing, and accounting, cannot be sensibly divided. An attempt to encompass such activities in the project would create enormous facility or operating problems, and increase project costs significantly.

A better understanding of the problem can be gained by considering the experience of one Southwest aerospace company. Its management wanted to establish certain procurement functions in the project organization, with the object of combining all the elements that affect cost, schedule, and performance in the unit. The company thought it had found a solution in assigning to the project organization the responsibility of procuring major systems and equipment items, while leaving procurement of raw stock and standard hardware to the functional organization. This, however, only settled the issue of who did the buying; it left unanswered which organization would perform other necessary functions. An analysis indicated that it was also necessary to identify those units which would:

- Determine the quantities and source of hardware to be procured.
- Receive and stock shipments from vendors.
- Issue and control inventories in support of manufacturing and customer service activities.

- Procure repair parts and spares to support manufacturing and customer deliveries.
- Conduct pricing, estimating, and make-or-buy analyses on potential procurements.
- Process and negotiate repair of purchased recoverable parts and systems.
- Package and ship items to be delivered or repaired.

One aircraft company with several projects going on at the same time attempted to avoid dividing functions and yet create an inter-mix project organization. Management ordered the engineering department to report to the project organization having the greatest task while it continued to provide service to the other projects. This scheme is objectionable because it

. . . causes major priority problems, except in cases where a company has only one very large project and one or more very small ones;

. . . forces the manager of the largest project to worry about serving other smaller projects, thus defeating the purpose of the project organization.

Some management practitioners have proposed that the project manager be permitted to take his business outside the company if he is dissatisfied with the quality of work of a functional organization on the project. Most companies, however, would hesitate to grant their project managers so much authority. For one reason, the work of the functional unit in question may be necessary to the company's future. Also, a decision by one project manager to sub-contract a task could seriously impair work on other projects by upsetting task loads and causing loss of critical skills. Furthermore, providing facilities and skills to complete existing projects and compete for future ones remains the responsibility of functional departments. Decisions of this kind should be made by the company president, to protect the long-range interests of the company.

Personnel Matters

The project manager is often selected during the proposal phase of an undertaking. In those instances, he plays a major role in determining the project organization's functions and responsibilities. In other cases, top management makes these decisions after the project is initiated, then names the project manager. His first task, and one of his most important tasks, is selecting—and getting—the personnel needed to accomplish the job.

MANAGER'S QUALITIES

It is, of course, essential that the project manager have superior leadership ability. He must have administrative experience in engineering and manufacturing. And he must be skilled in planning, budgeting, scheduling, and other control techniques.[2] A weak project manager cannot be made strong and effective by creating additional controls or a top-heavy project organization structure.

Sometimes a functional executive is designated project manager in addition to his normal duties. In such cases, he must have time available to devote to the project, and care must be taken so that the project does not conflict with his functional responsibilities. Otherwise, the project will suffer from lack of attention or biased decision making.

It must be kept in mind that veteran functional managers cannot be expected to accept direction readily from some lesser executive who is suddenly promoted to project manager. Top management can avoid this problem by:

Selecting a man who already has a high position of responsibility, or placing him high enough in the organization.

Assigning him a title as important-sounding as those of functional unit managers.

Supporting him in his dealings with functional managers.

If the project manager is expected to exercise project control over the functional departments, then he must report to the same level as the department managers, or higher.

STAFFING THE UNIT

Usually the manpower for a project organization comes from functional departments or from other project organizations which are phasing out. The project manager often encounters difficulty, however, in getting the people he wants, because:

1. Several projects may be competing for talent at the same time, and there may not be enough to go around.
2. Functional department executives may be unwilling to make the requested personnel available.
3. The selected employees may be unwilling to transfer.

One project manager found that publicizing his project, mixing in professional societies, and inviting important people to inspect his project were successful techniques for attracting and holding personnel. This indirect approach, however, is more likely to be necessary in attracting talent from other companies in more glamorous industries.

Within a company, the direct approach, in which the project manager discusses his requirements with the functional organization head who has the talent, usually solves the problem. In companies with several ongoing projects, where there are shortages of talent or a particular talent cannot be applied full-time to one project, the best solution may be to leave the talent in a central functional organization to serve all projects.

One of the most serious problems that the project manager may face is the reluctance of employees to join a project organization because they fear that at the completion of the job their employment may be terminated, or they may be transferred to other, less desirable jobs. An employee with a record of good progress and an established reputation in a functional department is likely to turn down an offer to join a project unit; he may be influenced by functional executives' often-held view that the establishment of a project organization is a reflection of inadequate performance on their part. In short, an employee may feel that in leaving the relative stability and security of a functional group he will have burned his bridges behind him and have no "home" to return to at the conclusion of the project.

Another factor affecting an employee's decision is the division of responsibilities between a functional organization and its counterpart in the project organization. A survey conducted by the Aerospace Industries Association revealed that when part of the procurement function has been placed in a project, the functional organization has retained either complete control or partial control of personnel selection and placement, coordination of salary grades, and coordination of salary increases.[3] The employee who becomes a part of the project organization in this circumstance finds that the project manager has little or no control over pay increases and promotions.

Management can do a number of things to encourage employees to transfer to project organizations. For instance, salary increases can be offered to employees as inducements to accept the risks involved. Furthermore, a number of promotional opportunities will usually result from forming a project organization, since additional management structure is being created. The company can make special efforts to relocate personnel phasing out of existing project organizations, and thereby create an atmosphere of security. (Incidentally, if a project manager does not look after his staff during phase-out of a project, he may not get them back on another project.) The use of financial incentives and a policy of "taking care" of people could, however, increase cost excessively.

In many cases, the excitement and glamour of a project with some promise of longevity is all that is needed to attract the personnel required. If the project manager is unable to complete his staffing within the company, he may want to seek talent outside the company.

Cost Considerations

The cost of a project organization varies, of course, according to its size, extent of new facilities and equipment needed, and its duration, among other factors. How much cost control a project manager has, or should have, is sometimes difficult to determine. Here are some aspects of cost worthy of consideration.

GREATER EFFICIENCY

Added cost from reduced manpower utilization is incurred when functions counterpart to those in the project organization continue to exist in the functional groups or in other project units. Dividing the work will cause loss of efficiency, particularly when it involves functions such as program planning, budgeting, and contracts administration, where the task to be accomplished is harder to identify and the performance is harder to measure. (Some companies, to their chagrin, have suffered unwarranted cost resulting from failure to reduce manpower levels in functional units when tasks are transferred to the project group.)

While increases in costs from reduced manpower utilization, from added management, and from expanded facilities probably cannot be avoided, they are likely to be small compared to other project costs. In any case, they may be offset by reduced costs in procurement, engineering, tooling, and manufacturing. For example, one survey of aerospace companies revealed that inclusion of the procurement function in a project organization results in improved performance sufficient to offset the usually higher operating costs.[4] Another survey, which dealt only with the engineering function, reported that 8 out of 19 large companies found that contract overruns had decreased or were eliminated by incorporating the function in project units.[5]

Since it is doubtful whether any company ever has managed identical projects under functional and project forms of organization, a company often finds it difficult to determine the effects on costs from use of the project approach. Nearly always, however, companies find they are exercising better cost control. They are applying more management to the project; tasks and budgets are better defined, changes more rigidly controlled, performance more closely watched; and management initiates action sooner to prevent or correct problems.

MANAGERIAL CONTROLS

While cost control is a key part of managerial supervision of a project, it is not always necessary for the project manager to oversee all expenditures directly. For example:

Company X did not try to give the project manager direct control over costs; instead it established a staff-type project organization. The project manager had control over funds allocation on all matters except burden costs outside the project organization. The various functional departments were incrementally funded for the task in current periods, and the project manager watched project progress to ensure task accomplishment in accordance with funds allocation. The project manager reallocated funds for task changes, but let the functional unit managers worry about controlling costs within the funds allocated. This system worked well for Company X.

Putting all feasible cost matters under the control of the manager while maintaining other project objectives does not always turn out as envisioned. In one situation:

> Company Y gave the project manager as much direct control over costs as possible, while trying to minimize the cost of the project. It established an intermix project organization containing the unique, control, and primary functions that could be divided economically without undue loss of efficiency or without incurring large facility expense. For example, the project manager had total responsibility for subcontract management, but procurement of sheet metal and standard parts was left in the functional material organization. Engineering design was transferred to the project organization, but research laboratories, drawing, and other services were still performed on a centralized basis by the functional units. Other key functions were similarly divided.
>
> After this arrangement was in operation a while, Company Y analyzed its costs and found them to be categorized as shown in Exhibit I. All its efforts to give the project manager cost supervision had resulted in giving him control over only 63% of the

Exhibit I. Breakdown of Costs for Project and Extent Controlled by Project Organization in Company Y

Area of cost		Percent of dollars spent	Percent of dollars under direct control of project organization
Subcontracted task		50%	50%
Purchased parts and materials		10	0
Direct labor (inplant)	Engineering	6	4
	Manufacturing	8	4
	Tooling	4	0
	Other	2	1
Indirect labor and overhead (inplant)		20	4
Total		100%	63%

total. Without direct control over subcontracting, he would have exercised control over only 13% of total project costs.

Effects on Company

However a company operates its project organizations, they are bound to affect the company while the units are carrying on their missions and even after they have been disbanded.

MAINTAINING CAPABILITY

An undesirable impact on company capabilities may result from using project organizations, because of these factors:

Project priorities and competition for talent may interrupt the stability of the organization and interfere with its long-range interests by upsetting the traditional business of functional organizations.

Long-range planning may suffer as the company gets more involved in meeting schedules and fulfilling the requirements of temporary projects.

Shifting people from project to project may disrupt the training of new employees and specialists, thereby hindering their growth and development within their fields of specialization.

Lessons learned on one project may not be communicated to other projects. One executive who was transferring from a project being phased out to a new project found the same mistakes being made that he had encountered on his former assignment three years earlier. He felt that the problem resulted from splitting normal functional responsibilities among project organizations and from not having enough qualified, experienced employees to spread among all organizations.

An individual-type project organization has of course the least impact on developing and maintaining company capability. The functional departments are doing the work; the resources and skills they develop on one project can be applied to current and succeeding projects.

In a staff-type project organization, however, the problem of maintaining capability may arise. Unique functions, such as site construction and testing, have no permanent impact, since the groups created for these tasks are usually disbanded at the conclusion of the task or project. Primary tasks, such as engineering, procurement, and manufacturing, are not affected, since they are accomplished by the functional organizations. Some of the project support functions, however, such as financial control, contract administration, program planning, and customer coordination, are performed by the staff-type project organizations as control activities. When these functions are divided among several project organizations or between project organizations and functional departments, there is some danger of losing efficiency—not having enough talent or the right talent on a particular project—and losing the capability at the end of phase-out of the project.

The same problem, with greater magnitude, has been experienced by intermix and aggregate project organizations, since primary functions such as engineering, procurement, and manufacturing are also assigned to the project organizations.

STRUCTURAL CHANGES

A predictable result of using the project approach is the addition of organization structure and management positions. Thus:

> One aerospace company, Company Z, compared its organization and management structure as it existed before it began forming projects units with the structure that existed afterward. The results are shown in Exhibit II. The number of departments had increased from 65 to 106, while total employment remained practically the same. The number of employees for every supervisor had dropped from 13.4 to 12.8. The company concluded that a major cause of this change was the project groups.
>
> Company Z uncovered proof of its conclusion when it counted the number of second-level and higher management positions. It found it had 11 more vice presidents and directors, 35 more managers, and 56 more second-level supervisors. Although the company attributed part of this growth to an upgrading of titles, the effect of the project organizations was the creation of 60 more management positions.

Conclusion

Before establishing a project organization, a company should assess the nature of the job and its requirements. Then the company should evaluate its existing structure to pinpoint any organizational

Exhibit II. **Management Structure Changes in Company Z from Project Organizations**

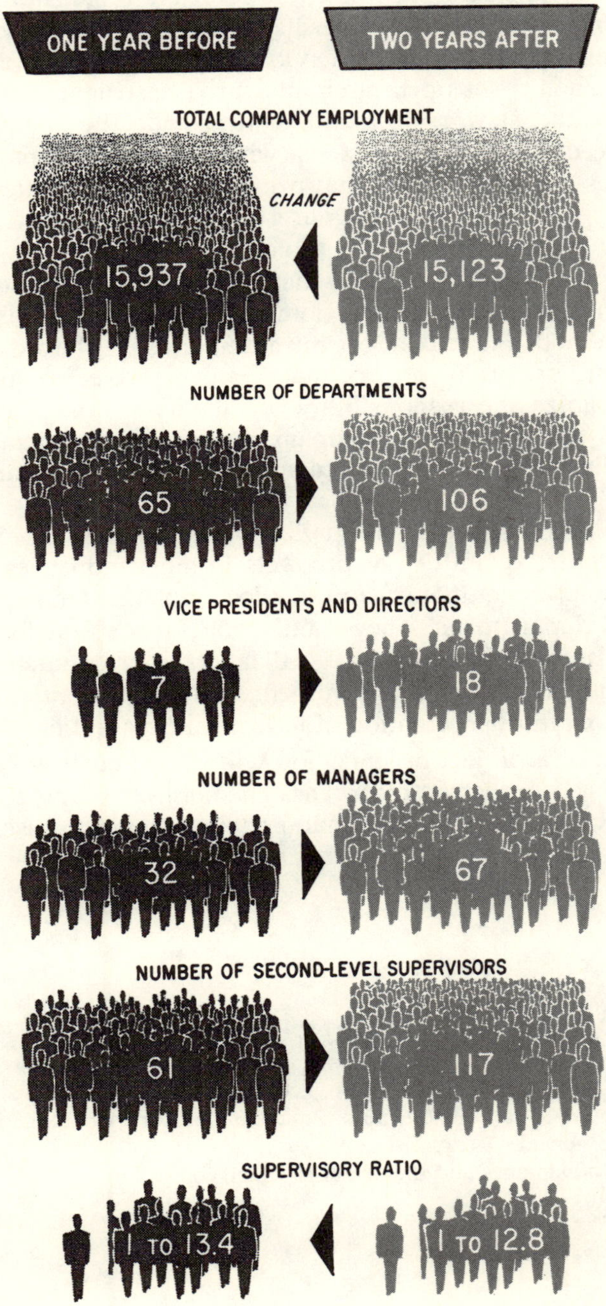

ONE YEAR BEFORE   TWO YEARS AFTER

TOTAL COMPANY EMPLOYMENT

CHANGE

15,937   15,123

NUMBER OF DEPARTMENTS

65   106

VICE PRESIDENTS AND DIRECTORS

7   18

NUMBER OF MANAGERS

32   67

NUMBER OF SECOND-LEVEL SUPERVISORS

61   117

SUPERVISORY RATIO

1 TO 13.4   1 TO 12.8

weaknesses that might inhibit successful accomplishment of the project. The project organization should be assigned any functions needed to compensate for known or probable organizational deficiencies. The scale of project organization is determined by the kind and scope of the organization functions assigned to it. Naturally a company should set up the minimal project structure necessary. Individual and staff project units can provide the emphasis and control needed for most missions, without the problems and disadvantages inherent in dividing primary functions. Intermix and aggregate project organizations are required rarely, and only for extremely critical and complex projects.

Neither the role of the project manager nor that of the functional manager can be permitted to dominate in a company using the project method. Functional organizations must perform tasks and services in support of project management. Project management must recognize the responsibility of functional organizations for developing and maintaining company capabilities. Top management must resolve conflicts between them to protect the company's best interest.

Functional organization specialization is the most efficient way to manufacture quantities of products in most industries. Project organizations are temporary and should complement or supplement functional departments. They should not replace functional organizations because functional specialization in areas such as engineering, manufacturing, and procurement is essential for the preservation and perpetuation of industrial capabilities.

Creation of a project organization will not automatically ensure successful accomplishment of an assigned objective. It is not a panacea for overcoming all functional organization weaknesses. But it can be a great asset to those companies which possess the acumen to exploit its strengths.

Appendix

Advantages and Disadvantages
of the Project Management Approach

How well have companies using project organizations met their objectives? To get some insight on this question, I made a mail survey of aerospace companies and received 47 responses.

The main advantages and the extent to which companies agree on them are listed in Figure I.

Other benefits reported by some companies include:

1. Better project visibility and focus on results.
2. Improved coordination among company divisions doing work on the project.
3. Higher morale and better mission orientation for employees working on the project.
4. Accelerated development of managers due to breadth of project responsibilities.

Figure I. Major Advantages

Advantages	Percent of respondents
Better control of the project	92%
Better customer relations	80
Shorter product development time	40
Lower program costs	30
Improved quality and reliability	26
Higher profit margins	24
Better control over program security	13

Figure II. Major Disadvantages

Disadvantages	Percent of respondents
More complex internal operations	51%
Inconsistency in application of company policy	32
Lower utilization of personnel	13
Higher program costs	13
More difficult to manage	13
Lower profit margins	2

Not all of the results have been advantageous, however. Some aerospace companies have had difficulty using project organizations. The main disadvantages reported are listed in Figure II.

Several companies reported other disadvantages from their own experience. These include:

1. Tendency for functional groups to neglect their job and let the project organization do everything.
2. Too much shifting of personnel from project to project due to priorities.

3. Duplication of functional skills in the project organization.

In evaluating the results of the survey, it appears that a company taking the project organization approach can be reasonably certain that it will improve controls and customer relations (if this is a factor), but internal operations will be more complex.

Notes

1. See John M. Stewart, "Making Project Management Work," *Business Horizons,* Fall 1965, p. 54.

2. For a full discussion of his role, see Paul O. Gaddis, "The Project Manager," HBR May–June 1959, p. 89.

3. *Summary of Project vs. Functional Organization Survey,* a report prepared by the Materials Procurement Committee, Aerospace Industries Association, February 1963.

4. Aerospace Industries Association, op. cit.

5. General Dynamics/Astronautics, *Impact of a Project Structured Organization on Administrative Matters,* Eighth Engineering Administrative Conference (San Diego, California, June 1, 1963).

2
The New New
Product Development Game

Hirotaka Takeuchi and Ikujiro Nonaka

The rules of the game in new product development are changing. Many companies have discovered that it takes more than the accepted basics of high quality, low cost, and differentiation to excel in today's competitive market. It also takes speed and flexibility.

This change is reflected in the emphasis companies are placing on new products as a source of new sales and profits. At 3M, for example, products less than five years old account for 25% of sales. A 1981 survey of 700 U.S. companies indicated that new products would account for one-third of all profits in the 1980s, an increase from one-fifth in the 1970s.[1]

This new emphasis on speed and flexibility calls for a different approach for managing new product development. The traditional sequential or "relay race" approach to product development—exemplified by the National Aeronautics and Space Administration's phased program planning (PPP) system—may conflict with the goals of maximum speed and flexibility. Instead, a holistic or "rugby" approach—where a team tries to go the distance as a unit, passing the ball back and forth—may better serve today's competitive requirements.

Under the old approach, a product development process moved like a relay race, with one group of functional specialists passing the baton to the next group. The project went sequentially from phase to phase: concept development, feasibility testing, product design, development process, pilot production, and final production. Under this method, functions were specialized and segmented: the marketing people examined customer needs and perceptions in

Authors' note: We acknowledge the contribution of Ken-ichi Imai in the development of this article. An earlier version of this article was coauthored by Ken-ichi Imai, Ikujiro Nonaka, and Hirotaka Takeuchi. It was entitled "Managing the New Product Development Process: How Japanese Companies Learn and Unlearn" and was presented at the seventy-fifth anniversary Colloquium on Productivity and Technology, Harvard Business School, March 28 and 29, 1984.

developing product concepts; the R&D engineers selected the appropriate design; the production engineers put it into shape; and other functional specialists carried the baton at different stages of the race.

Under the rugby approach, the product development process emerges from the constant interaction of a hand-picked, multidisciplinary team whose members work together from start to finish. Rather than moving in defined, highly structured stages, the process is born out of the team members' interplay (see Exhibit I). A group of engineers, for example, may start to design the product (phase three) before all the results of the feasibility tests (phase two) are in. Or, the team may be forced to reconsider a decision as a result of later information. The team does not stop then, but engages in iterative experimentation. This goes on in even the latest phases of the development process.

Exhibit I illustrates the difference between the traditional, linear approach to product development and the rugby approach. The sequential approach, labeled A, is typified by the NASA-type PPP system. The overlap approach is represented by type B, where the overlying occurs only at the border of adjacent phases, and type C, where the overlap extends across several phases. We observed a type B overlap at Fuji-Xerox and a type C overlap at Honda and Canon.

This approach is essential for companies seeking to develop new products quickly and flexibly. The shift from a linear to an integrated approach encourages trial and error and challenges the status quo. It stimulates new kinds of learning and thinking within the organization at different levels and functions. Just as important, this strategy for product development can act as an agent of change for the larger organization. The energy and motivation the effort produces can spread throughout the big company and begin to break down some of the rigidities that have set in over time.

In this article, we highlight companies both in Japan and in the United States that have taken a new approach to managing the product development process. Our research examined such multinational companies as Fuji-Xerox, Canon, Honda, NEC, Epson, Brother, 3M, Xerox, and Hewlett-Packard. We then analyzed the development process of six specific products:

FX-3500 medium-sized copier (introduced by Fuji-Xerox in 1978)

PC-10 personal use copier (Canon, 1982)

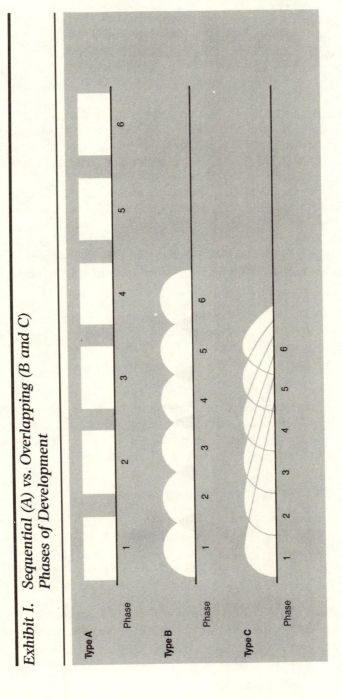

Exhibit I.   Sequential (A) vs. Overlapping (B and C)
Phases of Development

City car with a 1200 cc engine (Honda, 1981)

PC 8000 personal computer (NEC, 1979)

AE-1 single-lens reflex camera (Canon, 1976)

Auto Boy, known as the Sure Shot in the United States, lens shutter camera (Canon, 1979)

We selected each product on the basis of its impact, its visibility within the company as part of a "breakthrough" development process, the novelty of the product features at the time, the market success of the product, and the access to and availability of data on each product.

Moving the Scrum Downfield

From interviews with organization members from the CEO to young engineers, we learned that leading companies show six characteristics in managing their new product development processes:

1. Built-in instability
2. Self-organizing project teams
3. Overlapping development phases
4. "Multilearning"
5. Subtle control
6. Organizational transfer of learning

These characteristics are like pieces of a jigsaw puzzle. Each element, by itself, does not bring about speed and flexibility. But taken as a whole, the characteristics can produce a powerful new set of dynamics that will make a difference.

BUILT-IN INSTABILITY

Top management kicks off the development process by signaling a broad goal or a general strategic direction. It rarely hands out a clear-cut new product concept or a specific work plan. But it both offers a project team a wide measure of freedom and also establishes extremely challenging goals. For example, Fuji-Xerox's top management asked for a radically different copier and gave the FX-3500 project team two years to come up with a machine that could be produced at half the cost of its high-end line and still perform as well.

Top management creates an element of tension in the project team by giving it great freedom to carry out a project of strategic importance to the company and by setting very challenging requirements. An executive in charge of development at Honda remarked, "It's like putting the team members on the second floor, removing the ladder, and telling them to jump or else. I believe creativity is born by pushing people against the wall and pressuring them almost to the extreme."

SELF-ORGANIZING PROJECT TEAMS

A project team takes on a self-organizing character as it is driven to a state of "zero information"—where prior knowledge does not apply. Ambiguity and fluctuation abound in this state. Left to stew, the process begins to create its own dynamic order.[2] The project team begins to operate like a start-up company—it takes initiatives and risks, and develops an independent agenda. At some point, the team begins to create its own concept.

A group possesses a self-organizing capability when it exhibits three conditions: autonomy, self-transcendence, and cross-fertilization. In our study of the various new product development teams, we found all these conditions.

AUTONOMY. Headquarters' involvement is limited to providing guidance, money, and moral support at the outset. On a day-to-day basis, top management seldom intervenes; the team is free to set its own direction. In a way, top management acts as a venture capitalist. Or, as one executive said, "We open up our purse but keep our mouth closed."

This kind of autonomy was evident when IBM developed its personal computer. A small group of engineers began working on the machine in a converted warehouse in remote Boca Raton, Florida. Except for quarterly corporate reviews, headquarters in Armonk, New York, allowed the Boca Raton group to operate on its own. The group got the go-ahead to take unconventional steps such as selecting outside suppliers for its microprocessor and software package.

We observed other examples of autonomy in our case studies.

The Honda City project team, whose members' average age was 27, had these instructions from management: to develop "the kind of car that the youth segment would like to drive." An engineer said, "It's incredible how the company called in young engineers like ourselves to design a car with a totally new concept and gave us the freedom to do it our way."

A small group of sales engineers who originally sold microprocessors built the PC 8000 at NEC. The group started with no knowledge about personal computers. "We were given the go-ahead from top management to proceed with the project, provided we would develop the product by ourselves and also be responsible for manufacturing, selling, and servicing it on our own," remarked the project's head.

SELF-TRANSCENDENCE.   The project teams appear to be absorbed in a never-ending quest for "the limit." Starting with the guidelines set forth by top management, they begin to establish their own goals and keep on elevating them throughout the development process. By pursuing what appear at first to be contradictory goals, they devise ways to override the status quo and make the big discovery.

We observed many examples of self-transcendence in our field work. The Canon AE-1 project team came up with new ideas to meet the challenging parameters set forth by top management. The company asked the team to develop a high-quality, automatic exposure camera that had to be compact, lightweight, easy to use, and priced 30% lower than the prevailing price of single-lens cameras. To reach this ambitious target, the project team achieved several firsts in camera design and production: an electronic brain consisting of integrated circuits custom-made by Texas Instruments; modularized production, which made automation and mass production possible; and reduction in the number of parts by 30% to 40%. "It was a struggle because we had to deny our traditional way of thinking," recalled the head of the AE-1 team. "But we do that every day in the ongoing parts of our business," responded another Canon executive. The entire organization makes daily, incremental improvements to strengthen what the president calls "the fundamentals": R&D, production technology, selling prowess, and corporate culture.

The Honda City project team also achieved a breakthrough by transcending the status quo. The team was asked to develop a car with two competitive features for the youth segment: efficiency in resources and fuel, and uncompromising quality at a low price. The team's natural instinct was to develop a scaled-down version of Honda's best-selling Civic model. But after much debate, the team decided to develop a car with a totally new concept. It challenged the prevailing idea that a car should be long and low and designed a "short and tall" car. Convinced that an evolution toward a "machine minimum, man maximum" concept was inevitable, the team was willing to risk going against the industry norm.

CROSS-FERTILIZATION. A project team consisting of members with varying functional specializations, thought processes, and behavior patterns carries out new product development. The Honda team, for example, consisted of hand-picked members from R&D, production, and sales. The company went a step further by placing a wide variety of personalities on the team. Such diversity fostered new ideas and concepts.

While selecting a diverse team is crucial, it isn't until the members start to interact that cross-fertilization actually takes place. Fuji-Xerox located the multifunctional team building the FX-3500—consisting of members from the planning, design, production, sales, distribution, and evaluation departments—in one large room. A project member gave the following rationale for this step: "When all the team members are located in one large room, someone's information becomes yours, without even trying. You then start thinking in terms of what's best or second best for the group at large and not only about where you stand. If everyone understands the other person's position, then each of us is more willing to give in, or at least to try to talk to each other. Initiatives emerge as a result."

OVERLAPPING DEVELOPMENT PHASES

The self-organizing character of the team produces a unique dynamic or rhythm. Although the team members start the project with different time horizons—with R&D people having the longest time horizon and production people the shortest—they all must work toward synchronizing their pace to meet deadlines. Also, while the project team starts from "zero information," each member soon begins to share knowledge about the marketplace and the technical community. As a result, the team begins to work as a unit. At some point, the individual and the whole become inseparable. The individual's rhythm and the group's rhythm begin to overlap, creating a whole new pulse. This pulse serves as the driving force and moves the team forward.

But the quickness of the pulse varies in different phases of development. The beat seems to be most vigorous in the early phases and tapers off toward the end. A member of Canon's PC-10 development team described this rhythm as follows: "When we are debating about what kind of concept to create, our minds go off in different directions and list alternatives. But when we are trying to come to grips with achieving both low cost and high reliability, our minds work to integrate the various points of view. Conflict tends to occur when some are trying to differentiate and others are trying to integrate. The knack lies in creating this rhythm and knowing when to move from one state to the other."

Under the sequential or relay race approach, a project goes through several phases in a step-by-step fashion, moving from one phase to the next only after all the requirements of the preceding phase are satisfied. These checkpoints control risk. But at the same time, this approach leaves little room for integration. A bottleneck in one phase can slow or even halt the entire development process.

Under the holistic or rugby approach, the phases overlap considerably, which enables the group to absorb the vibration or "noise" generated throughout the development process. When a bottleneck appears, the level of noise obviously increases. But the process does not come to a sudden halt; the team manages to push itself forward.

Fuji-Xerox inherited the PPP system (see type A in Exhibit I) from its parent company, but revised it in two ways. First, it reduced the number of phases from six to four by redefining some of the phases and aggregating them differently. Second, it changed the linear, sequential system into the so-called "sashimi" system. Sashimi is slices of raw fish arranged on a plate, one slice overlapping the other (see Exhibit II).

The sashimi system requires extensive interaction not only among project members but also with suppliers. The FX-3500 team invited them to join the project at the very start (they eventually produced 90% of the parts for the model). Each side regularly visited the other's plants and kept the information channel open at all times. This kind of exchange and openness—both within the project team and with suppliers—increases speed and flexibility. Fuji-Xerox shortened the development time from 38 months for an earlier model to 29 months for the FX-3500.

If sashimi defines the Fuji-Xerox approach, then rugby describes the overlapping at Honda. Like a rugby team, the core project members at Honda stay intact from beginning to end and are responsible for combining all of the phases.

Exhibit II. Fuji-Xerox's Product Development Schedule

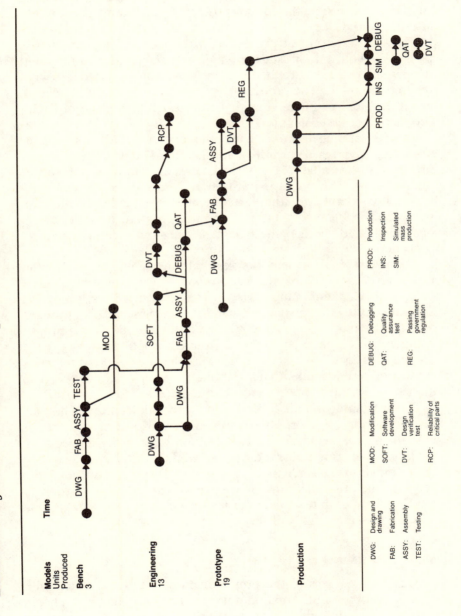

Models
Units
Produced

Bench
3

Engineering
13

Prototype
19

Production

DWG: Design and drawing

FAB: Fabrication

ASSY: Assembly

TEST: Testing

MOD: Modification

SOFT: Software development

DVT: Design verification test

RCP: Reliability of critical parts

DEBUG: Debugging

QAT: Quality assurance test

REG: Passing government regulation

PROD: Production

INS: Inspection

SIM: Simulated mass production

In the relay-like PPP system, the crucial problems tend to occur at the points where one group passes the project to the next. The rugby approach smooths out this problem by maintaining continuity across phases.

The Auto Boy project proceeded with much overlapping across phases as well. Canon's design engineers stayed alert throughout the process to make sure their design was being converted into what they had in mind. The production people intruded onto the design engineers' turf to make sure that the design was in accord with production scale economies.

The overlapping approach has both merits and demerits. Greater speed and increased flexibility are the "hard" merits. But the approach also has a set of "soft" merits relating to human resource management. The overlap approach enhances shared responsibility and cooperation, stimulates involvement and commitment, sharpens a problem-solving focus, encourages initiative taking, develops diversified skills, and heightens sensitivity toward market conditions.

The more obvious demerits result from having to manage an intensive process. Problems include communicating with the entire project team, maintaining close contact with suppliers, preparing several contingency plans, and handling surprises. This approach also creates more tension and conflict in the group. As one project member aptly put it, "If someone from development thinks that 1 out of 100 is good, that's a clear sign for going ahead. But if someone from production thinks that 1 out of 100 is not good, we've got to start all over. This gap in perception creates conflict."

The overlaping of phases also does away with traditional notions about division of labor. Division of labor works well in a type A system, where management clearly delineates tasks, expects all project members to know their responsibilities, and evaluates each on an individual basis. Under a type B or C system, the company accomplishes the tasks through what we call "shared division of labor," where each team member feels responsible for—and is able to work on—any aspect of the project.

MULTILEARNING

Because members of the project team stay in close touch with outside sources of information, they can respond quickly to changing market conditions. Team members engage in a continual process of trial and error to narrow down the number of alternatives that they must consider. They also acquire broad knowledge and diverse skills, which help them create a versatile team capable of solving an array of problems fast.

Such learning by doing manifests itself along two dimensions: across multiple levels (individual, group, and corporate) and across multiple functions. We refer to these two dimensions of learning as "multilearning."

MULTILEVEL LEARNING.   Learning at the individual level takes place in a number of ways. 3M, for example, encourages engineers to devote 15% of their company time to pursuing their "dream." Canon utilizes peer pressure to foster individual learning. A design engineer for the PC-10 project explained, "My senior managers and some of my colleagues really study hard. There is no way I can compete with them in the number of books they read. So whenever I have time, I go to a department store and spend several hours in the toy department. I observe what's selling and check out the new gadgets being used in the toys. They may give me a hint or two later on."

Learning is pursued emphatically at the group level as well. Honda, for example, dispatched several members of the City project team to Europe for three weeks when the project reached a dead end at the concept development phase. They were told simply to "look around at what's happening in Europe." There they encountered the Mini-Cooper—a small car developed decades ago in the United Kingdom—which had a big impact on their design philosophy.

While it was developing the PC-10 copier, Canon team members left the project offices to hold a number of meetings in nearby hotels. In one of the early meetings, the entire project team broke up into subgroups, each with a representative from the design team and the production team. Each subgroup was told to calculate the cost of a key part and figure out ways of reducing that cost by one-third. "Since every subgroup faced the same mandate and the same deadline, we had no choice," recalled one project member. Learning took place in a hurry.

Learning at the corporate level is best achieved by establishing a company-wide movement or program. Fuji-Xerox, for example, used the total quality control (TQC) movement as a basis for changing the corporate mentality. TQC was designed to heighten the entire organization's sensitivity toward simultaneous quality and productivity improvement, market orientation, cost reduction, and work simplification. To achieve these goals, everyone in the organization had to learn the basics of techniques like statistical quality control and value engineering.

Hewlett-Packard embarked on a four-phased training program in marketing as part of the corporation's aim to become more market-oriented. The company now brings in top academics and business consultants to spread the marketing message. It also applies techniques borrowed from the consumer packaged goods industry, such as focus group interviews, quantitative market research, and test marketing. Further, the company has created a corporate marketing division to accelerate what one insider calls "the transition from a company run by engineers for engineers to one with a stronger marketing focus."

MULTIFUNCTIONAL LEARNING.   Experts are encouraged to accumulate experience in areas other than their own. For instance:

All the project members who developed Epson's first miniprinter were mechanical engineers who knew little about electronics at the start. So the leader of the project team, also a mechanical engineer, returned to his alma mater as a researcher and studied electrical engineering for two years. He did this while the project was under way. By the time they had completed the miniprinter project, all the engineers were knowledgeable about electronics. "I tell my people to be well-versed in two technological fields and in two functional areas, like design and marketing," the leader said. "Even in an engineering-oriented company like ours, you can't get ahead without the ability to foresee developments in the market."

The team working on NEC's PC 8000 consisted of sales engineers from the Electronic Devices Division. They acquired much of the know-how to develop the company's first personal computer by putting together TK 80, a computer kit, and introducing it on the market two years in advance of the PC 8000; and by stationing themselves for about a year, even on weekends, at BIT-IN, an NEC service center in the middle of Akihabara, talking with hobbyists and learning the user's viewpoint.

These examples show the important role that multilearning plays in the company's overall human resource management program. It fosters initiative and learning by doing on the part of the employees and helps keep them up to date with the latest developments. It also serves as a basis for creating a climate that can bring about organizational transition.

SUBTLE CONTROL

Although project teams are largely on their own, they are not uncontrolled. Management establishes enough checkpoints to prevent instability, ambiguity, and tension from turning into chaos. At the same time, management avoids the kind of rigid control that impairs creativity and spontaneity. Instead, the emphasis is on "self-control," "control through peer pressure," and "control by love," which collectively we call "subtle control."

Subtle control is exercised in the new product development process in seven ways:

1. Selecting the right people for the project team while monitoring shifts in group dynamics and adding or dropping members when necessary. "We would add an older and more conservative member to the team should the balance shift too much toward radicalism," said a Honda executive. "We carefully pick the project members after long deliberation. We analyze the different personalities to see if they would get along. Most people do get along, thanks to our common set of values."

2. Creating an open work environment, as in the case of Fuji-Xerox.

3. Encouraging engineers to go out into the field and listen to what customers and dealers have to say. "A design engineer may be tempted to take the easy way out at times, but may reflect on what the customer had to say and try to find some way of meeting that requirement," noted an engineer from Fuji-Xerox.

4. Establishing an evaluation and reward system based on group performance. Canon, for example, applied for patents for products from the PC-10 project on a group basis.

5. Managing the differences in rhythm throughout the development process. As mentioned earlier, the rhythm is most vigorous in the early phases and tapers off toward the end.

6. Tolerating and anticipating mistakes. Engineers at Honda are fond of saying that "a 1% success rate is supported by mistakes made 99% of the time." A Brother executive in charge of R&D said, "It's natural for young engineers to make a lot of mistakes. The key lies in finding the mistakes early and taking steps to correct them immediately. We've taken steps to expedite the trial production cycle

for that reason." A 3M executive noted, "I believe we learn more from mistakes than from successes. That's not to say we should make mistakes easily. But if we do make mistakes, we ought to make them creatively.

7. Encouraging suppliers to become self-organizing. Involving them early during design is a step in the right direction. But the project team should refrain from telling suppliers what to do. As Xerox recently found out, suppliers produce better results when they have the problem explained to them and are allowed to decide how to furnish the parts.

TRANSFER OF LEARNING

The drive to accumulate knowledge across levels and functions is only one aspect of learning. We observed an equally strong drive on the part of the project members to transfer their learning to others outside the group.

Transfer of learning to subsequent new product development projects or to other divisions in the organization takes place regularly. In several of the companies we studied, the transfer took place through "osmosis"—by assigning key individuals to subsequent projects. A Honda executive explained, "If the factory is up and running and the early-period claims are resolved, we dismantle the project team, leaving only a few people to follow through. Since we have only a limited number of unusually able people, we turn them loose on another key project immediately."

Knowledge is also transmitted in the organization by converting project activities to standard practice. At Canon, for example, the Auto Boy project produced a format for conducting reviews that was used in later projects. One team member recalled, "We used to meet once a month or so to exchange notes on individual subprojects in progress and once in three months or so to discuss the project from a larger perspective. This pattern later became institutionalized into the monthly and quarterly progress reviews adopted from the PC-10 minicopier project."

Naturally, companies try to institutionalize the lessons derived from their successes. IBM is trying to emulate the personal computer development project—which was completed in 13 months with outside help—throughout the company.

At Hewlett-Packard, the personal computer group is reprogramming the way the entire company develops and sells new products.

In the past, the company was famous for designing a machine for a particular customer and charging a premium price. But it recently engineered its ThinkJet—a quiet inkjet printer—for low-cost mass production and priced it low. Within six months of its introduction, the printer captured 10% of the low-end market. Hewlett-Packard began to apply what it had learned from designing and pricing ThinkJet to its minicomputer line. Within months of putting ThinkJet on the market, the company introduced a minicomputer system for a broad corporate audience at a modest price.

But institutionalization, when carried too far, can create its own danger. Passing down words of wisdom from the past or establishing standard practices based on success stories works well when the external environment is stable. Changes in the environment, however, can quickly make such lessons impractical.

Several companies have tried to unlearn old lessons. Unlearning helps keep the development team in tune with the realities of the outside environment. It also acts as a springboard for making more incremental improvements.

Much of the unlearning is triggered by changes in the environment. But some companies consciously pursue unlearning. Consider these examples:

Epson's target is to have the next-generation model in development stages as a new model is being introduced on the market. The company tells its project teams that the next-generation model must be at least 40% better than the existing one.

When Honda was building the third-generation Civic model, its project team opted to scrap all the old parts and start anew. When the car made its debut before the public, all the new parts were displayed right next to the car at the request of the project members. The car won the 1984 Car of the Year Award in Japan.

Fuji-Xerox has refined its sashimi approach, first adopted for the FX-3500. Compared with that effort, a new product today requires one-half of the original total manpower. Fuji-Xerox has also reduced the product development cycle from 4 years to 24 months.

Some Limitations

Some words of caution are in order. The holistic approach to product development may not work in all situations. It has some built-in limitations:

It requires extraordinary effort on the part of all project members throughout the span of the development process. Sometimes, team members record monthly overtime of 100 hours during the peak and 60 hours during the rest of the project.

It may not apply to breakthrough projects that require a revolutionary innovation. This limitation may be particularly true in biotechnology or chemistry.

It may not apply to mammoth projects like those in the aerospace business, where the sheer project scale limits extensive face-to-face discussions.

It may not apply to organizations where product development is masterminded by a genius who makes the invention and hands down a well-defined set of specifications for people below to follow.

Some limitations also stem from the scope of our research. Our sample size was limited to a handful of companies and our findings were drawn, for the most part, from observing how the development process was managed in Japan. General conclusions, therefore, must be made with some caution. But as new approaches to product development gain acceptance in the United States, the difference between the two countries may not be so much a difference of kind as a difference of degree.

Managerial Implications

Changes in the environment—intensified competition, a splintered mass market, shortened product life cycles, and advanced technology and automation—are forcing managements to reconsider the traditional ways of creating products. A product that arrives a few months late can easily lose several months of payback. A product designed by an engineer afflicted with the "next bench" syndrome—the habit of designing a product by asking the coworkers on the next bench what kind of a product he or she would like—may not meet the flexible requirements of the marketplace.

To achieve speed and flexibility, companies must manage the product development process differently. Three kinds of change should be considered.

First, companies need to adopt a management style that can promote the process. Executives must recognize at the outset that product development seldom proceeds in a linear and static manner. It involves an iterative and dynamic process of trial and error. To manage such a process, companies must maintain a highly adaptive style.

Because projects do not proceed in a totally rational and consistent manner, adaptability is particularly important. Consider, for example, situations where:

> Top management encourages trial and error by purposely keeping goals broad and by tolerating ambiguity. But at the same time, it sets challenging goals and creates tension within the group and within the organization.

> The process by which variety is amplified (differentiation) and reduced (integration) takes place throughout the overlapping phases of the development cycle. Differentiation, however, tends to dominate the concept development phase of the cycle and integration begins to take over the subsequent phases.

> Operational decisions are made incrementally, but important strategic decisions are delayed as much as possible in order to allow a more flexible response to last-minute feedback from the marketplace.

Because management exercises subtle forms of control throughout the development process, these seemingly contradictory goals do not create total confusion. Subtle control is also consistent with the self-organizing character of the project teams.

Second, a different kind of learning is required. Under the traditional approach, a highly competent group of specialists undertakes new product development. An elite group of technical experts does most of the learning. Knowledge is accumulated on an individual basis, within a narrow area of focus—what we call learning in depth.

In contrast, under the new approach (in its extreme form) non-experts undertake product development. They are encouraged to acquire the necessary knowledge and skills on the job. Unlike the experts, who cannot tolerate mistakes even 1% of the time, the non-experts are willing to challenge the status quo. But, to do so, they must accumulate knowledge from across all areas of management, across different levels of the organization, functional specializations, and even organizational boundaries. Such learning in breadth serves as the necessary condition for shared division of labor to function effectively.

Third, management should assign a different mission to new product development. Most companies have treated it primarily as a generator of future revenue streams. But in some companies, new product development also acts as a catalyst to bring about change in the organization. The personal computer project, for example, is said to have changed the way IBM thinks. Projects coming out of Hewlett-Packard's personal computer group, including ThinkJet, have changed its engineering-driven culture.

No company finds it easy to mobilize itself for change, especially in noncrisis situations. But the self-transcendent nature of the project teams and the hectic pace at which the team members work help to trigger a sense of crisis or urgency throughout the organization. A development project of strategic importance to the company, therefore, can create a wartime working environment even during times of peace.

Changes affecting the entire organization are also difficult to carry out within highly structured companies, especially seniority-based companies like the ones commonly found in Japan. But unconventional moves, which may be difficult to pull off during times of peace, can be legitimized during times of war. Thus management can uproot a competent manager or assign a very young engineer to the project without encountering much resistance.

Once the project team is formed, it begins to rise in stature because of its visibility ("we've been hand-picked"), its legitimate power ("we have unconditional support from the top to create something new"), and its sense of mission ("we're working to solve a crisis"). It serves as a motor for corporate change as project members from a variety of functional areas begin to take strategic initiatives that sometimes go beyond the company's conventional domain and as their knowledge gets transferred to subsequent projects.

The environment in which any multinational company—from the United States or Japan—operates has changed dramatically in recent years. The rules of the game for competing effectively in today's world market have changed accordingly. Multinationals must achieve speed and flexibility in developing products; to do so requires the use of a dynamic process involving much reliance on trial and error and learning by doing. What we need today is constant innovation in a world of constant change.

Notes

[1] Booz, Allen & Hamilton survey reported in Susan Fraker, "High-Speed Management for the High-Tech Age," *Fortune,* March 5, 1984, p. 38.

[2.] See, for example, Ilya Prigozine, *From Being to Becoming* (San Francisco, Calif.: Freeman, 1980); Eric Jantsch, "Unifying Principles of Evolution," in Eric Jantsch, ed., *The Evolutionary Vision* (Boulder, Colo.: Westview Press, 1981); and Devendra Sahal, "A Unified Theory of Self-Organization," *Journal of Cybernetics,* April–June, 1979, p. 127. See also Todao Kagono, Ikujiro Nonaka, Kiyonari Sakakibara, and Akihiro Okumura, *Strategic vs. Evolutionary Management: A U.S.-Japan Comparison of Strategy and Organization* (Amsterdam: North-Holland, 1985).

3
Manufacturing by Design

Daniel E. Whitney

In many large companies, design has become a bureaucratic tangle, a process confounded by fragmentation, overspecialization, power struggles, and delays. An engineering manager responsible for designing a single part at an automobile company told me recently that the design process mandates 350 steps—not 350 engineering calculations or experiments but 350 workups requiring 350 signatures. No wonder, he said, it takes five years to design a car; that's one signature every $3\frac{1}{2}$ days.

It's not as if companies don't know better. According to General Motors executives, 70% of the cost of manufacturing truck transmissions is determined in the design stage. A study at Rolls-Royce reveals that design determines 80% of the final production costs of 2,000 components.[1] Obviously, establishing a product's design calls for crucial choices—about materials made or bought, about how parts will be assembled. When senior managers put most of their efforts into analyzing current production rather than product design, they are monitoring what accounts for only about a third of total manufacturing costs—the window dressing, not the window.

Moreover, better product design has shattered old expectations for improving cost through design or redesign. If managers used to think a 5% improvement was good, they now face competition that

Author's note: I am indebted to my colleagues James L. Nevins, Alexander C. Edsall, Thomas L. De Fazio, Richard E. Gustavson, Richard W. Metzinger, Jonathan M. Rourke, and Donald S. Seltzer for their contributions to this article. We have worked together for many years developing the ideas expressed here.

is reducing drastically the number of components and subassemblies for products and achieving a 50% or more reduction in direct cost of manufacture. And even greater reductions are coming, owing to new materials and materials-processing techniques. Direct labor, even lower cost labor, accounts for so little of the total picture that companies still focusing on this factor are misleading themselves not only about improving products but also about how foreign competitors have gained so much advantage.

In short, design is a strategic activity, whether by intention or by default. It influences flexibility of sale strategies, speed of field repair, and efficiency of manufacturing. It may well be responsible for the company's future viability. I want to focus not on the qualities of products but on development of the processes for making them.

Converting a concept into a complex, high-technology product is an involved procedure consisting of many steps of refinement. The initial idea never quite works as intended or performs as well as desired. So designers make many modifications, including increasingly subtle choices of materials, fasteners, coatings, adhesives, and electronic adjustments. Expensive analyses and experiments may be necessary to verify design choices.

In many cases, designers find that the options become more and more difficult; negotiations over technical issues, budgets, and schedules become intense. As the design evolves, the choices become interdependent, taking on the character of an interwoven, historical chain in which later decisions are conditioned by those made previously.

Imagine, then, that a production or manufacturing engineer enters such detailed negotiations late in the game and asks for changes. If the product designers accede to the requests, a large part of the design may simply unravel. Many difficult and pivotal choices will have been made for nothing. Where close calls went one way, they may now go another; new materials analyses and production experiments may be necessary.

Examples of failure abound. One research scientist I know, at a large chemical company, spent a year perfecting a new process—involving, among other things, gases—at laboratory scale. In the lab the process operated at atmospheric pressure. But when a production engineer was finally called in to scale up the process, he immediately asked for higher pressures. Atmospheric pressure is never used in production when gases are in play because maintaining it requires huge pipes, pumps, and tanks. Higher pressure reduces the volume of gases and permits the use of smaller equipment. Unfortunately, the researcher's process failed at elevated pressures, and he had to start over.

Or consider the manufacturer whose household appliance depended on close tolerances for proper operation. Edicts from the styling department prevented designs from achieving required tolerances; the designers wanted a particular shape and appearance and would not budge when they were apprised of the problems they caused to manufacturing. Nor was the machine designed in modules that could be tested before final assembly. The entire product was built from single parts on one long line. So each finished product had to be adjusted into operation—or taken apart after assembly to find out why it didn't work. No one who understood the problem had enough authority to solve it, and no one with enough authority understood the problem until it was too late. This company is no longer in business.

Finally, there was the weapon that depended for its function on an infrared detector, the first of many parts—lenses, mirrors, motors, power supplies, etc.—that were glued and soldered together into a compact unit. To save money, the purchasing department switched to a cheaper detector, which caused an increase in final test failures. Since the construction was glue and solder, bad units had to be scrapped. Someone then suggested a redesign of the unit with reversible fasteners to permit disassembly. But this time more reasonable voices prevailed. Reversible fasteners would have actually increased the weapon's cost and served no purpose other than to facilitate factory rework. Disassembly would not have been advisable because the unit was too complex for field repair. It was a single-use weapon—with a shelf life of five years and a useful life of ten seconds. It simply had to work the first time.

Manufacturers can avoid problems like this. Let's look at a success story. One company I know wanted to be able to respond in 24 hours to worldwide orders for its electronic products line—a large variety of features in small-order batches. Engineers decided to redesign the products in modules, with different features in each module. All the modules are plug compatible, electrically and mechanically. All versions of each module are identical on the outside where assembly machines handle them. The company can now make up an order for any set of features by selecting the correct modules and assembling them, all of this without any human intervention, from electronic order receipt to the boxing of final assemblies.

In another company, a high-pressure machine for supplying cutting oil to machine tools requires once-a-day cleaning. Designers recently reconfigured the machine so that normal cleanout and ordinary repairs can be accomplished without any tools, thus solving some bothersome union work-rule problems.

There are no guarantees, of course, but the experiences of these companies illustrate how design decisions should be integrated, informed, and balanced, and how important it is to involve manufacturing engineers, repair engineers, purchasing agents, and other knowledgeable people early in the process. The product designer asks, "What good is it if it doesn't work?" The salesperson asks, "What good is it if it doesn't sell?" The finance person asks, "What good is it if it isn't profitable?" The manufacturing engineer asks, "What good is it if I can't make it?" The team's success is measured by how well these questions are answered.

The Design Team and Its Task

Multifunctional teams are currently the most effective way known to cut through barriers to good design. Teams can be surprisingly small—as small as 4 members, though 20 members is typical in large projects—and they usually include every specialty in the company. Top executives should make their support and interest clear. Various names have been given to this team approach, like "simultaneous engineering" and "concurrent design." Different companies emphasize different strengths within the team. In many Japanese companies, teams like this have been functioning for so long that most of the employees cannot remember another way to design a product.

Establishing the team is only the beginning, of course. Teams need a step-by-step procedure that disciplines the discussion and takes members through the decisions that crop up in virtually every design. In traditional design procedures, assembly is one of the last things considered. My experience suggests that assembly should be considered much earlier. Assembly is inherently integrative. Weaving it into the design process is a powerful way to raise the level of integration in all aspects of product design.

A design team's charter should be broad. Its chief functions include:

1. Determining the character of the product, to see what it is and thus what design and production methods are appropriate.
2. Subjecting the product to a product function analysis, so that all design decisions can be made with full knowledge of how the item is supposed to work and all team members understand it well enough to contribute optimally.
3. Carrying out a design-for-producibility-and-usability study to determine if these factors can be improved without impairing functioning.
4. Designing an assembly process appropriate to the product's particular character. This involves creating a suitable assembly sequence, identifying subassemblies, integrating quality control, and designing each part so that its quality is compatible with the assembly method.
5. Designing a factory system that fully involves workers in the production strategy, operates on minimal inventory, and is integrated with vendors' methods and capabilities.

THE PRODUCT'S CHARACTER. Clearly it is beyond the scope of this article to establish by what criteria one judges, develops, or revamps the features of products. Recently, David A. Garvin has analyzed eight fundamental dimensions of product quality; and John R. Hauser and Don Clausing have explored ways to communicate to design engineers the dimensions consumers want—in the engineers' own language.[2]

Character defines the criteria by which designers judge, develop, or revamp product features. I would only reiterate that manufacturing engineers and others should have something to say about how to ensure that the product is field repairable, how skilled users must be to employ it successfully, and whether marketability will be based on model variety or availability of future add-ons.

An essential by-product of involving manufacturing, marketing, purchasing, and other constituencies in product conception, moreover, is that diverse team members become familiar enough with the product early in order to be able to incorporate the designers' goals and constraints in their own approaches. As designers talk with manufacturing or field-service reps, for example, they can make knowledgeable corrections. ("Why not make that part out of plastic? I know a low-cost source." "Because the temperature there is 1,000°; plastic will vaporize." "Oh.")

PRODUCT FUNCTION ANALYSIS.   This used to be the exclusive province of product designers. But now it is understood that to improve a product's robustness, to "design quality in" in Genichi Taguchi's good phrase, means thoroughly understanding a product's function in relation to production methods. Product designers and manufacturing engineers used to try to understand these relations by experience and intuition. Now they have software packages for modeling and designing components to guide them through process choices—software that would have been thought fantastic a generation ago.

Recently I worked on a product containing delicate spinning parts that had to be dynamically balanced to high tolerances. In the original design, partial disassembly of the rotating elements after balancing was necessary before the assembly could be finished, so the final product was rarely well balanced and required a lengthy adjustment procedure. Since total redesign was not feasible, the team analyzed the reassembly procedure solely as it pertained to balance and concluded that designers needed only to tighten various tolerances and reshape mating surfaces. Simple adjustments were then sufficient to restore balance in the finished product.

Another important goal of product function analysis is to reduce the number of parts in a product. The benefits extend to purchasing (fewer vendors and transactions), manufacturing (fewer operations, material handlings, and handlers), and field service (fewer repair parts).

When a company first brings discipline to its design process, reductions in parts count are usually easy to make because the old designs are so inefficient. After catching up, though, hard, creative work is necessary to cut the parts count further. One company I know saved several million dollars a year by eliminating just one subassembly part. The product had three operating states: low, medium, and high. Analysis showed that the actions of one part in the original design always followed or imitated the actions of two others. Designers eliminated the redundant part by slightly altering the shapes of the other two parts.

This change could never have been conceived, much less executed, if the designers hadn't had deep knowledge of the product and hadn't paid attention to the actions underlying its engineering.

DESIGN FOR PRODUCIBILITY.   Recently, a company bragged to a business newsweekly about saving a mere $250,000 by designing its bottles for a new line of cosmetics to fit existing machines for filling, labeling, and capping. This plan seems so obvious, and the savings were so small as compared with what is possible, that the celebration seemed misplaced. But it's a better outcome than I remember from my first job with a drug company. It spent a fortune to have a famous industrial designer create new bottles and caps for its line. They were triangular in cross section and teardrop shaped, and they would not fit either existing machines or any new ones we tried to design. The company eventually abandoned the bottles, along with the associated marketing campaign.

Obviously, nothing is more important to manufacturing strategy than designing for the production process. In the past, this has meant designing for manufacturing and assembly, and value engineering, which both strive to reduce costs. But now we have to go beyond these goals.

To take the last point first, value engineering aims chiefly to reduce manufacturing costs through astute choice of materials and methods for making parts. Does the design call for metal when a ceramic part will do? If metal, should we punch it or drill it? Value engineering usually comes into play after the design is finished, but the thoroughness we seek in design can be achieved only when decisions are made early.

Moreover, design for producibility differs from design for assembly, which typically considers parts one by one, simplifies them, combines some to reduce the parts count, or adds features like bevels around the rims of holes to make assembly easier. Valuable as it is, this process cannot achieve the most fundamental improvements because it considers the product as a collection of parts instead of something to satisfy larger goals, such as reducing costs over the product's entire life cycle.

Nippondenso's approach vividly illustrates how an overriding strategy can determine a product's parts and the production process. The Delco of Japan, Nippondenso builds such car products as generators, alternators, voltage regulators, radiators, and anti-skid brake systems. Toyota is its chief customer. Nippondenso has learned to live with daily orders for thousands of items in arbitrary model mixes and quantities.

The company's response to this challenge has several components:

The combinatorial method of meeting model-mix production requirements.

In-house development of manufacturing technology.

Wherever possible, manufacturing methods that don't need jigs and fixtures.

The combinatorial method, carried out by marketing and engineering team members, divides a product into generic parts or subassemblies and identifies the necessary variations of each. The product is then designed to permit any combination of variations of these basic parts to go together physically and functionally. (If there are 6 basic parts and 3 varieties of each, for example, the company can build $3^6 = 729$ different models.) The in-house manufacturing team cooperates in designing the parts, so the manufacturing system can easily handle and make each variety of each part and product.

Jigless production is an important goal at this point, for obvious reasons. Materials handling, fabrication, and assembly processes usually employ jigs, fixtures, and tools to hold parts during processing and transport; the jigs and fixtures are usually designed specifically to fit each kind of part, to hold them securely. When production shifts to a different batch or model, old jigs and tools are removed and new ones installed. In mass-production environments, this changeover occurs about once a year.

In dynamic markets, however, or with just-in-time, batches are small, and shifts in production may occur hourly—even continually. It may be impossible to achieve a timely and economical batch-size-of-one production process if separate jigs are necessary for each model. Nippondenso's in-house manufacturing team responds to this problem by showing how to design the parts with common jigging features, so that one jig can hold all varieties, or by working with designers to make the product snap or otherwise hold itself together so that no clamping jigs are needed.

By cultivating an in-house team, Nippondenso also solves three difficult institutional problems. First, the company eliminates proprietary secrecy problems. Its own people are the only ones working on the design or with strategically crucial components. Second, equipment can be delivered without payment of a vendor's markup, thus reducing costs and making financial justification easier. Third, over the years the team has learned to accommodate itself intuitively to the company's design philosophy, and individual team members have learned how to contribute to it. Designers get to know each other too, creating many informal communication networks that greatly shorten the design process. Shorter design periods mean less lead time, a clear competitive advantage. (It is worth noting that many Japanese companies follow this practice of designing much of their automation in-house, while buying many product components from outside vendors. American companies usually take the opposite tack: they make many components and buy automation from vendors.)

Nippondenso uses combinatorial design and jigless manufacturing for making radiators. Tubes, fins, headers, and side plates comprise the core of the radiator. These four snap together, which obviates the need for jigs, and the complete core is oven soldered. The plastic tanks are crimped on. The crimp die can be adjusted to take any tank size while the next radiator is being put in the crimper, so radiators can be processed in any model order and in any quantity. When asked how much the factory cost, the project's chief engineer replied, "Strictly speaking, you have to include the cost of designing the product." A factory isn't just a factory, he implied. It is a carefully crafted fusion of a strategically designed product and the methods for making it.

Without a guiding strategy, there is no way to tell what suggestions for improvement really support long-range goals. Some product-design techniques depend too much on rules, including rule-based systems stemming from expert systems. These are no substitute for experienced people. Volkswagen, for example, recently violated conventional ease-of-assembly rules to capture advantages the company would not otherwise have had.

In the company's remarkable Hall 54 facility in Wolfsburg, Germany, where Golfs and Jettas go through final assembly, robots or special machines perform about 25% of the final-stage steps. (Before Hall 54 began functioning, Volkswagen never did better than 5%.)[3]

To get this level of automation, VW production management asked to examine every part. It won from the board of directors a year-long delay in introducing the new models. Several significant departures from conventional automotive design practices resulted, the first involving front-end configuration. Usually, designers try to reduce the number of parts. But VW engineers determined that at a cost of one *extra* frame part the front of the car could be temporarily left open for installation of the engine by hydraulic arms in one straight, upward push. Installing the engine used to take a minute or longer and involved several workers. VW now does it unmanned in 26 seconds.

Another important decision concerned the lowly screw. Purchasing agents usually accept the rule that low-cost fasteners are a competitive edge. VW engineers convinced the purchasing department to pay an additional 18% for screws with cone-shaped tips that go more easily into holes, even if the sheet metal or plastic parts were misaligned. Machine and robot insertion of screws thus became practical. Just two years later, so many German companies had adopted cone-pointed screws that their price had dropped to that of ordinary flat-tip screws. For once, everyone from manufacturing to purchasing was happy.

ASSEMBLY PROCESSES.   Usually assembly sequence is looked at late in the design process when industrial engineers are trying to balance the assembly line. But the choice of assembly sequence and the identification of potential subassemblies can affect or be affected by—among other factors—product-testing options, market responsiveness, and factory-floor layout. Indeed, assembly-related activities with strategic implications include: subassemblies, assembly sequence, assembly method for each step, and integration of quality control.

Imagine a product with six parts. We can build it many ways, such as bottom up, top down, or from three subassemblies of two parts each. What determines the best way? A balance of many considerations: construction needs, like access to fasteners or lubrication points; ease of assembly (some sequences may include difficult part matings that risk damage to parts); quality control matters, like the operator's ability to make crucial tests or easily replace a faulty part; process reasons, like ability to hold pieces accurately for machine assembly; and, finally, production strategy advantages, like making subassemblies to stock that will be common to many models, or that permit assembly from commonly available parts.

Again, software now exists to help the designer with the formidable problem of listing all the possible assembly sequences—and there can be a lot, as many as 500 for an item as simple as an automobile rear axle. It would be impossible for a team to attack so complex a series of choices without a computer design aid to help, according to a preestablished hierarchy of goals like that just discussed—access to lubrication points, etc. Another virtue of this software is that it forces the team to specify choices systematically and reproducibly, for team members' own edification but also in a way that helps justify design and manufacturing choices to top management.

Consider then, automatic transmissions, complex devices made up of gears, pistons, clutches, hydraulic valves, and electronic controls. Large transmission parts can scrape metal off smaller parts during assembly, and shavings can get into the control valves, causing the transmission to fail the final test or, worse, fail in the customer's car. Either failure is unacceptable and terribly expensive. It is essential to design assembly methods and test sequences to preempt them.

With respect to assembly machines and tooling, manufacturers should consider the following questions:

Can the product be made by adding parts from one direction, or must it be turned over one or more times? Turnovers are wasted motion and costly in fixtures.

As parts are added in a stack, will the location for each subsequent part drift unpredictably? If so, automatic assembly machines will need expensive sensors to find the parts, or assembly will randomly fail, or parts will scrape on each other too hard.

Is there space for tools and grippers? If not, automatic assembly or testing isn't an option.

If a manufacturing strategy based on subassemblies seems warranted, are the subassemblies designed so they do not fall apart during reorientation, handling, or transport?

There are clear advantages to combining consideration of these assembly procedures and/or quality control strategy with design. Designers who anticipate the assembly method can avoid pitfalls that would otherwise require redesign or create problems on the factory floor. They can also design better subassemblies to meet functional specifications—specifications that will be invaluable when the time comes to decide whether to take bids from outside vendors or make the part on the company's own lines, specifications that will determine how to test the subassembly before adding it to the final product.

Designers concerned about assembly must ask:

What is the best economic combination of machines and people to assemble a certain model-mix of parts for a product line (given each machine's or person's cost and time to do each operation, plus production-rate and economic-return targets)?

How much time, money, production machinery, or in-process inventory can be saved if extra effort is put into design of the product, its fabrication and assembly processes, so that there are fewer quality control failures and product repairs? A process that yields only 80% successful assemblies on the first try may need 20% extra capacity and inventory—not to mention high-cost repair personnel—to meet the original production goals.

Where in the assembly process should testing take place? Considerations include how costly and definitive the test is, whether later stages would hide flaws detectable earlier, and how much repaired or discarded assemblies would cost.

These are generic problems; they are hard to answer, and they too are stimulating the development of new software packages. This new software enhances the ability of manufacturing people to press their points in (often heated) debates about design. Hitherto, product designers, more accustomed to using computer modeling, have had somewhat of an upper hand.

FACTORY SYSTEM DESIGN.   Many features of good product design presuppose that machines will do the assembly. But automation is not necessary to reap the benefits of strategic design. Indeed, sometimes good design makes automatic assembly unnecessary or uneconomic by making manual assembly so easy and reliable. Regardless of the level of automation, some people will still be involved in production processes, and their role is important to the success of manufacturing.

Kosuke Ikebuchi, general manager of the General Motors–Toyota joint venture, New United Motors Manufacturing Inc. (NUMMI), believes that success came to his plant only after careful analysis of the failures of the GM operation that had preceded it: low-quality parts from suppliers, an attitude that repair and rework were to be expected, high absenteeism resulting in poor workmanship, and damage to parts and vehicles caused by transport mechanisms.[4] The assembly line suffered from low efficiency because work methods were not standardized, people could not repair their own equipment, and equipment was underutilized. Excess inventory, caused by ineffective controls, was another problem. Work areas were crowded. Employees took too much time to respond to problems.

NUMMI's solutions focused on the Jidoka principle—quality comes first. According to NUMMI's factory system today, workers can stop the line if they spot a problem; the machinery itself can sense and warn of problems. Two well-known just-in-time methods of eliminating waste—the kanban system of production control and reductions in jig and fixture change times—are important to NUMMI's manufacturing operation.

But lots of other things also contribute to this plant's effectiveness: simplified job classifications, displays and signs showing just how to do each job and what to avoid, self-monitoring machines. NUMMI has obtained high-spirited involvement of the employees, first by choosing new hires for their willingness to cooperate, then by training them thoroughly and involving them in decisions about how to improve the operations.

Design Means Business

The five tasks of design bring us back to the original point. Strategic product design is a total approach to doing business. It can mean changes in the pace of design, the identity of the participants, and the sequence of decisions. It forces managers, designers, and engineers to cross old organizational boundaries, and it reverses some old power relationships. It creates difficulties because it teases out incipient conflict, but it is rewarding precisely because disagreements surface early, when they can be resolved constructively and with mutual understanding of the outcome's rationale.

Strategic design is a continual process, so it makes sense to keep design teams in place until well after product launching when the same team can then tackle a new project. Design—it must be obvious by now—is a companywide activity. Top management involvement and commitment are essential. The effort has its costs, but the costs of not making the effort are greater.

Notes

1. J. Corbett, "Design for Economic Manufacture," *Annals of C.I.R.P.*, vol. 35, no. 1, 1986, p. 93.

2. David A. Garvin, "Competing on the Eight Dimensions of Quality," HBR November–December 1987, p. 101; and John R. Hauser and Don Clausing, "The House of Quality," HBR May–June 1988, p. 63.

3. E. H. Hartwich, "Possibilities and Trends for the Application of Automated Handling and Assembly Systems in the Automotive Industry," International Congress for Metalworking and Automation, Hanover, West Germany, 1985, p. 126.

4. Kosuke Ikebuchi, unpublished remarks at the Future Role of Automated Manufacturing Conference, New York University, 1986.

4
You *Can* Manage
Construction Risks

John D. Macomber

Colossal County Hospital was coming apart at the seams. With dozens of newly hired doctors, nurses, and technicians, millions of dollars of equipment on the road, and patient appointments backed up for months, the new facility was impossible to use. For one thing, construction wasn't finished, and much of what was complete was faulty. Worse yet, the contractor had placed liens on the property for nonpayment, preventing occupancy. Costs had greatly outdistanced available financing. The hospital staff was frantic; the bank was apoplectic; the board of trustees was in despair.

How had it happened? The chairman of the board—head of the local branch of a financial services company—was baffled. He tried to trace the history of the project.

Two years earlier, the board members had voted to build an important new facility and renovate an adjoining older one. They hired the best available hospital architect. One group of trustees went on to focus its attention on a special bond issue to provide low-cost financing, while another group put together and executed a detailed marketing strategy to position the hospital as a world leader in several areas of care and research. Working closely with the doctors who would direct the various programs, the architect designed a state-of-the-art medical facility and a splendid building that would serve as a symbol for the hospital and as a landmark for the city.

On the architect's recommendation, a local contractor was retained to begin pricing the preliminary plans. As the drawings and budgeting progressed, the hospital was confident enough to apply for bank financing, and the bank, on the basis of the contractor's estimates and the proposed bond issue, agreed to make the loan.

Then the contractor presented his final budget. To the board's surprise, the estimate had grown by $3.5 million—and the detailed construction drawings still weren't complete. The contractor claimed the architect was upgrading the quality and scope of construction. The architect insisted he was only complying with the growing wish list of the trustees, doctors, and marketing experts hired by the board. But the bond issue was based on the original budget, and it wasn't big enough to accommodate the higher price. The hospital could not proceed. The trustees and the doctors held a meeting.

The doctors insisted they had added very little, and they refused to eliminate any of the medical features designed into the building. The trustees were convinced that the overall increase in scope was much smaller than the new price indicated. Everyone suspected the contractor of taking advantage of the hospital. The chairman decided it was time to act.

"In my industry—financial services," he reasoned, "all services are bid for. We give all aspirants a chance to say what they will charge. That's the way to get the lowest price."

A local manufacturer on the board agreed. "I had one of these 'trust me' contractors do my warehouse on a time-and-materials basis, and he soaked me good. He put his worst workers on the job, he didn't fight for purchase discounts, and he did everything he could to get costs up so his fee would go up. Let's not make the same mistake I made."

So the project was put out to bid with no modifications in scope and still without completed blueprints and specifications. Five companies submitted bids. The hospital's chief financial officer awarded the contract to a builder whose price was within the original budget. The original contractor was banished in disgrace, despite his protestations that his estimate was the right price for all the work the hospital would need.

Conflicts developed at once. The new builder had assumed that the space to be renovated would be vacated to work in, but the hospital couldn't do that. The builder threatened to stop work, so the board caved in and gave him an increase. The architect and the contractor fought constantly over interpretation of the drawings and specifications. The trustees, distracted by questions of finance and marketing, did not always make timely decisions. The contractor cut every possible corner to hold down costs, and the architect overruled him again and again.

Just as the building was nearly finished, the board was shocked to receive a huge change-order request from the contractor alleging inaccurate specifications, changed conditions, and decision delays by the owner. The hospital refused to pay. The builder shut the job down and placed mechanic's liens on the property.

This was where the project now stood. The members of the board—successful local businesspeople, educators, and public servants—were angry and embarrassed; the architect was bitter; the original contractor was full of I-told-you-so's for anyone who'd listen. The chairman of the board was still baffled.

This story is exaggerated, of course, but parts of it are familiar to anyone who has been involved in a construction project. Building headaches are a fact of business life. Companies move. Businesses modernize old quarters. Growing organizations need more space. Companies incur some of their largest and longest term debts to finance these investments, while occupancy delays and construction quarrels can rank among the most debilitating problems a company can face. It is often impossible to predict exactly what a project will cost and how long it will take to complete, and it is always difficult to coordinate a dozen professionals—architects, engineers, contractors, bankers, lawyers, consultants, many with their own hidden agendas—and scores of subcontractors, suppliers, and workers.

All in all, the risks involved in a construction project are as great as any a company normally faces, and these risks are very different from the kind companies are used to. Yet many corporate officers and directors who consistently analyze and manage every other controllable risk fail to use all the tools available to control construction risk.

One reason CEOs and directors overlook or underestimate construction risk—and delegate it to subordinates to handle—is that construction is old technology. Buildings have been built before— what's so different about this one? The CFO is the watchdog for other expenses—why can't she watch these dollars too? The company has a department that does its purchasing—why can't it purchase a building? The facilities manager shares a vocabulary with the contractor—why not let him oversee the process? It seems foolish not to delegate a procedure that has been repeated a million times since the pyramids were finished.

But it is the exceptional CFO who can get beyond the first few summary numbers to understand what services a prospective contractor is really proposing; it is the unusual purchasing agent who can oversee completion of a product containing tens of thousands of parts delivered over a period of up to several years; and facilities managers seldom have the expertise to defend their employers against contractors' claims. Finally, most companies do not go through the building process frequently. Construction skills are simply not part of a normal manager's repertoire.

Construction is a confusing process governed by complicated contracts and involving complex relationships in several tiers. The customer is really buying a service, not a product. At one relationship level, the contractor performs an essential service by directing and coordinating the work of dozens or hundreds of subcontractors, suppliers, craftspeople, and laborers. At the next level, someone—sometimes the contractor or the architect—must also coordinate the builder's services with those of the architects, engineers, and consultants. Finally, someone must take control of the entire process and coordinate the coordinators. At this level, the CEO and the board of directors will either manage the project and its risks or let the risks manage them. There is no substitute for responsibility at the top.

There are seven steps in the analysis and management of construction risk:

1. Understanding the types and phases of risk.
2. Assessing the risks of a particular construction project.
3. Matching risks with in-house capabilities and building a construction team.
4. Defining a building strategy.
5. Picking the right kind of contract.
6. Choosing the builder.
7. Monitoring construction.

Understanding the Types and Phases of Risk

There are three kinds of construction risk, and they surface in two phases. The first kind of risk is financial—the project exceeds its budget and endangers the financial health of the company. Budget overruns are not always a matter of poor construction supervision. They are often the result of bad planning, wishful pricing, or poor coordination.

The second kind of risk has to do with time—the building is finished behind schedule. Delays can have devastating financial consequences. What damage will your retail outlet suffer if its space is ready on January 4 instead of November 15? How will your organization function if the computer room is not ready because no one was ever assigned responsibility for ensuring uninterruptible power? What is the toll on your business if your CFO has to spend 40 days in a construction arbitration case?

The third type of risk is design-related—the completed building does not meet the organization's needs. For example, a health care organization with a fixed budget might elect to build a small addition with above-average finishwork and systems, only to discover on completion that it doesn't have enough space. (Perhaps it should have built a larger but plainer facility for the same money.) Or an office developer might pick an air-conditioning system that allows individual controls for each office but turns out to be too noisy. (A better match might have been to sacrifice individual controls to gain acoustic value or perhaps to spend more money to get both.)

All three kinds of risks can be addressed in both the *preconstruction phase* and the *construction-and-settlement phase*. The preconstruction phase is often the most grueling for the owner and often the most important. The organization must now make projections about marketing, budget, space, and schedule, and make actual decisions about design, zoning requirements, traffic, and other environmental concerns. The risks in this phase are small in one sense because no one is actually building anything. But the risks are large in other ways. For one thing, consultants are expensive, and, since the construction loan is not yet in place, the company has to pay them out-of-pocket with unleveraged, highly speculative money. Also, a planning mistake or a piece of budgetary wishful thinking at this moment can cause big problems later on.

At this stage, Colossal County Hospital was already in trouble on three counts. First, the trustees were focusing on their individual specialties in marketing and finance, leaving the other preconstruction responsibilities to subordinates and doctors. Second, the architect dominated the preconstruction team and led it toward a design that would make more architectural and medical history than business sense. Third, the original contractor did not anticipate the growing wish lists, and, once he saw them, he was unable to convince the trustees that his new price was indeed reasonable—in fact, inescapable. The preconstruction team was poorly selected for the real needs of the project, and no one was in a position to monitor the team in detail and with authority.

There is a great deal of uncertainty and ambiguity in the preconstruction phase because the design-cost equation is constantly changing. A lot of hands-on specialists deal poorly with this lack of definition, and a poorly managed team can degenerate into chaos if the participants are allowed to hide behind their disciplines and stonewall or ignore each other.

The design-cost picture that emerges from this phase is the foundation on which great construction-period risk will rest, yet the work done now is the most manageable of the whole. Market and financial risks are external and uncontrollable. Preconstruction risk is internal to the team and can be controlled. The key to success in this phase, as elsewhere, is picking the right team—then providing coordination and central direction. The health care space and air-conditioning noise examples could both be best addressed in the preconstruction phase. Good use of the architect's and contractor's expertise at this juncture can save lots of problems later on.

In the construction-and-settlement phase, the risk factors move from planning to supervision. The design is mostly fixed; time risk no longer depends on creating a realistic schedule but on sticking to it; budgetary risk is no longer a matter of pricing but of cost control.

Yet appearances are deceptive. Depending on the contract, cost control is now mostly or entirely the contractor's responsibility. If your contract specified liquidated damages for late delivery, then schedule is the contractor's responsibility too, although most contracts allow several cost and schedule exceptions. What's more, a construction loan is now in place, so the bank reimburses the contractor directly for construction costs—usually on a monthly basis, always after carefully checking that the work has actually been done and the materials actually delivered, and almost always after holding back 5% to 10% of the total as a kind of performance guarantee until the entire project is complete and final settlement takes place. So where is the owner's risk?

Let's go back to Colossal County Hospital, a large institution brought to its knees at this very stage of the project. First of all, poor planning in the preconstruction phase came home to roost as the project drew to a close. For instance, the trustees had put the project out to bid on the basis of incomplete construction documents (blueprints and specifications), so the contractor had a right to adjust the price as the architect added new details. Second, while the bond issue set a limit on funds, the doctors and the architect fought to spend more, and the trustees never confronted the disparity. Third, the conditions of construction (the hospital's continued use of the space being renovated) and the trustees' repeated failure to make prompt decisions cost the contractor time, and such delays are legitimate grounds for a schedule extension. Finally, the mechanic's lien allows a contractor or subcontractor with a payment dispute to tie up a project in the courts and prevent its use or sale until the dispute is settled. And these are only a few of the problems that can crop up even after price, schedule, financing, payment mechanisms, and delivery date have supposedly been established once and for all.

As complex and as great as all these risks appear—particularly in the egregious case of Colossal County Hospital—it would be a waste of effort to try to eliminate every one of them, because that simply couldn't be done. The goal is to control and manage construction risk within reasonable limits.

Assessing the Risks of a Particular Construction Project

No two projects, no two sites, and no two construction teams are ever exactly the same. In order to pick the right team members, the right group of consultants, the right architect, the right contractor, and the right kind of contract, you need to understand the risks of your particular project. The crucial consideration is project complexity.

What are the company's needs for the project? Is there a rush for occupancy? Do you have time to develop complete blueprints and specifications before you put the project out to bid, or will you have to overlap this document preparation time with the start of construction? Are the mechanical systems routine, or will the contractor need to coordinate their design as well as installation? Is the quality of construction critical, as in a hospital, or do you need only a roof and walls? What about project financing? Some lenders will not make a commitment until they have seen the contracts and all of the completed drawings.

What about the site? There is a world of difference between building on a piece of well-drained farmland and building on a downtown site with an uncertain history and unknown conditions. Hazardous waste and the remains of old foundations are just two of the invisible surprises that are entirely the owner's responsibility in most contracts.

What about the structure? A new building will have many more components than an old one will, but a rehabilitation project will mean more unknowns and greater risks.

Evaluating the risk is the first step to controlling it. Exhibit I, "Assessing Construction Risk," lists the chief risk elements and shows how three hypothetical projects might have rated them.

Matching Risks with Capabilities and Building a Construction Team

Once you've estimated the risks of your project, the next step is to assess your organization's capacities. Building the construction team involves a series of classic make-or-buy decisions: What do we need? Can we provide it in-house? Should we buy it from outside? Exhibit II, "Assessing In-House Capability," will help give you an idea of your organization's capacity to deal with the hundreds of construction headaches that will come up during the project.

Everyone knows that building a building requires a contractor and usually an architect, a couple of engineers, a lender, several consultants, and sometimes a lawyer. (Of all these professionals, there is only one you will have the freedom to choose as you please—the architect. See the Appendix, "Choosing an Architect," for suggestions.) For the purposes of controlling risk, however, the principal players are your own board of directors, CEO, and senior staff, one or more of whom will actually oversee the entire project.

This person or persons—whom we might call the owner's representative (or even the developer)—will be at the center of a highly charged tangle of big egos, great stress, and high financial stakes. While the architect makes erudite speeches on aesthetics and design, the contractor may communicate mostly in profanities. While the banker speaks financial double-talk in hopes of reducing the lender's risk to zero, the heads of marketing and operations tear their hair out at the prospect of getting the wrong space at the wrong time. It takes a tough leader to coordinate everyone's efforts. If the CEO has the time and expertise, so much the better. If not, then he or she will have to delegate the responsibility to some unusual subordinate with the necessary breadth of knowledge and experience, or carefully assign parts of it to the architect or the contractor. But under no circumstances should coordination be delegated casually. Construction is one of the most argumentative industries on earth and the home of Murphy's Law—"If something can go wrong, it will."

Defining a Building Strategy

The exhibits have two important implications. First, they show how to identify and address the various individual elements of risk. Second, they define a strategy for the selection of a contractor and consultants. A concentration of high-risk components suggests you should look for the *performance* benefits of *cooperation* and try to find a contractor able to work as a team player. Predominantly low-risk components point instead to the *price* benefits of *competition*. Both kinds of contractors are readily available virtually everywhere.

The construction industry is highly fragmented and comparatively unsophisticated. Company strategies are often more intuitive than deliberate. Still, by choice or accident, construction companies lie somewhere on the spectrum between low-cost product providers at one end of the scale and highly differentiated service providers at the other. The challenge for clients is to identify the objective of each project and to pick the right fit.

Colossal County Hospital had a high-risk job and should have built a strong, cooperative team, including a contractor who would have worked closely with the board to solve problems. Instead, a board oriented too strongly toward competition made a decision solely on the basis of price and suffered the ill effects of an adversarial relationship with the builder. By contrast, the trustee who felt he'd been "soaked" on a time-and-materials contract for a warehouse did in fact waste money on cooperation. He should have had a competitive hard-money bid based on complete construction documents.

If your project is a simple, one-story building on a flat piece of vacant land, a low-cost provider is probably appropriate. The builder will not add much value beyond getting the material to the site and erecting it. If, on the other hand, your project is a complicated, fast-paced rehab, the noncraft services offered by a highly differentiated contractor may have great potential value. Your project may place special requirements on the contractor, like building

Exhibit I.　Assessing Construction Risk

Although many projects will have special risk factors of their own, this table lists the most important things to consider in assessing the risks of your project. The table is filled in for the situations of three hypothetical buildings. Colossal County Hospital is adding a new wing and renovating some older space on a crowded site in the middle of a city. Allperils Insurance is building a new, moderate-rise office structure in a suburban office park. Goodgoods Inc. is putting up a warehouse on former agricultural land near an interstate highway well away from populated areas.

H = High risk　　M = Moderate risk　　L = Low risk

Risk Elements	Colossal County Hospital	Allperils Insurance Company	Goodgoods Warehouse
Product			
Site			
Maneuvering room	H No staging area	M Office park; some constraints	L Plenty of room
Neighbors	H Residential and politicized	L Cooperative	L None
Soils	L Sand and gravel	H Peat and organics	M Sand and gravel, some boulders
Traffic	H Congested city streets	M Coordinate with neighbors	L Easy freeway access
Previous uses	M Old foundations	H Gas station site, buried tanks	L None
Foundation			
Excavation	H Retaining walls and underpinning	M Open cut, some shoring	L Open cut
Technology	L Backhoe and steam shovel	H Pressure-injected footings	L Simple concrete mat
Structure			
Design	L Beams and floors	L Columns, beams, and floors	L Bearing walls, joists, and deck
Materials	M Cast-in-place concrete	L Steel and concrete composite	L Masonry, steel, concrete
Exterior			
Design	H Complex: variety and details	M Prefabricated metal panels	L Stucco
Materials	M Brick, stone, glass	H Stainless steel	L Stucco
Dimensional tolerance	M Moderate	H Low tolerance	L High tolerance
Mechanical and electrical			
Heating-and-cooling plant	H Cogeneration steam and electric	L Gas-fired boiler and chiller	L Electric heat, no A.C.
Distribution	L Hot-and-cold-water fan-coil units	M Heat pumps	L None

Communications	H Hospital monitoring systems	H Fiber-optic voice and data	L None
Finishes			
Complexity	M Moderate	L Straightforward	L Spartan
Materials	M Moderate: paint and plaster	H Marble and mahogany lobby	L Paint, paneling, drywall
On-site craftsmanship	M Durable more than memorable	H Close tolerances	L Serviceable
Sourcing	L Local warehouse stock	M Some special-order items	L Local warehouse stock
End uses			
Flexibility intended	L No: floor plans fixed	M Partitions changeable	M Highly flexible
Impact on business	H Can't operate without it	L Moving day can wait	H Can't afford warehouse delay
Special situations	H Renovation while space in use	L None	L None
Process			
Financing			
Preconstruction sources	M Limited	L In-house funds	L In-house funds
Permanent financing	H Reliable but inflexible	L In-house funds	M Traditional mortgage
Lender requirements	M Strict; bonded contractor	L Strict but self-administered	M Lenient
Time			
Preconstruction time allowed	L Years	M Months	H Weeks
Construction pace	H Fast-track	M Normal	H Selected overtime work
Architecture			
Complexity of project	H High	M Suburban office standards	L Low
Focus of designer	M Make architectural history	M Promote client image	L Economy and ease of construction
Completeness of plans	H Not enough for bid confidence	L Complete	M Essential items shown
Compensation to architect	M High pay for quality designer	M Moderate fee	L Low fee for standard product
Owner's decision structure	H Many committees and users	M One small committee	L One person

Exhibit I. (continued)

Risk Elements		Colossal County Hospital	Allperils Insurance Company	Goodgoods Warehouse
Need for "cooperative" input	Rethinking of design option	H Many preliminary designs	M General program known	L Few, if any
	Relative number unknowns	M Moderate; mostly new construction	L Few	L Very few
	Budgeting expertise needed	H Complex schedule and cost issues	M Some (atrium, lobby pricing)	L None beyond architect
Approvals	Regulations and codes	H Many agencies and rules	M Standard life-safety codes	L Basic building codes
	Politics	L Strong community support	L Conformity standards	L No issues

Exhibit II. Assessing In-House Capability

To make an adequate assessment of how much outside help you will need to get your building built, you need to look at your staff's talents. Basically, more in-house talent means less risk.

Capability	Colossal County Hospital	Allperils Insurance Company	Goodgoods Warehouse
Budgeting talent	M One physical-plant veteran	H Nobody	L One former contractor in-house
Design talent	H Nobody in-house	H Nobody	H Nobody
Team-building talent	H No focus on this project	M Moderate	L One strong CEO
Monitoring talent	M Finance experts, no construction experience	M Finance experts, no construction experience	H Nobody
Appetite for conflict	H Board doesn't like conflicts	L Well-developed	L CEO happy to knock heads
Fund resources	H No money for overruns	L Can fund overruns in-house	M Need to borrow more for overruns

one phase while the next is still being designed and priced; anticipating discovery of unknown conditions, like concealed rotting timbers; doing a workmanlike job from inadequate design documents; or working around existing occupants. Contractors who can do all this will charge more, but they will also act more like members of your team.

Another service the differentiated contractor can provide is to help you take advantage of the fragmentation of the building business by getting good competition among subcontractors. The commercial building industry is made up of thousands of subcontractors in several hundred specialized trades. These small companies tend to be entrepreneurial and fiercely independent, and their fractiousness can be a problem or an asset. Subcontracts and purchase orders can amount to 70% or 80% of the total cost of a commercial building project. Builders skilled at handling competition at the trade level may charge a higher fee for their own services and still produce the lowest total final cost.

Some contractors are also adept at forming value-adding partnerships with the subcontractors they use most often. Teams like these can gain efficiencies from shared design and production information as well as from a good understanding of each other's work styles. In this kind of cooperative setting, the game can have a sum higher than zero. Teamwork reduces friction, uncertainty, inefficiency, and duplication of effort.

Such teamwork is what Colossal County Hospital needed at every level. Of course, building teamwork requires energy and trust. As always, the question for management is whether the added value is worth the added cost. Colossal County didn't expend the energy or money to build the right team when it should have. Other owners may not need to.

Picking the Right Kind of Contract

The disparities among the levels of service outlined here have led to three main contract types. All three have been around for years, but many owners don't understand their relation to risk control. In most cases, a good evaluation of the kind and level of risk will point clearly to one of these three contracts.

The *lump-sum* contract is easy to understand. Each contractor bidding on the project estimates a total cost, adds a profit margin, and bids a fixed price for the job. The owner picks the lowest bid. If costs go up, the price to the owner remains the same. If costs go down—and the incentive to *make* them go down by cutting corners can be considerable—the extra margin goes to the contractor. This contract is truly a zero-sum game. Whatever the contractor gets is something you don't get.

With a lump-sum contract, the contractor takes all the visible risk, and the owner takes none. This seems like a good bet for high-risk projects, but just the opposite is true. First, should costs rise unexpectedly above the price that was bid and accepted, your contractor's dedication to the job may abruptly vanish. Second, with a lump-sum contract, the price may be fixed, but so is the scope of the work. Even a small change in the project can throw the whole contract out the window, and you cannot afford to renegotiate that contract once the work is under way. By avoiding risk, you also give up most of your decision-making power. In other words, you pay your money and you take your chances—which is no way to build a hospital or any other highly differentiated structure. Still, the lump-sum contract is the right contract for simple jobs where price is more important than collaboration.

Most people are familiar with *time-and-materials* contracts—based on the cost of work plus a fee. Lawyers bill this way, and so do auto mechanics. The builder gets reimbursed for the actual costs of the work, whatever they are, plus a percentage fee or markup. So, in other words, the owner takes all the risk and the contractor none. The customer can be fairly certain that work will be properly done, because there is no incentive to cut corners. Of course, the more the contractor spends, the more the contractor makes—and we know from experience that auto mechanics and lawyers have no particular incentive to hurry.

Despite the obvious disadvantages in terms of risk, there are three fairly common situations—and one fairly uncommon one—where time-and-materials is nevertheless the right contract for the owner. The first is when quality matters more than money. The second is when time is very limited and the contractor will have to work extensive overtime. The third is when construction documents are incomplete or missing, which leaves the contractor nothing on which to base a bid. The fourth situation comes up when owners have so much construction expertise and so much time to devote to supervision that they can get exactly what they want and still hold down costs by directing the location and quality of every brick and nail.

For most situations, one of these two contracts will fit the bill. But for many large construction users, a hybrid form called *guaranteed-maximum-price* is more appropriate. It is often the best contract for performing the work identified as high-risk in the two exhibits.

Like time-and-materials, guaranteed-maximum-price is also based on the cost of work plus a fee, but risk is shared. Up to the predetermined maximum price, the contractor passes along all costs to the owner, but once that price is reached, all risk belongs to the builder.

As in a time-and-materials contract, the owner benefits when direct costs are less than expected. But when costs go up too far, contractors absorb the overrun, as they would in a lump-sum contract. Generally, this arrangement keeps the best features of both other contract types and allows the owner to have his cake and eat it too. Most often, the guaranteed-maximum price will be set higher than the lump-sum price for the same project because the contractor's profit is capped.

The goal in this case is to make contractors team players without giving them carte blanche. The construction company's profit does not depend on cost cutting but rather on good performance of this service for the owner. What the customer gets is a limit on exposure and a cooperative relationship instead of an adversarial one.

Exhibit III, "Cost vs. Price with Three Contract Types," shows price in relation to actual construction cost in lump-sum, time-and-materials, and guaranteed-maximum-price contracts.

These three contract types all assume the traditional owner-architect-contractor configuration. There are three less common ways to assign these roles. With a *turnkey* contract, the owner buys site, design, and finished building as a package. The supplier secures the construction financing and plays the role of owner and contractor (and sometimes architect) during construction. Turnkey contracts are suited to situations where the needs of the user are easily described.

A *design-build* contract is very like a turnkey contract in that the architect and contractor work under one contract, giving one source of responsibility. This fosters cooperation at the cost of eliminating traditional checks and balances. But in design-build, as opposed to turnkey, the owner is responsible for financing.

Construction management, in its simplest form, is merely a consulting service. Construction managers often supplement the own-

Exhibit III.   Cost vs. Price with Three Contract Types (in thousands of dollars)

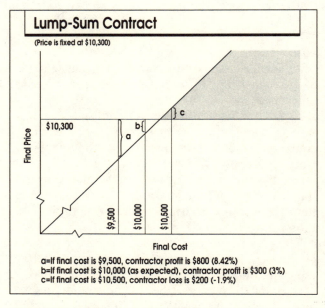

Lump-Sum Contract
(Price is fixed at $10,300)

Final Price — Final Cost

$10,300

a=If final cost is $9,500, contractor profit is $800 (8.42%)
b=If final cost is $10,000 (as expected), contractor profit is $300 (3%)
c=If final cost is $10,500, contractor loss is $200 (-1.9%)

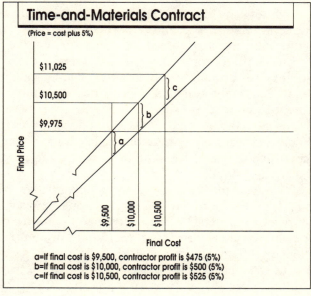

Time-and-Materials Contract
(Price = cost plus 5%)

$11,025

$10,500

$9,975

Final Price — Final Cost

a=If final cost is $9,500, contractor profit is $475 (5%)
b=If final cost is $10,000, contractor profit is $500 (5%)
c=If final cost is $10,500, contractor profit is $525 (5%)

Assume that the contractor believes your project will wind up costing just about $10 million to build. These three graphs show the price to you and the profit or loss to the contractor for three different kinds of contracts at three different actual final cost levels. At point *a* in each diagram, the contractor has shaved $500,000 from the anticipated cost. At *b*, costs have run as expected. At *c*, there has been a cost overrun of $500,000. Basically, with a *lump-sum*, the contractor gets all the savings and takes all the risk. With *time-and-materials*, the owner gets the savings and takes the risk. And with *guaranteed-maximum-price*, the owner gets the savings, the builder takes the risk.

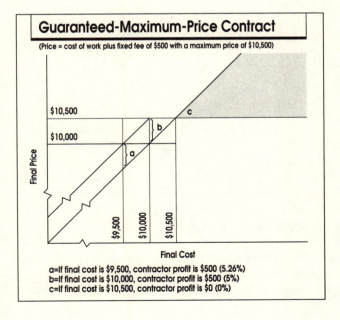

Guaranteed-Maximum-Price Contract

(Price = cost of work plus fixed fee of $500 with a maximum price of $10,500)

Final Price

$10,500
$10,000

$9,500
$10,000
$10,500

Final Cost

a=If final cost is $9,500, contractor profit is $500 (5.26%)
b=If final cost is $10,000, contractor profit is $500 (5%)
c=If final cost is $10,500, contractor profit is $0 (0%)

er's in-house construction team by giving advice and providing supervision for a fee. They take no fiduciary responsibility, and they do not guarantee price, results, or schedule. (Be aware that architects, engineers, contractors, and consultants all use the phrase "construction management" a little differently. Before you contract for construction management, make sure you know exactly what you're getting.)

Choosing the Builder

It sounds elementary at this point to say that the way a company chooses a builder should match its project-risk level and contract type. But the old practice of bidding out contracts is so well established that organizations resort to it even when it makes no sense. Each kind of project and contract should have its own selection criteria.

LUMP-SUM.   The builder for a lump-sum contract can be chosen almost entirely by means of an open bid based on construction documents—blueprints and specifications—that clearly define the scope of the work. (Never put partial documents out to bid. In fact, if you must choose a contractor before the documents are done, lump-sum may be the wrong type of contract.) Beyond requiring bidders to satisfy some minimum level of experience, reputation, and financial strength, price is really all you care about.

One warning: Resist the temptation to take advantage of a very low bid. It may be a mistake based on misinterpreted construction documents, and the ensuing fight won't be worth it.

TIME-AND-MATERIALS.   For a so-called cost-plus or time-and-materials contract, reputation, ability, and trust are paramount. Check references, look for the right chemistry between all parties, make sure you are comfortable with the builder. Whatever you do, don't try to make a selection on the basis of some kind of estimated bid. If the contract has no cap, the bid means nothing. It can only tempt you to choose the lowest of several meaningless numbers, and that is a good way to pick the least competent candidate.

GUARANTEED-MAXIMUM-PRICE.   The process here is much like the one above. Your guide should be the contractor's experience, references, and integrity, and the chemistry between you. You are planning to pay a fee to a company for its competence in managing construction, meeting schedules, maintaining quality, providing construction services, and treating its clients honestly and fairly. Establishing that competence should be your only criterion.

Any company in the running for this type of contract will be able to give you the names of previous customers who can tell you just how well it performed in the past. Ask about the accuracy of the cost estimates and the extent of the savings returned to the owner (or the size of the overrun absorbed by the contractor). Ask how many serious fights there were and whether they were settled satisfactorily. Find out if the space was delivered on time. Ask for references from former subcontractors as well, and find out what they thought of the company they worked for. You are buying a value-added service. Make sure you will get what you're paying for.

Monitoring Construction

Everybody likes to watch excavating equipment and play sidewalk superintendent when the big steel flies. Monitoring the team and the contract is much less fun—and much more important. Once again, the scope and method of supervision depends on the kind of contract.

On a lump-sum contract, the developer or the owner's representative must monitor both materials and workmanship to make sure the contractor does not pad his or her own profit by delivering less than what was contracted for. This level of attention calls for a construction supervisor who understands specifications, details, workmanship, and materials gradation and handling.

On a time-and-materials contract, the construction supervisor's job is to see that the contractor doesn't waste the owner's money. The builder will not likely cut corners, but cost control probably won't be a top priority either. This kind of contract needs a monitor who understands labor productivity, effective use of raw materials, and cost accounting.

In theory, the structure of a guaranteed-maximum-price contract reduces the degree of supervision the owner will need. The contractor assumes the risk of a cost overrun and earns a predetermined fee to make sure that the work and the materials are right. Still, a prudent owner will keep an eye on workmanship and accounting. The skills of an experienced construction supervisor must still be available, but the need is less urgent.

Clearly, the person who acts as construction supervisor needs experience and expertise. Few CEOs—and few members of the board—would qualify. If the project coordinator is not a construction expert, it may sometimes be worthwhile to hire a construction consultant. Often the architect is used for construction supervision, and sometimes this works very well. But architects are trained to design, and their capacity and willingness to check on workmanship, monitor materials, and oversee accounting is at best uneven.

Then, too, as projects grow more complex, the architect has a progressively greater need to work with, not against, the contractor. There will always be issues of interpretation, aesthetics, even cost, for them to consider together. And in a project with many unknown risks—a building with marine foundations, say, or the renovation of a historic structure—the contractor's experience and judgment are crucial assets for the architect. An owner's insistence on police duty can impair an architect's ability to work with the builder.

Colossal County Hospital survived its ordeal—the city intervened with an emergency loan and a supplemental bond issue—and learned from the experience. For its next addition, the board built a team from the beginning and stayed abreast of the process. The new chairman of the board, head of a local management consulting firm, took on the role of in-house developer. She led the team through a preconstruction analysis of complexity and risk that then drove the choice of contract, builder, financing, and schedule. The chosen contractor had a reputation for accurate pricing and cooperative problem solving. The project came in on time and even slightly under budget.

The manufacturing trustee learned his lesson too. For his new distribution center, he hired an architect who could provide him with dependable, detailed drawings; he put the project out to bid only when all of the specifications and blueprints were complete; and he chose the low bidder from a field of 12 prequalified builders. The space cost him 50% less than with the earlier time-and-materials contract.

Construction is a major obligation for many growing companies. The initial estimates of cost, time, and trouble are bound to change dramatically as work progresses. The construction team itself may be volatile and problematic. But the directors and top management of your company can identify, analyze, and rationally control these risks.

Appendix

Choosing an Architect

Kathy A. Spiegelman

Even if you've never managed a building project, you can still help your company find a suitable architect. Here are some tips for making the right choice:

1. *Name a design committee.* As soon as you've established the need for a building project, set up a committee. Members will likely include the CEO, the CFO, probable users, and maintenance staff. Decide how the architect will be chosen—by consensus, majority vote, or executive decision.

2. *Outline the project.* The committee must start by agreeing on a project program. Clarify what you need and want in a building. Think about goals, schedule, budget, and locations. Decide what matters most—speed, cost, design—and make a preliminary assessment of risk. For all its technical expertise, the design firm is only a consultant. There is no substitute for the owner's overall direction.

3. *Decide on a selection process.* Expensive design competitions are appropriate for museums and multinational headquarters buildings. The usual method—much preferred by architects—is prequalification and interview.

4. *Make a preliminary list of architects.* Get a list of local design firms. Ask friends, business associates, and your facilities managers for names. Prestige is less important than matching the architect with the scope of the challenges. Send a "request for qualifications" (RFQ) to likely firms. This can simply be a letter describing the project and asking interested design firms to submit their credentials.

5. *Shorten the list.* When the RFQ responses have come in and you've reduced the list to no more than about a dozen candidates, follow up with an RFP (request for proposals) to help you decide which firms to interview. Of course, the amount of detail you can expect from design firms in response to an RFP will depend on how much information you give them and how many contenders have a shot at the job. In assessing proposals, consider the following (the first two are the most important):

☐ Proposed project team. Will the firm's principals work on your project day-to-day? If not, who will?

☐ Budget-and-schedule track record. Staying within the financial and time constraints is critical.

☐ Size of firm and length of practice. Big firms have depth, but a small firm just might give you more personalized service.

☐ Recent project history. Look for similar clients and building types, but remember that no two projects are ever exactly the same.

☐ Location. Local firms have a decided advantage in dealing with local authorities and regulations. Distant firms can reduce their disadvantage by working with a local architect.

☐ Special expertise. Rehabs are different from new construction; urban and suburban areas are different; historic preservation is a special skill.

☐ Knowledge of codes. Coordination of electrical and mechanical systems with layout and furnishings is the architect's responsibility before it becomes the contractor's.

☐ Supervisory experience. If the design firm will be supervising construction, make sure it knows how.

☐ Fee proposal. Architects can propose a fee only if you've defined project goals and scope enough to give them a clear sense of the job.

6. *Interview the short list.* The interviews will be interesting and entertaining—design firms are good at this—but don't be seduced by slides, models, and a lot of talk about the design process. Ask about the firm's approach to cost estimating and cost control; experience in getting local government approvals and handling public hearings; procedures for solving design problems; relations with the special technical consultants the project will require. Otherwise, the interview should be an elaboration of the RFP response. Make a particular point of discussing the firm's experience with construction bidding and the different kinds of contracts. Finally, make sure that the key figures on the project team are at the interview, and be sure

you're comfortable with the personalities you'll be working with. From time to time, your architect will probably have to read your mind in order to turn your wishes into blueprints. Ask yourself if this is the firm that can translate your personal vision into concrete detail.

7. *Check references.* Interviewing will give you specific questions to ask of references. Ask particularly about cost control, schedule compliance, and problem solving. Find out which individuals worked on the project, and speak to them. Your principal question is whether the previous client would use the same architect again, and why or why not. Visit finished buildings and talk to their users.

8. *Get off to a good start.* Once you understand your own goals, choosing the right architect is a matter of combining thoughtful questions with common sense. When your decision is made, notify the unsuccessful candidates and give each an explanation of your choice. Then the real challenge begins—working with the chosen architect to satisfy your company's needs.

PART III

III

Leading

1
The Project Manager

Paul O. Gaddis

In new and expanding fields like electronics, nucleonics, astronautics, avionics, and cryogenics, a new type of manager is being bred. Although he goes by many titles, the one most generally used is *project manager*. His role in modern industry deserves more scrutiny than it has received from students of management and professional managers.

Generally speaking, the project manager's business is to create a *product*—a piece of advanced-technology hardware. The primary tool available to him is the brainpower of men who are professional specialists in diverse fields. He uses this tool in all the phases of the creation of his product, from concept through the initial test operation and manufacturing stages.

This article will consider those functions of management which receive special emphasis in advanced-technology industry:

What does a project manager in advanced-technology industry do?

What kind of man must he be?

What training is prerequisite for success?

Before going into these topics, let us first take a look at this new industry in which the project manager works.

Meeting Specifications

Advanced-technology industry is the kind of business where a complex product is designed, developed, and manufactured to meet predetermined performance specifications. The advanced-technology company is committed at the outset to succeed in meeting these performance specifications or acceptable modifications thereof.

In this kind of work the development phase is always substantial, since the essential function of the new industry is the adaptation of recent research findings to the solution of specific problems in creating a new product. But operating groups in advanced-technology companies do not themselves perform fundamental research. While advanced-technology practitioners recognize the essential need for a vital output of fundamental research, and are in fact dependent on this output for survival as an industry, they do not work in the fundamental areas.

UNIT ORGANIZATION

A project is an organization unit dedicated to the attainment of a goal—generally the successful completion of a developmental product on time, within budget, and in conformance with predetermined performance specifications.

The project staff will be a "mix" of brainpower, varying with the project's mission. For example, a project involving a high degree of development, such as one devoted to achieving a practical demonstration of ionic propulsion that can later be applied in rocketry, will have a high proportion of scientists to engineers and a high proportion of theoretically inclined personnel. In contrast, a project committed to attaining a successful full-power trial of a propulsion engine utilizing a proven solid propellant will have more engineers than scientists.

Projects are typically organized by task (vertical structure) instead of by function (horizontal organization). The relative advantages of "project" and "systems" organizations have been the subject of widespread controversy, and it is not my intent here to elaborate on this issue. The obvious organizational goal is to seek the advantages of both—the vertical structure in which the control and performance associated with autonomous management are maintained for a given project, and the horizontal in which better continuity, flexibility, and use of scarce talents may be achieved in a technical group.

Unique Characteristics

A study of the project manager function must examine these topics: what he does, what he must be, and what training he needs. In considering these, I shall limit myself to the more or less autonomous project in which "real" management and personnel responsibility resides with the project manager. This autonomy is in contrast to the organization in which the project function is maintained by a "project engineer," who often is relegated to a staff position with responsibilities far outweighing his authority, and who must pursue tenuous relationships with a great deal of skill and persistence to achieve even modest performance goals.

How does the job of the advanced-technology project manager differ from the picture of the conventional manager in modern industry? For one thing, he is managing a higher proportion of *professionals,* from the working level of the "journeyman engineer" up through his subordinate managers. Even in manufacturing operations on advanced-technology products it is often necessary to introduce engineers and scientists to the laboratory floor in large numbers. As further evidence of the technological infiltration, note that purchasing groups for these projects are likely to be staffed by a substantial proportion of engineers.

In view of this, the project manager needs a different attitude regarding the classic management functions of control, coordination, communication, and the setting of performance standards. Moreover, the professional attitude and approach is steadily gaining emphasis and more widespread acceptance throughout all of the engineering industries.

In learning to manage a group of professional employees, the usual boss-subordinate relationship must be modified. Of especial importance, the *how*—the details or methods of work performance by a professional employee—should be established *by the employee.* It follows that he must be given the facts necessary to permit him to develop a rational understanding of the *why* of tasks assigned to him.

Moreover, if this kind of employee is to be treated as a professional, he must have established for him performance standards of the highest order, and must be accountable for productivity at the professional level. He may be granted the prerogatives of a professional—independence of detailed supervision, freedom from administrative routine where feasible, and working quarters which afford privacy and comfort. But at the same time he must never be excused from the responsibility of having to *produce* in accordance with the exacting requirements of his profession.

These points are illustrated by the actions of a line engineer in a West Coast company:

This manager had cut his teeth on the air-frame assembly lines, but was now leading a group which was assembling and checking out highly complex air-borne electronics equipment. He decided that there was a real need in his group for a young electronics engineer who would assist in the interpretation of quality control tests.

After obtaining the necessary approval from management, he made several requests to the "professional employment office" to get such an engineer.

Following about two weeks of waiting, however, he saw that there seemed to be no intention to start action on his behalf in the personnel office. In exasperation, he finally called on the supervisor of professional employment, who was a doctor of engineering placed in this position to expedite the acquisition of key scientific personnel. The manager was told somewhat blandly by the young academician that the employment office had never been informed of the *reasons* why an assembly and test group should require the services of an additional professional electronics engineer.

After the manager had finished sputtering about line authority not needing reasons, he finally came to realize that his best course of action would be to explain in painful detail his need for the additional engineer. The supervisor accepted his reasons, and he got his new engineer in a week.

Another unique aspect of the project manager's job is that his task is finite in duration. He cannot see a reasonably long line of repetitive or similar functions stretching ahead of him as his management counterparts in manufacturing or sales do. Nor can he modify his assembly line to manufacture a new product. He is managing a specific group of advanced specialists; the professional mix of his group is tailored specifically for the accomplishment of an assigned mission. If he and his group are successful performers, they will complete all facets of their job, and so work themselves out of a job, as quickly as possible. This may be a year or less in some projects, and may run to five years and upward for long-range, high-budget projects.

In any case, the project manager must trust his corporate management, implicitly in most cases, to provide him and his forces with continuity of work on successive projects. Needless to say, the record of top management in achieving this continuity will affect the peace of mind, if not the performance, of the project manager and his entire staff.

Another feature of the project manager's job is the absence of feedback information during the early stages and often other stages of his project. Under the servomechanism analogy of management control, a manager establishes a closed loop in which the performance output of his group is fed back to him, compared with performance standards, and corrective control action is then directed into the system.

However, in advanced-technology work, during the design phase of a project and before test results of newly developed equipment are available, the project manager often finds himself like a pilot flying blind, assisted by a relatively unproven set of instruments. His experience, judgment, and faith must carry him through until early test results become available; from this first feedback he can modify the design approach in a direction most likely to meet the acid requirements of further proof tests. Meanwhile, during these periods of blind flying, he may be forced to make long-term decisions which commit substantial funds.

It is because of these "facts of life" in project work that crisis, uncertainty, and suspense are continually recurring to test the mettle of the manager and his staff. To illustrate:

A project group was developing a small liquid fuel missile for a military mission. Early in the project it became apparent that a new high-capacity pump for the propulsion system was going to be needed.

After an exhaustive analysis of the problem, it was decided that the prospects for developing and proving the kind of pump needed, in the time interval permitted by the project schedule, were good enough to warrant committing the project to the use of this pump.

A pump vendor was selected, and this vendor in turn set up his own subproject under a rigorous time schedule to develop the new pump in time for the missile application. As a matter of prudence an alternate pump supplier was also charged with the mission of producing a pump to meet the requirements, using a different design approach from that of the first supplier.

During the months which ensued, the responsibility for the validity of the initial decision never rested lightly on the management personnel in the project. In the normal course of progress, substantial funds were committed to the propulsion system design and to the procurement of other components for the system. Moreover, it was at times necessary to make partly intuitive decisions based on the engineers' progress on the pump under development. These decisions in turn affected the design of the other components in the system.

For a period of five months, the entire progress in design and procurement of hardware was based on faith in the integrity of the original pump decision. This foundation became more substantial only when one of the two pump suppliers was able to place a prototype of his pump in a test loop and prove its performance. And even here there was risk, since many new components have worked beautifully in the prototype test stage but have been subject to failures when the manufactured versions were placed in use.

One of the two developmental pumps proved clearly unsuccessful, while the other just barely met performance requirements on the test stand. This necessitated a vigorous redesign effort in the project. The pump performance specifications were somewhat relaxed, and the remainder of the system was altered to accommodate the new piece of equipment. Late changes had to be accepted, both on the drawing boards and in the shops, in the other components being procured for the system. In short, the project staff went through a period of technological "crisis." In this case, fortunately, the crisis was successfully resolved. The project's prototype missile was ready for test with only a minor delay in schedule.

Authority and Responsibility

Essential to the project management concept is a clear delineation of authority and responsibility. The manager knows that his basic responsibilities are to deliver his end product (1) in accordance with performance requirements, (2) within the limitations of his budget, and (3) within the time schedule that his company or customer has specified. In general, the manager will delegate by tasks, so that subordinate managers in his group will have these same three responsibilities for subprojects.

Success or failure may well hinge on the manager's ability to discern fine variations in emphasis among performance, budget, and time schedule needs and to resolve the continuous apparent conflicts which occur between them. During the life of an average project the relative importance of each of his three responsibilities may change several times. It can be fatal to overemphasize the schedule when dollars have become the governing requirement, or vice versa. Likewise, performance requirements must be met or trimmed to fit reality. The skillful project manager will aim for a balanced emphasis; he will try to stay flexible so he can shift and adapt to new circumstances as they occur.

Like the line manager, the project manager is at once a man of action, a man of thought, and a front man. As a man of action, his most important function will be the establishment and the preservation of a sense of momentum throughout all layers of his project. What he will strive hardest to avoid is "dead center" situations in which general inertia seems to become overpowering and his technical people for the moment see no direction in which to advance. Thus, the usual management function of trouble shooting, or of unraveling the knots, will occupy a great deal of his time.

The first-line supervisors—the "supervising engineers"—are by definition the men who play the key roles in guiding the day-by-day progress of a project toward its goals. Such a supervisor often bears the same range of burdens borne by his manufacturing counterpart; demands on his time can easily be overpowering if the project manager does not act to shield him from diversionary requirements.

At the same time it should be borne in mind that in attempting to shield a supervisor, to free him to concentrate chiefly on the vital engineering job at hand, the project manager can unknowingly deal a severe blow to the supervisor's advancement potential. The supervisor is at a critical point in his career, at which leadership capability and administrative potential can blossom or be blighted. A general and basic tenet of management—the training of individuals for leadership—must not be shelved merely because the pace of an advanced-technology project seems at times to be overpowering. Instead the project manager must walk the middle course. For example, he may shield the supervisor from poorly founded requests for detailed information by a staff office, while at the same time letting him resolve with the personnel department a tough question in personnel administration involving one of his engineers.

In pursuing his objective of maintaining momentum, the project manager must be constantly aware of the apparent disdain for time commitments which prevails on the part of the more theoretically inclined scientists and engineers. While this attitude is a rather deep study in itself, one part of it that must be understood is the drive for perfection that so often characterizes the professional mind. Any kind of promised delivery date inevitably involves a compromise with perfection, in that the product or study must be cut off, wrapped up, and delivered at that point, thereby leaving dangling the further improvements which the scientist would like to make. The tendency to finish the job to a *T*, if allowed to run rampant, can result in continuous postponements of output and reduce the productivity of the project as a whole.

In the nuclear power industry, one can find in almost any reactor project a common example of the perfectionist and his tribulations:

A nuclear reactor core—representing an investment of hundreds of thousands of dollars—must be loaded with a specific amount of fissionable fuel (usually uranium). The decision of just how much fuel is correct is one of the more agonizing which must be faced by industry technologists.

Typically, the loading is set by the designers using early calculations based on a series of simplified reactor experiments with varying quantities of nuclear fuel. While this first loading figure is adequate, it varies from the *optimum* depending on the performance of the nuclear designers in their highly complex and difficult art. Nevertheless, the prolonged processes of reactor core manufacture must be commenced without further delay, and during the ensuing year or longer the scientists undertake a detailed performance analysis of the reactor core with the established loading. This analysis is conducted by means of the most advanced high-capacity digital computers, and hopefully yields a confirmation of the fuel loading. Specifically it tells the designers how close they have come to the optimum loading; the nearer the optimum, the greater the reliability of the reactor, and the more economic its performance.

The perfectionist problem first arises when preliminary information about the fuel loading is requested by the manufacturing engineers from the designers. The nuclear designers are reluctant to part with what they feel are "premature" data. From this point on, the project manager faces a tough series of decisions—he will have to balance the demands of the schedule with the incremental improvements in data to be gained by continuing the design study "one more week." The designers will be quite articulate in expressing the gains to be realized by deferring the schedule.

In every nuclear project the time must come when, by management decree if necessary, the first loading data are released and further improvement is considered unwarranted. At this point the manufacturing engineers commence to build the reactor, while the scientists begin the detailed, confirmatory analysis of the reactor they have just designed. In the nuclear industry, fortunately, the detailed analysis generally confirms that the originally established loading was near optimum, thanks largely to the very high caliber of scientists and engineers in this field.

In addition to his everyday job of keeping the work moving, the project manager should put a good deal of thought into planning. The crux of effective performance of any project lies in the interrelationship between organizational structure and individuals. The art of organization planning involves the correct tailoring of organizational structure to available individuals, and vice versa. An often-repeated thought in the literature of scientific administration is that although the organizational structure of a project is important, if not vital, it will not make up for inadequate caliber of technologists in the organization. On the other hand, poor organization structure can tie up the output of topnotch engineers and scientists.

In advanced-technology industries, sound organization planning requires adroitness in recruiting scarce talent both from within and without the parent organization. It also involves the ability to utilize engineers and scientists who in some cases do not measure up to reasonable requirements for the project—the ability to shape a team which can "play over its head" when it has to. Sound organization planning in a project cannot be done without a thorough understanding of the personalities, the characteristics, and the attitudes of all the technologists, both as individuals and as members of their particular professional methodologies.

Advance planning is vital in a project. In this area, an important duty of the project manager is to avoid the crises that often manifest themselves during the design, manufacturing, and checkout stages. Perfection will never be attained, and the best efforts of the manager can serve only to reduce, never to eliminate, these crises. Still, advance planning pays for itself many times over.

While technological crises have become accepted as an inherent part of our advanced-technology projects, it must always be realized that each of these crucial periods leaves residual effects throughout the remaining course of the project. Thus, the resolution of such a

crisis generally involves a sacrifice of engineering principle for ex-
pediency, which may in turn lead to subsequent crises. Further,
each crisis, with its resultant need for immediate solution, erodes
the constructive attitude of the project's engineers and scientists,
particularly the theoreticians.

Clearly, therefore, the more that can be done to avoid or alleviate
these situations in advance, the better. It is unfortunately true that
most crises that arise during the course of a project can be traced
to lack of adequate advance planning.

At any time during the course of the project, the manager may
be called on to act as front man to help shape or reshape the policies
that affect his project relative to the corporate structure and the
company's development objectives. Contrary to much opinion about
the advanced-technology industries, "selling" is a never-ending job
of a project manager, as it is of most other senior managers in the
corporate organization. In the matters of acquiring scarce funds,
people, and materials, the project manager must always be able to
make an effective presentation, often on short notice. Many project
managers have suddenly found themselves, in mid-course, fighting
for the very existence of their project.

While the outcome of many such struggles is often beyond the
influence of any actions taken by the manager, it is true that in
numerous other cases his actions as a fully informed representative
of the project will have a profound influence on the outcome.

Individual in Between

As the foregoing may suggest, life is not dull for a project manager.
He is the man in between management and the technologist—the
one man in the organization who must be at home in the front office
talking about budgets, time schedules, and corporate policies *and*
at home in the laboratory talking about technical research and development problems. But he is not a superman. He cannot be expected to double as a member of the executive committee and as a
scientist equally well. Being a little of both, he is different from
both—and it is precisely this quality which makes him so valuable.
In his own right he does what neither the front-office executive nor
the scientist can do: accomplish the aims of his corporate management, while serving as a perpetual buffer so that the engineers and
scientists can meet the technological objectives that only they can
define and only their output can meet.

Clearly, therefore, the job is an unusual one. What manner of man is needed to fill it? What aptitudes should he have? What special difficulties should he be willing and able to handle?

REASONABLE "PROJECTITIS"

The subject of "projectitis" may appropriately be examined here; it is a seeing of all things as though a particular project were the center of the corporate universe—the alpha and the omega of the development effort. This phenomenon of organizational beings as observed in World War II was called "theateritis." The late General Henry H. Arnold, in his autobiography *Global Mission,*[1] remarked that the disease of theateritis—the inability of an Air Force commander to be cognizant of the problems of war in any theater other than his own—caused him great concern and trouble in his personal dealings with his top field commanders. However, General Arnold noted at the same time that he would not have under his command any general who did not suffer from this disease.

The project manager on his own battleground needs a modicum of "projectitis" to generate the necessary drive and momentum to spark the project to success. These symptoms of projectitis will be observed by top corporate executives, but they will expect this malady and will themselves suffer with acute outbreaks from time to time, depending on which and how many of their projects are in the limelight.

However, when dealing with his engineers and scientists, the project manager must not suffer, or appear to suffer, from any blind or extreme case of projectitis in establishing schedular aims and policy objectives. If he does succumb to this tendency, perhaps as a result of pressure from an afflicted management, at least two adverse results may occur: (1) technological advancement in the development of his product, which in actuality is the most basic of the project's responsibilities, will suffer; (2) the human resources of the project (the most important resources in advanced-technology industry) will be reduced in efficiency and productivity.

FREE COMMUNICATION

The subject of communication deserves much attention in project management, just as in all management.

The theoretically inclined technologist, generally a man of imaginative creativity, as well, often, as his engineering brother with the more factual kind of creativity, inherently regards the right to communicate as the bread of life for an adequate scientific career. To this principle is related the cherished right to publish scientific work for the judgment of one's scientific peers.

Yet there is a contradictory element in the attitude of scientists toward communication. It may be suspected, based on observations in any professional technological group, that there are some who pay only lip service to the ideal of free communication and who in reality are more than hesitant in communicating the results of their work, or their attitudes on any topic, to anyone connected with administration.

Vannevar Bush, in his book *Modern Arms and Free Men,*[2] noted the distinctly different reactions to communication which he observed among military men and academicians:

> In the military there is vigorous and open debate on proposed actions before the decision. But when an office with clearly constituted authority makes the decision, the antagonists, acting under a basic doctrine of their profession, swing around to support actively the idea they had opposed.
>
> In contrast, under the customs which prevail in academic circles, the duly established decision signals the start of the fight. In this environment, it is very difficult to learn the nature of the opposition to administrative planning, since academicians are not inclined to communicate freely in such matters. Consequently, after decisions are drawn there tends to be considerable passive and sometimes active resistance in the execution of the ideas.

The lessons here for the project manager are plain. He must expend considerable active effort in learning to communicate adequately with his scientists and in developing the communicative attitudes of his engineers. It has been clearly demonstrated that scientists and engineers who work in the operating environment *can* adapt their output to mesh with corporate schedules and budgets, if they are *adequately informed* regarding corporate policies and objectives. Budgets and schedules must not be mere edicts, but should be carefully prepared with the cognizance of and with the aid of the technologists who must live by them. Whenever occasional arbitrary actions originate in the realms of policy, they should be explained as carefully as possible, and on this basis they will be accepted and implemented.

THE NEXT PROJECT

The temporal aspect of a project manager's task may strain his capacities in dealing with people. Because the duration of a project is well defined, it is only human for the scientists and engineers who work on it to come to anticipate their next assignment, even though it may be a year or more away. This can result in a kind of divided allegiance, in which the engineers look to others outside the project who may be able to help them in gaining their next assignment.

The project manager must counter this tendency to cast about for the next task, for it will diminish his effective control of the present task. In this effort he must be bulwarked by a potent company sales policy that has provided and will continue to provide new projects for professional employees. When he has this backing, the manager then need only follow a basic rule of managerial conduct—that of letting his people know where they stand. Frankness and integrity, when used in discussing the future, will allay their instinctive concern about the job that is over the horizon. It will convince them their role in future projects is assured unless they have been told otherwise.

QUALIFICATIONS FOR SUCCESS

Some of the qualifications that a successful project manager must possess proceed logically from the preceding discussion:

1. His career must have been molded in the advanced-technology environment.
2. He must have a working knowledge of many fields of science, the fundamental kind of knowledge which he can augment when necessary to delve into the intricacies of a specific technology.
3. He must have a good understanding of general management problems—especially marketing, control, contract work, purchasing, law, and personnel administration. The concept of *profitability* should be familiar to him.
4. He must have a strong, continuous, active interest in teaching, training, and developing his supervisors.

In reviewing these qualifications, one can observe the emphasis on the *integrative* function in the operations of the project manager. There is an ever-present requirement for the joining of many parts into a systematic whole. Describing the processes by which the integrative mind works is, of course, difficult, for they are largely indefinable, just as the requisite qualities for managerial personnel are not subject to scientific definition. It is clear, however, that the integrative mind must deal with intangible factors as well as the tangible, and that there is need also at times for an intuitive process in the formulation of judgment and decision (especially where men's reactions are an important factor). It is perhaps in this respect that the outlook of a good project manager differs most sharply from that of the researcher:

> The methodology of scientific analysis and experimentation has been carefully developed over many years and is a part of the indoctrination of young men in training for a scientific career. This indoctrination breeds a distrust of intuition and a tendency to disregard intangibles. Further, the analytical mind will not draw its hypothesis until all relevant data have been observed and interpreted. If a hypothesis must be drawn before this, it must be thoroughly qualified and hedged in the interests of scientific accuracy.

In project organizations, it is recognized that the analytical mind produces the concepts by which the project advances toward its goal. But without the integrative function, often nothing would be done with the concepts originating in the analytical function. The topnotch manager of an advanced-technology project must be capable of both integration and analysis, and must understand that the rigorous training of professional technologists with its emphasis on analysis sometimes impairs their integrative ability.

Friendly Differences

In discussing the attributes of the project manager, it soon becomes apparent that he has much in common with his corporate brethren in research administration. The research director also works in advanced technologies and holds similar responsibilities. His usual task is to lead research groups in planning and developing new products which will fit into his company's future marketing plans.

However, there are subtle, yet substantive, differences in the managerial approach of the advanced-technology project manager and that of the research administrator. In military parlance, the former is primarily a tactician, the latter essentially a strategist.

These differences may be illustrated by a look at the typical kinds of meetings in which these two managers are likely to be engaged:

For the project manager, it is a clutch meeting with officials of a key supplier—a meeting which is the result of previous efforts falling short of their goals. The chief engineer and the manufacturing superintendent of the supplier firm are present, well primed with absolute reasons why they cannot make scheduled delivery of a critical piece of hardware, without which the project manager cannot complete his product.

After the opening formalities are over, this meeting begins to resemble a kind of combat. The enemy is inertia. There is a persevering, chips-down type of resourcefulness on the part of the project representatives. They must cross-examine all of the advocates who say that the key component cannot be made—the supplier's designers who say the design cannot be completed as intended, or the accountant who says it cannot be built for anywhere near the original cost estimate, or the manufacturing engineer who says it cannot be built the way the denizens of the ivory tower designed it. Then these reasons must be refuted, or if they stand up under this scrutiny, the project's designs must be altered to accommodate a simpler component. In *some* way the project must acquire a usable component, and the threatened loss of schedule or budget must be recouped.

The research administrator's first meeting may be with a budget committee. The controller proclaims that while he can measure the input to the new research program well enough in terms of its cost, he cannot measure the output very well at all (and really is it worthwhile anyway?).

The second meeting is with a marketing committee. The sales manager states that he cannot understand why a certain research group after two years has not produced the widget which he is sure will revolutionize the market.

The third meeting is with a staff committee, where the research manager is straining to acquaint policy people with the company's

technical problems so that they may appreciate the broad implications of these problems.

Both these roles require resourcefulness. It might be said, however, that the project manager's task requires an *intensive* resourcefulness, in which his efforts are ever directed against obstacles to
progress. Conversely, the research administrator must display an
extensive resourcefulness in meeting his primary objective—i.e.,
supplying his company with enough new products, and at the right
time, to protect its market position against the competitive forces
of product obsolescence. This requires him to handle some tough
intangibles: How do you measure the output of a research group,
or its impact on the company's market position? How do you evaluate the feasibility and potential payoff of new product concepts?

The project manager, in his tactical role, is closely related to line-
operating management. In the research administrator's strategic
role, there are many elements of the key staff adviser's functions,
as well as the requirement for leading engineers and scientists in
a research program. This program generally represents a wider
road, traveled under less exigent circumstances, than the narrow
road and fast pace followed by the advanced-technology project.

A further insight into the differences between these two types of
managers may be gained by considering the way that status accounting is handled. Enlightened research administration has generally learned that it is unwise to burden a research team by
requiring from it regular status reports on a periodic basis. Rather,
it is preferable to require the team to submit a report only when it
has something to report, since research advances do not come by
regular increments of the calendar.

However, in the advanced-technology project, periodic status reports are appropriate and valuable. A report showing the absence
of advance during a reporting period is an important indicator of
trouble to project management.

Thinkers and Doers

Before the Sputnik era, William H. Whyte, Jr., leveled a very
penetrating criticism against attempts to make scientists conform
to the organization in U.S. industry.[3] Since the Sputniks, others
have jumped on this rolling bandwagon and have generated an
impressive indictment of the smothering of individuality and in-

hibition of creativity resulting from the integration of scientists and engineers with organized corporate groups.

While most of this criticism has validity, it should not be interpreted to reflect adversely on the project method of getting advanced-technology results. Project people know and understand that basic and fundamental research is being slighted in this country; they realize that project staffs—the doers—will run out of work to do unless the storehouse of basic scientific knowledge is effectively and continuously replenished. They are also keenly aware that the laissez-faire environment, the unorganized structure, of the world's great laboratories has been the origin of technological advancement.

The project method has proved to be an effective way of *utilizing* the scientific output of the thinkers in the laboratories. The project— i.e., group, organization, team, task force, or whatever name it may go by—has piled up a fine record of accomplishment since the days of the famed Manhattan Project. Certainly there has been a requirement of conformity; and, usually, little latitude has been allowed the scientists and engineers in determining the areas in which they will work or the subject which they will investigate, because of requirements for interlocking efforts on a large scale. Yet the records of achievement remain.

For those men with the mental and personal endowment for the project kind of work—the men of factual creativity, the applied scientists, the practicing technologists—there is no element of professional degradation in this work. On the contrary, this type of professional finds the project pace challenging and exhilarating, as can be easily verified by observation—and far preferable to the apparent aimlessness of the pure research environment.

The real indictment of the organization can come only when professional technologists are misused, when the group tries to fit the square peg into the round hole. Those scientists who are genuinely creative, and who can justifiably exhibit the individualism of a fundamental researcher, are rare. It is a shameful waste to attempt to use such men in a project—a waste to the nation, in that their output is hobbled and misapplied, and a loss to the project effort, in that they probably will not contribute to its progress.

Discerning men have long observed that "project people" are inspired by more immediate, if less exalted, goals. In the words of Francis Bacon, penned about 1620 in the preface to his *Novum Organum:*

Let there be therefore (and may it be for the benefit of both) two streams and two dispensations of knowledge; and in like manner two tribes or kindreds of students in philosophy—tribes not hostile or alien to each other, but bound together by mutual services . . . let there in short be one method for the cultivation, another for the invention, of knowledge.

And for those who prefer the former, either from hurry, or from consideration of business, or for want of mental power to take in and embrace the other (which must needs be most men's case), I wish that they may succeed to their desire in what they are about, and obtain what they are pursuing. But if any man there be who, not content to rest in and use the knowledge which has already been discovered, aspires to penetrate further . . . I invite all such to join themselves, as true sons of knowledge, with me, that passing by the outer courts of nature, which numbers have trodden, we may find a way at length into her inner chambers.

Role in the Future

The United States today faces the enormous problem of how to regain undisputed technological leadership. The character of American technological advancement during the next five years will shape our future and determine our survival or extinction.

The role to be played by project management in these years ahead will be challenging, exciting, and crucial. Truly it will be the acid test of the project manager and the project concept, but it will be much more than that. It will be a momentous trial of free enterprise, business administration, and progressive industrial management as we know them today.

Notes

1. New York, Harper & Brothers, 1949.
2. New York, Simon and Schuster, Inc., 1949.
3. *The Organization Man* (New York, Simon and Schuster, Inc., 1956), Part V, "The Organization Scientist."

2
Harvard Business School Note: Managing a Task Force

James P. Ware

Companies establish task forces to work on problems and projects that cannot be easily handled by the regular functional organization. Typically the problems cut across existing departmental boundaries or are simply so time-consuming that working on them would disrupt routine department tasks.

A task force can be a powerful management tool for resolving complex and challenging problems. Several factors contribute to this strength:

1. The group is usually very task-oriented because it was formed to solve a specific problem or achieve a well-defined outcome. When the problem is solved or the task is accomplished, the group disbands.
2. If the task force brings together managers from the affected functional areas, it will possess a diversity of skills and understanding that can potentially produce a high-quality solution.
3. If group members are selected on the basis of their individual competence relative to the problem, there is rarely any "deadwood."

These same characteristics, however, can present a task force leader with several difficult managerial problems:

1. The group represents an inherent criticism of the regular organization's failure to deal with the problem, so there may be significant tensions and even battles between members and non-members.
2. Individual task force members who come from different parts of the organization usually bring with them a wide diversity of view-

points, goals, and loyalties. The task force can become a battle-ground for fighting out longstanding departmental conflicts.

3. The temporary nature of the task force may limit members' willingness to commit personal time and energy to the project.

4. Managers who are personally ambitious often view a task force assignment as a major opportunity to "score points" with upper management. These private agendas can seriously interfere with the group's problem-solving effectiveness.

5. If the group members do not know each other well, or are competing with each other—either personally or as departmental representatives, the leader will find it very difficult to create the shared sense of purpose and mutual respect that is so necessary for issue-oriented problem solving.

Clearly, the success of a task force's efforts depends heavily on the way its activities are managed. This note will suggest a number of simple operating guidelines for increasing the effectiveness of any temporary management group. These suggestions have been grouped into four categories, based on the sequence in which the leader will confront the problems:

1. Starting Up the Task Force
2. Conducting the First Meeting
3. Running the Task Force
4. Completing the Project

These guidelines apply primarily to a task force leader. However, the most effective groups are often those in which several members carry out the leadership activities. Thus, you may find many of these ideas useful even in groups where you do not have formal leadership responsibilities.

Starting Up the Task Force

Your work as task force leader begins the moment you accept the responsibility for chairing the group. The period before the first formal meeting presents several opportunities for making decisions that will affect many of the group's later activities. Careful attention to details at the very beginning will pay subsequent dividends as the group confronts tough issues during the course of its deliberations. In fact, these "front-end" activities probably represent your greatest opportunity for defining the group's working style.

These start-up activities should focus on the following basic tasks:

1. **CLARIFY WHY THE TASK FORCE IS BEING FORMED.**   Although the specific circumstances surrounding each project will be unique, most task forces are established to accomplish one or more of the following general objectives:

a. Investigate a poorly understood problem
b. Recommend and/or implement a high-quality solution to a recognized problem
c. Respond to a crisis that results from a sudden change in the organization's business conditions
d. Bring together the people with the knowledge and skills to work on the problem
e. Gain commitment to a decision by involving the people who will be affected by its implementation
f. Develop managers by providing them with exposure to other functional areas and people
g. Force resolution of a longstanding problem, or work around an obstacle (such as a particular individual or group)

Usually the commissioning executives will have several purposes in mind. ("Commissioning executives" refers to the upper-level management group that determines a task force should be established.) For example, a new product development project can also be an excellent training experience for junior marketing managers. Similarly, a study of excessive inventories could be part of a strategy to reduce the power of an ineffective but well-entrenched purchasing manager.

Often, however, multiple objectives are incompatible, in that one objective may be attainable only at the expense of another. Additionally, the various commissioning executives may have differing objectives, or differing priorities for conflicting objectives. In many cases these differences will not be openly expressed or even recognized.

Thus, one of your first critical tasks will be to meet with the commissioning executives and with other managers who have an interest in the project's outcome. In those meetings you will want to explore the relevance and relative importance of each possible objective. You may even find it necessary to define alternative objectives and possible conflicts yourself. You can be a very active participant in the process of clarifying the task force's mission.

It is also important for you to determine whether the task force will be expected to conduct a preliminary investigation, to engage in problem solving and decision making, or to implement an already agreed-upon change. The choice of emphasis will obviously depend upon the history and nature of the particular problem, but you should seek an explicit statement about the boundaries of the project.

The nature of the work to be done will influence decisions about who should be on the task force, and about what kinds of operating and decision-making procedures will be appropriate.

For example, an exploratory investigation of a customer service department's efficiency would require very different analytic skills and working procedures from the installation of a computerized invoicing and inventory control system. Consequently, you will want to select task force members whose skills match the project requirements.

A useful technique for confronting these issues is to write out a proposed statement of purpose, and then to engage each of the commissioning executives in an assessment of how well your statement reflects their expectations. As the executives help you revise the statement, they will develop personal commitment to it and thus to the task force's success.

2. **DEFINE GENERAL OPERATING PROCEDURES.**

a. Will members be assigned to the group on a full-time or part-time basis?
b. When should the task be completed?
c. What will the group's budget be?
d. What organizational reports and other information will be available to the group?
e. How much decision-making power is being delegated to the group?
f. What information should be reported to functional managers, and how often?

There is no way to anticipate all the procedural issues that the group will face, and many of those that can be anticipated will have to be worked out by the whole task force group. Again, however, you should discuss these questions in advance with the executives who are establishing the task force. It is far better to be told explicitly that some topics and decisions are beyond the group's charter than to discover those boundaries only by crossing over them.

One of the most important procedural issues to be resolved concerns the way in which the group will make task-related decisions. The more exploratory and open-ended the basic project is, the more open and participative the decision-making procedures should be. There is considerable research evidence to suggest that task-oriented groups prefer relatively directive leaders, and that decision making is usually most efficient in a structured climate. However, if the problem requires an imaginative or wholly new perspective, then a more unstructured climate will generally produce more innovative ideas.

Although you should discuss leadership and decision-making styles with both the commissioning executives and prospective task force members, this is not a decision to make once for the entire project. The effectiveness of each approach depends very much on the nature of the current problem, and you will probably want to vary your procedures as the project progresses.

3. **DETERMINE WHO SHOULD BE ON THE TASK FORCE.**   As much as possible, individuals who are asked to join the task force should be people who

a. Possess knowledge and skills relevant to the task
b. Are personally interested in the problem
c. Have, or can get, the time to devote to the task force
d. Enjoy working in groups and are effective in group settings
e. Will not dominate the meetings or decisions solely on the basis of personality or power

While individual competence is important, however, it is not an adequate basis for constructing the project group. It is equally important to consider the overall composition of the group. Does each member possess organizational credibility and influence relative to the problem? Is each of the functional areas that will be affected by the group's work represented? The exclusion of important departments will not only generate resentment and resistance, but may also reduce both the quality of the task force's recommendations and the probability that the recommendations will eventually be implemented.

A major membership selection dilemma is whether to include persons who are likely to obstruct the group's investigations and to slow down progress toward a consensus solution. Although including such individuals may reduce problem-solving efficiency, it will increase substantially the probability of their later supporting (or at least not actively opposing) the group's recommendations. Lowered efficiency in early deliberations is usually more than compensated for by a smoother implementation experience. In addition, when individual resistance is based on valid information or experience, a solution that ignores the sources of that resistance is likely to be suboptimal or even unworkable.

It is vitally important that you be involved in the membership selection process. You may have information about prospective members that will have a direct bearing on the appropriateness of their involvement. In addition, your participation in the selection process adds your personal commitment to the group's effectiveness. Finally, your involvement in selecting task force members provides you with an additional opportunity to learn more about upper management's expectations about the way the task force will operate.

4. **CONTACT PROSPECTIVE MEMBERS.**   Your first contact with each prospective task force member gives you an opportunity to begin defining not only the problem the group will be addressing but also the procedures it will be using. Whenever possible this contact should be made in person. You may want to include the prospective member's functional boss in the same meeting. Having the boss there ensures that all three of you agree on the basic purpose of the task force and on the prospective member's level of involvement.

These first contacts also provide an opportunity for you to explore each person's current knowledge and feelings about the problem, and to build a productive personal relationship if one does not already exist. This information and experience can prove invaluable as you prepare for the first full task force meeting.

5. **PREPARE FOR THE FIRST MEETING.**   Because the quality of the first meeting sets the tone for all later activities, you will want to prepare a careful agenda. There are two major objectives for this first meeting:

a. Reaching a common understanding of the group's task
b. Defining working procedures and relationships

Since the most important function of the first meeting will be to define the problem and the organization's expectations for the group's output, the commissioning executives should be asked to attend the meeting if at all possible. Be certain to review everything you have learned about the problem and the group members with your boss in advance of the meeting in order to ensure that the group begins with a positive, productive experience.

It is highly unlikely that you will be able to carry out all these start-up activities as thoroughly as you would want to. Time pressures, physical separation of group members, and prior relationships may all prevent the kind of thorough, rational analysis these suggestions imply. In addition, the commissioning executives may find it very hard to give you a clear statement of the problem. After all, most task forces are established because the organization actually does not fully understand the nature of its problem.

You have to accept some of the responsibility for defining the problem. But you also have to know when to stop *discussing* and start *doing*. That is a difficult managerial judgment that you can make only within the context of a specific situation. These suggestions can get you off to a good start, but you may not be able to follow them all. Often you will have no choice; other decisions will limit your alternatives. But you *can* become aware of the risks you incur by omitting a preparatory step and thereby be more alert to potential future problems.

Conducting the First Meeting

This meeting is important not only because it is the first time all task force members will be together, but because patterns of interactions begun here will influence all later group activities.

The two major objectives for this first meeting have already been suggested. Each will be discussed briefly below:

1. **REACHING A COMMON UNDERSTANDING OF THE GROUP'S TASK.** This goal is clearly the most important item on the agenda; yet in most instances it will be the most difficult to accomplish. Few of the other members will have devoted as much time or attention to the task as you have. Until they get "up to speed" and see the problem in the same general terms that you do, they will be a group in name only.

Each manager will come into this meeting feeling a responsibility to represent his or her own department's interests. Each will interpret the problem in terms of those interests, and each will possess a unique combination of ideas and information about the problem.

Furthermore, many of the group members will be feeling highly defensive, as they anticipate that other managers will blame their departments for the problems. These feelings are not only natural, but are very likely based on past personal experiences. If you know or suspect that such feelings exist within the group, try to find a positive way to bring them to the surface. Encourage everyone to participate by expressing their opinions and offering their suggestions, but ask them to withhold judgments until all the relevant information is out in the open. You can serve as the role model for other group members by asking questions that focus on facts, by maintaining strict neutrality on the issues, and by eliciting ideas from all members.

At this point the group probably does not possess enough information to achieve a deep understanding of the problem and its probable causes. Indeed, the lack of information and understanding is generally one of the major reasons for establishing a task force. Nevertheless, it is essential for the group to achieve at least a general agreement that the problem exists, and where its boundaries lie.

Your most difficult task at this first meeting, however, may be to prevent a premature consensus on an appropriate solution. Most experienced managers are sure they know what the problems are and what actions are required. Thus, even though you are seeking some level of agreement on the nature of the *problem,* you do not want the group to settle on a *solution* yet.

You *do* want group members to develop a sense of their joint responsibilities, and of what the appropriate next steps are. An explicit recognition of the area in which group members differ is also highly desirable. Member participation in a task-focused discussion of this kind will serve to generate commitment to the group and its general goals, even if differences of opinion as to appropriate strategies are openly recognized.

2. **DEFINING WORKING PROCEDURES AND RELATIONSHIPS.**   A second essential topic for the first meeting is the question of how the group will work on its task. Among the issues that require explicit attention are the following:

a. Frequency and nature of full task force meetings
b. Structure of subgroups
c. Ground rules for communication and decision making within the task force between meetings

d. Ground rules or norms for decision making and conflict resolution

e. Schedules and deadlines for accomplishing subtasks and for completing the final report

f. Ground rules for dealing with sensitive issues; agreement on which ones require involving other managers

g. Procedures for monitoring and reporting progress, both within the task force and to functional area managers

h. Explicit processes for critiquing and modifying task force working procedures

Spending time on these procedural issues serves two primary purposes. First, the discussion will help group members form clear expectations concerning their projected activities and working relationships. These expectations will reduce the tensions inherent in an otherwise very unstructured situation. Second, the process of reaching agreement on procedural matters can become a model of how the task force will resolve other problems.

Resolution of these issues at the first meeting can provide all participants with a positive experience associated with the group. However, this is obviously a full agenda, and you will probably need to carry these topics over into subsequent meetings; but try to end the first meeting on a note of agreement. If you can achieve a solid consensus on some portion of these procedural matters at the first meeting, you will have taken a major step toward a successful project no matter how deeply divided the group is on substantive issues.

Running the Task Force

Once the front-end work has been completed, your efforts will focus on keeping the project moving and on monitoring and reporting the group's progress. Although specific circumstances will vary, there are several general principles to keep in mind:

1. **HOLD FULL TASK FORCE MEETINGS FREQUENTLY ENOUGH TO KEEP ALL MEMBERS INFORMED ABOUT GROUP PROGRESS.** Though each meeting should have a specific purpose, periodic meetings should be scheduled well in advance, and all members should be required to attend. A meeting can always be canceled if there is nothing substantial to discuss. However, full meetings do have an important symbolic value. They are the only time the full group is physically together, and anything said there is heard simultaneously

by everyone. Very often the most valuable and creative discussions are those that evolve spontaneously in response to someone's raising a nonagenda item. For example, the most successful fund-raising project in the history of public television (the cast party following the final episode of *Upstairs, Downstairs*) grew out of two spontaneous comments during an informal staff meeting at WGBH in Boston.

While that kind of creativity cannot be purposefully planned, you can most definitely create opportunities for unstructured, exploratory discussions.

2. **UNLESS THE TASK FORCE IS VERY SMALL (FEWER THAN 5–7 MEMBERS), DIVIDING UP INTO GROUPS WILL BE MANDATORY.**   You must manage this process very carefully, however. Dividing the project into separate tasks that can be worked on simultaneously can be a very efficient mechanism for achieving rapid progress. But remember that one of the virtues of the task force approach is the synergy that results from new combinations of individuals investigating problems in areas they are not overly familiar with. If you permit the task force members to work only in their own areas, or with persons they already know and work well with, you are throwing away one of your major advantages.

Of course, when strange managers go poking around in parts of the company they are unfamiliar with, they may ask "stupid" questions that insult or unintentionally threaten the functional managers they work with. Warn your group members of this danger, and then be prepared to spend some of your time both telling functional managers about your group's work and smoothing ruffled feathers as they occur.

You must also recognize that working in subgroups can cause individuals to lose their overall perspective. If the task force becomes too differentiated, the various subgroups may form their own identities and develop an advocacy style of pushing for "their" solutions. The more the total job is broken down for subgroup work, the more you must encourage formal intergroup sharing of problems, findings, and ideas as the project moves along.

3. **BE CAREFUL NOT TO ALIGN YOURSELF TOO CLOSELY WITH ONE POSITION OR SUBGROUP TOO EARLY.**   This principle is particularly important if there are clearly opposing and mutually exclusive sides to the issue. Although you will eventually have to make a commit-

ment to a plan of action, you will serve the group most effectively by being as concerned with the problem-solving *process* as you are with the specific outcomes of that process.

4. SET INTERIM PROJECT DEADLINES AND DEMAND ADHERENCE TO THEM. When you are in charge of the schedule and know how arbitrarily some of the key checkpoints were set, it becomes far too easy to assume you can make up lost time later. No matter how arbitrary the interim deadlines are, however, if you miss them you will miss your final deadline too.

Insistence on meeting deadlines is doubly important when the task force members are assigned to the project only on a part-time basis. If they are continuing to carry out functional responsibilities, they will feel pressures to spend their time on operating tasks with immediate outcomes. The pressure to accomplish immediate tasks will always outweigh the needs of the longer-range task force projects. Part-time task force members face a real dilemma and will be under continual stress. As the project leader, you must be prepared to spend a major portion of your time prodding your group members to complete their tasks on schedule. At the same time, however, you must remain sympathetic with the legitimate needs of the functional areas and be careful not to antagonize either your members or their functional bosses. Your task will be especially delicate in situations where you have no formal authority over these part-time members, or where the lines of authority have been spelled out only vaguely.

5. BE SENSITIVE TO THE CONFLICTING LOYALTIES CREATED BY BELONGING TO THE TASK FORCE. As task force members work together in group activities, they normally begin to develop commitments to the project and to each other. These commitments often become another source of stress, as members feel loyalties to both the task force and to their "home" departments. On the one hand, they continue to feel responsible for representing the interests of their functional areas, and on the other, they feel growing pressures to help the task force accomplish its goals.

Assisting the task force frequently requires group members to share confidential information with you or with other members. You must recognize the risk this sharing involves. Whenever feasible, the source of confidential information should remain anonymous. As task force leader you may be able to play a valuable intermediary role in this regard. But remember that once someone has entrusted you with confidential information, that person has become dependent on your integrity. If you are ever indiscreet, you are unlikely to be so trusted again, and your value to the organization will be seriously diminished.

6. **YOUR MOST IMPORTANT LEADERSHIP ROLE IS THAT OF COMMU-NICATING INFORMATION AMONG TASK FORCE MEMBERS AND BE-TWEEN THE TASK FORCE AND THE REST OF THE ORGANIZATION.** This communications role will be time-consuming, but it is absolutely essential to the success of the project. You must take personal responsibility for monitoring group progress, for bringing appropriate subgroups together to share information and ideas, and for reporting both progress and problems to your own boss and to the functional managers in whose areas the task force is working.

Very often your most important activities will involve listening to individual managers, passing information from one task force member to another, and bringing together managers who must exchange or share information and ideas. While these activities often seem inordinately time-consuming, they form the glue that binds the individual task force members together. As individuals and subgroups pursue their investigative tasks, you will probably become the only manager who retains an overall understanding of the total project. Communicating that understanding to others, and reminding them of their interdependence, is a critical responsibility.

Completing the Project

The work of an investigative task force typically culminates with a written report and a summary presentation of findings and recommendations to upper management. An implementation task force will normally have more concrete operating results to demonstrate its accomplishments, but even so, there is often a formal meeting at which the task force officially relinquishes its responsibilities to an operating group.

The written report documents the work of the task force, but its importance lies in the decision-making process it generates. In fact, the preparation of the final report can provide a structure and focus for the task force's concluding activities. You should prepare a tentative outline of this report early in the project and circulate it widely among group members. This outline can actually serve as a guide to the development of specific recommendations; the need to write the report will force the group to reach specific decisions.

Drafts of the report can then become the basis for working out any differences remaining among the task force members. Except in highly charged situations with major organizational consequences, you should strive to reach a group consensus before presenting any recommendations to upper management. Unless your group members are agreed on what actions are needed, you can hardly expect management acceptance or approval of the report.

The summary presentation of findings and recommendations to management is just as important an event as the task force's first meeting. The presentation should be carefully organized, with explicit attention to who will say what, in what sequence, and with what visual aids. The importance of these preparations varies in direct proportion with the extent to which the recommendations will be surprising, controversial, and/or expensive.

You should brief your own boss and other key executives before the formal presentation. This briefing does not necessarily require their approval or agreement, but their advance understanding can help to prevent defensive reactions or categorical rejections of your group's recommendations. This kind of briefing can be especially important if your recommendations involve major changes in organization structure, budget allocations, or strategic focus for any of the executives who will be present at the formal presentation.

As important as this formal presentation is, however, it rarely constitutes an adequate wrap-up of the task force project. Only if the recommendations are very straightforward and noncontroversial will the management group be able to understand and act on them at one sitting. A more effective strategy will be to plan *two* meetings. In the first, you summarize the findings and recommendations, as described above, and distribute the formal report. At the end of this presentation, you then schedule a second, decision-making meeting for the near future. The time period between the two meetings gives the executives an opportunity to read the report and consider its implications.

This period will be a busy time for the task force members, who can meet individually and in subgroups with key executives to clarify the report. Only when the report has been acted upon can the task force consider its work actually finished.

3
How to Make a Team Work

Maurice Hardaker and
Bryan K. Ward

Anyone who has ever run a business or organized a project has discovered how hard it can be to get the whole team on board to ensure that everyone knows where the enterprise is heading and agrees on what it will take to succeed.

At IBM we've used a method for some years that helps managers do just this. The technique, which we call PQM or Process Quality Management, grew out of many studies with customers to determine their needs and from internal studies as part of IBM's business quality program. PQM has been used successfully by service companies, government agencies, and nonprofit organizations, as well as manufacturers.

In PQM, managers get back to the often overlooked basics of an endeavor. IBM has had many successes abroad by paying attention to such details.

IBM Europe's manufacturing arm relied heavily on PQM when it launched a series of changes including continuous-flow manufacturing. First the vice president of manufacturing and his team made sure they understood the task ahead. Then they focused on new priorities for the company's major materials-management processes. As a result of their decisions, changes cascaded through the manufacturing organization's work force, leading not only to better interplant logistics but also to smooth introduction of continuous-flow manufacturing among IBM's 15 European plants. As this happened, manufacturing cycle times and inventory levels improved, costs dropped, quality rose, and the company became more flexible in meeting customer demand. That may not be the end of the rainbow, but it's not bad from a two-day PQM session.

PQM has also been the starting point for many IBM customers of a host of management decisions in such areas as strategy formulation, funding, human resource management, marketing, and resource allocation for large, complex projects. Often a PQM study is undertaken because something has happened—someone sees a new opportunity, a new technology, or new competitors. But it is useful any time.

PQM does not differ radically from other planning processes: we identify goals and the activities critical to their attainment, and we provide a way to measure success. But PQM demands an intensive one- or two-day session at which *all* the key managers concerned agree on what must be done and accept specific responsibility.

There's no guarantee that a unit will achieve its mission, of course. That requires competent follow-through by the entire organization. But PQM lays the groundwork for such success. And at least all the key players start off facing in the same direction.

Gather the Team

PQM begins with a person who is the leader of the management team—the boss, the one whose job depends on getting the team's mission accomplished. He or she should then involve everyone on the immediate management team and no one else—nobody missing and no hitchhikers. At most there should be 12 people, since more than that is just too unwieldy. And if even one member of the team cannot attend the study, wait. PQM requires a buy-in from everyone not only to identify what is needed but also to commit to the process.

By management team we usually mean a formal group of managers, a board of directors, say, or a divisional vice president and his or her top managers. But the team can also be a collection of individuals drawn from various sectors of the company for a specific project, like the team brought together at IBM to introduce continuous-flow manufacturing. In either case, the mission is normally too large or complex for one person, so the boss collects or inherits a team to work on it.

PQM demands spontaneity, so even though the boss convokes the team, a neutral outsider should lead the discussions. The leader could be a consultant or a manager or an officer from elsewhere in the company. What's important is that leaders not be the bosses' subordinates and that their livelihood should not depend on achieving the mission. Furthermore, the discussions are best held off premises; at the office, secretaries can fight their way through steel doors to deliver "urgent" messages.

Finally, and perhaps this goes without saying, the boss had better be ready to accept challenges to the status quo. We have presided at a few disasters where, despite assurances of open-mindedness, the boss turned the study into a self-justifying monologue. Fortunately, this is rare; it's a terrible waste of time.

Understand the Mission

The first step in the PQM effort is to develop a clear understanding of the team's mission, what its members collectively are paid to do. *Collectively* is important. A marketing vice president and a finance vice president will have different ideas about their separate functional missions. But when they meet together as part of the management team, they should know their job as members of that team.

If the mission statement is wrong, everything that follows will be wrong too, so getting a clear understanding is crucial. And agreeing on a mission may not be as easy as it may at first seem. People in well-run companies and government agencies tend to know their job descriptions, the benefits package, and their own job objectives. But even at the top, their ideas about the organization's mission are often pretty vague—to make profits or something like that. In part, this reflects the nature of management teams. People are appointed, stay awhile, do their jobs, and move on; each team includes long-serving members, new arrivals, and new leaders. As a group, they may never have articulated their mission to one another. A PQM study makes them stand back and ask fundamental questions like "Do we really understand our business well enough to form a mission statement?"

Our advice is to make the mission statement explicit—nail it to the wall. It shouldn't be more than three or four short sentences. For example, the following is a mission statement for one of IBM Europe's units:

> Prepare IBM World Trade Europe Middle East Africa Corporation employees to establish their businesses.
>
> Organize high-level seminars for IBM customers and make a significant contribution to IBM's image in Europe.
>
> Demonstrate the added value of the International Education Centre through excellence in advanced education, internationalism, innovation, and cross-functional exchanges.

The unit's mission statement defines the boundaries of the business (Europe, the Middle East, and Africa) and the customer population (all IBM employees within that area plus senior people from IBM's customers). It says what has to be done and says that achievement will be measured by the unit's demonstrable impact on IBM business successes, customer satisfaction, and company image in Europe.

The mission should be clear enough to let you know when you have succeeded and are entitled to a reward. "Increase profits" is not a rewardable mission. How much of an increase? .5%? 5%? 50%? But "generate positive cash flow" might well be a rewardable mission for a management team nursing a sick company. We did a study with one IBM customer whose mission was quite simply to survive until next year. It had a well-planned strategy for the future but a rough patch to negotiate for the next 12 months.

Once a team has defined its goal or mission, it could go straight to identifying its critical success factors (CSFs), the things it will have to do to succeed. But in our experience that's premature. At this point, few teams are relaxed enough to do the free associating needed to pinpoint their real CSFs. They are fixed on what they know and on today's problems, not on new possibilities.

To break out of old ways of thinking, we suggest a 10-minute brainstorming session in which team members list one-word descriptions of everything they believe could have an impact on achieving their mission. The usual brainstorming rules should apply:

Everyone should contribute.

Everything is fair game, no matter how crazy or outrageous.

Nobody is permitted to challenge any suggestion.

The facilitator should write everything down so the team can see the whole list.

While thinking about these dominant influences, each member should focus intently on the team's mission. Members should look inside and outside their bailiwicks, sometimes far outside to factors like national characteristics or public policy issues. The dominant influences that turned up in a brainstorming session for a Spanish company, for example, included the socialist government, the Basques, the Catalonians, regionalism, terrorism, and the mañana syndrome. Typically a team's list will contain 30 to 50 diverse items ranging from things like costs and supplier capabilities to jogging and the weather.

Spell Out Your Goals

Now the team should be ready to identify the critical success factors, a term used for many years in corporate planning to mean the most important subgoals of a business, business unit, or project. Here we define CSFs as what the team must accomplish to achieve its mission.

Consensus on these aims is vital. In one study, the top 10 managers in 125 European companies were asked individually to identify their companies' 5 most critical objectives. The minimum number from each company would be 5; the maximum, 50. Managers of the 40 most profitable companies agreed on 6 to 12 objectives. For the 40 worst companies, the range was 26 to 43. In other words, the top executives of the poor performers had no shared vision of what they were trying to do, while just the opposite was true of the successful companies' leaders. Significantly, a few years after the managers of one worst category company had agreed on its critical objectives, the company moved into the most profitable group.[1]

Like the mission, CSFs are not the how to of an enterprise, and they are not directly manageable. Often they are statements of hope or fear. The list in the first part of the Exhibit is typical. In a sense, every CSF should be viewed as beginning with the words "We need . . ." or "We must . . ." to express buy-in by all ("We") and agreed-on criticality ("need" or "must").

In naming its CSFs, a team should be guided by the necessary-and-sufficient rule. That is, the group must agree that each CSF listed is *necessary* to the mission and that together they are *sufficient* to achieve the mission. This is a stringent requirement. The CSF list must reflect the absolute minimum number of subgoals that have to be achieved for the team to accomplish its mission.

The seven CSFs in the Exhibit are designed for a fictitious enterprise that sells consumer products in the United States. It's a mature market, and the company's market share and profitability have eroded. The CEO's mission statement for this business might read:

> Restore market share and profitability over the next two years, and prepare the company and marketplace for further profitable growth.

To accomplish that mission, the management team must achieve all seven CSFs over the next two years. That's what we mean by necessary and sufficient.

Exhibit. Turning a Mission into an Agenda

Charting a project / Business processes	Best-of-breed product quality	New products that satisfy market needs	Excellent suppliers	Motivated, skilled workers	Excellent customer satisfaction	New business opportunities	Lowest delivered cost	Count	Quality
P1 Research the marketplace		■			■	■		3	C
P2 Measure customer satisfaction	■				■	■	■	4	D
P3 Advertise products				■	■	■		3	B
P4 Monitor competition	■	■	■		■	■	■	6	D
P5 Measure product quality	■	■		■	■		■	5	C
P6 Educate vendors		■	■	■	■			4	E
P7 Train employees		■		■	■	■	■	6	C
P8 Define new product requirements		■		■	■		■	4	C
P9 Process customer orders					■		■	2	B
P10 Develop new products	■	■	■	■	■		■	6	B
P11 Monitor customer complaints		■			■		■	3	D
P12 Negotiate manufacturing designs		■	■	■	■		■	5	D
P13 Define future skill needs	■	■		■				3	C
P14 Select and certify vendors	■	■	■		■		■	5	C
P15 Promote the company				■	■	■		3	C
P16 Support installed products	■				■		■	3	B
P17 Monitor customer or prospect's business		■			■		■	3	E
P18 Announce new products			■	■	■			3	C

Graphing makes priorities clear

Number of critical success factor impacts

Quality scale	E	D	C	B	A	Number of critical success factor impacts
						7
		P4	P7	P10		6
		P12	P5 P14			5
	P6	P2	P8			4
	P17	P11	P1 P18 P13 P15	P3 P16		3
				P9		2
						1
						0
	E	D	C	B	A	

Quality scale

Zone 1   E
          Embryonic stage

Zone 1   D
          Bad

Zone 2   C
          Fair

Zone 3   B
          Good

          A
          Excellent

P = business process number

In addition, each CSF must be devoted to a single issue—pure in the elemental sense, like hydrogen or gold. The word *and* is verboten. The team has to struggle to reduce its list honestly; it can't succumb when some creative manager says, "Why don't we combine numbers three and seven so we reduce product cost *and* improve morale?"

The list should be a mix of tactical and strategic factors. If the factors are all strategic (increase market share to 15% by 1992, for example), the business might founder while everybody concentrates on the blue skies ahead. Equally, if all are tactical (reduce the delivered cost of product ABC to $20.50 by year end), the business could kill itself on short-term success. The ratio depends on several considerations, of course, including the nature of the business unit doing the study. A regional sales office would likely have more tactical CSFs, while a corporate headquarters would have an almost entirely strategic list.

The maximum number of CSFs is eight. And if the mission is survival, four is the limit—you don't worry about whether your tie is straight when you are drowning. There is no magic about eight. It just seems to be the largest number of truly critical goals that a management team can focus on continuously.

Our rules on number and absolute consensus may be tough, but they work, and it's essential to follow them. Whenever we have been persuaded to relax either rule, we have ended up with a mess, a list of moans rather than the truly visceral issues affecting the business. If someone cries, "We can't agree, let's vote," don't do it. Insist on consensus; highly paid, experienced, businesswise people should be able to agree on what's vital to their business, after all.

Reaching agreement on the CSFs usually takes from one to three hours. The longest time we've seen was a day. In that case, the team was composed of the heads of nine quasi-independent business units and managers from headquarters. Understandably, they had a tough time reaching consensus.

Find What Matters Most

The third step in PQM is to identify and list what has to be done so that a company can meet its critical success factors. This might mean being more responsive to the market, exploiting new technologies, or whatever else is essential to accomplish the CSFs.

Ask almost any management team for a list of its business activities or processes, however, and you will often get a set of bland descriptions like maintenance or sales or customer service. These aren't business processes. They don't describe what is actually done in the business.

We recommend a more rigorous approach, one that draws on our necessary-and-sufficient rule. As with the CSFs' relation to the mission, each process necessary for a given CSF must be indicated, and together all those processes must be sufficient to accomplish it.

Other rules we find useful are:

Each business process description should follow a verb-plus-object sequence.

Every business process should have an owner, the person responsible for carrying out the process.

The owner should be a member of the management team that agreed to the CSFs.

No owner should have more than three or four business processes to manage.

To show how these rules work, think about the process "measure customer satisfaction," listed as P2 in the Exhibit. This process has an action verb and an object of the action. It can have an owner, and its quality or performance can be measured. Is this process currently being done? By whom? How often? How well? How well are competitors doing it? Since each team member shares collective responsibility for the affected CSFs, the entire team should be interested in the answers. But only one person owns that process—commitment by all, accountability by one.

"Bill customers" is another example of a business process—and it differs a lot from "invoicing," which is usually the title on the billing-office door. Invoicing is a simple process; bill customers describes a much richer field for disaster. Many functions contribute to billing: sales, field engineering, accounting, legal distribution, and information services. But the person responsible for the actual invoicing is rarely one who can coordinate all the activities needed to get an accurate, understandable, complete invoice at the right time and at the lowest cost. The invoicing manager isn't likely to have a broad enough view of the business or the power to effect needed change. The result is often customer dissatisfaction, bad cash flow, a lot of arguing and finger pointing, and low morale—in other words, poor competitiveness.

Once identified as an important process, however, billing customers can be assigned to a member of the management team, who will then be responsible for its performance.

Now suppose we have a complete list of important business processes, each of which has an owner. The list is exclusive, since a process has to be important to be there. But it still needs ranking to identify the most critical processes, those whose performance or quality will have the biggest impact on the mission. This is the penultimate stage of our PQM.

First place the processes and the CSFs in random order on a matrix as shown in "Charting a project" in the Exhibit. Then focus on the first critical success factor—in our example, "best-of-breed product quality"—and ask this question: Which business processes must be performed especially well for us to be confident of achieving this CSF? The object is to single out the processes that have a primary impact on this particular CSF. Many business activities will touch on it, of course; what you're after are the essential ones.

The facilitator fills in a box on the chart for each critical process identified for this CSF. In the Exhibit, for example, our team has listed "measure customer satisfaction," "monitor competition," "measure product quality," and seven other processes for its first CSF. Then the list must pass the sufficiency test. If all these activities are performed well, will the team achieve its first critical goal? If the team answers no, then it must identify what else is needed.

This is usually the stage at which teams begin to be really creative, looking beyond what is already being done and breaking new ground. There's a check, though, because each new process added for sufficiency must also have an owner within the management team. So it has to be important enough to feature on the matrix.

The team then repeats this process for each CSF in turn, being careful to apply the necessary-and-sufficient test before moving on to the next CSF. Then the number of CSFs that each process affects is totaled and placed in the count column on the right-hand side of the matrix.

By now the chart is a valuable document. The management team has agreed on its mission, on the subgoals, or CSFs, required to accomplish the mission, and finally, on the things that must be done to achieve those goals. Moreover, while each CSF is owned collectively by the entire team, each business process is owned by an individual member. Only one more step remains—identifying the most critical processes.

If companies had unlimited resources, each process could have equal attention for resources and management focus. But in practice, of course, managers' time and resources are always limited. So next pinpoint those activities that warrant the most attention.

Clearly, the most important processes are those that affect the most CSFs. "Monitor competition," for example, affects six of the seven CSFs, so it is a strong candidate for scrutiny. But to get a meaningful ranking for management's attention, we also need to know how well each process is being performed.

In our PQM studies, we use a subjective ranking, which is entered in the quality column on the matrix. A = excellent performance, B = good performance, C = fair performance, D = bad performance, and E = informal or embryonic performance or indicates a process that's not performed at all. It may seem surprising, but we hear very few arguments about process quality. By this stage in the PQM process, the managers are really working as a team.

"Graphing makes priorities clear," the second part of the Exhibit, shows the best way we've found to help the team translate its rankings into an action plan. The quality of each process is plotted horizontally and the number of CSFs the process impacts is plotted vertically. Then the team divides the graph into zones to create groups of processes. We can see immediately that Zone 1 contains the most critical processes. All the processes are important, by definition. But the higher risk (or higher opportunity) processes are found in Zone 1. These activities need the team's closest attention if the company is to improve market share and profitability within two years.

Follow-through

That's the PQM process—one way to conduct what is, in truth, a never-ending journey to zero defects.

But as we said up front, PQM requires follow-through. Decide the nature of the improvement needed, and establish relevant process measurements. Then apply the needed resources for the appropriate improvements.

We cannot stress follow-through enough. The decisions reached by the management team must cascade throughout the organization. And always there are surprises. During one PQM process, it was discovered that not only was the process "define management responsibilities" one of the most critical at that time, it was also agreed that it was just not being done. This is the kind of function that everyone assumes is being done and someone else is doing it. Yet its poor performance (or nonexistence) can be a major inhibitor to success. The CEO immediately accepted ownership of that process and responsibility for its quality improvement.

We recommend revisiting the CSF list about once a year or whenever a significant change has taken place in a team's mission, its makeup, or the marketplace. In a year's time, the mission usually stays the same, but the critical success factors and the most critical processes usually don't. Some of the processes will have moved from Zone 1 to Zone 2; others will be newly critical.

If a company's CSFs remained constant while all of its business processes were being attended to, it would end up with zero-defect processes—and a justified reputation as a highly competitive company. But all kinds of things can alter a company's mission and goals: government, competitors, reorganization, new technology, new opportunities, the marketplace. And when you change the CSFs, you necessarily change the grid.

The next time a new matrix is produced, however, the business should be stronger and more flexible. If PQM has been applied, fewer existing processes will fall in quality category D or C. The average quality of business activities will be higher, and the biggest focus will be on new categories, the E processes, that the new CSFs demand. Eventually, you may even find that all your basic business activities are clustered in category A. Then the only changes a new CSF list will provoke are those responding to a changing environment. Such adaptability is the ultimate goal of PQM.

But does this mean the list of important processes is getting longer and longer and the matrix deeper and deeper? Not necessarily. Over time, what was once a most critical process will become sufficiently stable and well performed to allow its ownership to be delegated. And that's as it should be.

Note

1. "Strategy and Innovation in the Firm," an unpublished study conducted in 1973 by Charles-Hubert Heyvaert, University of Leuven, Belgium.

4
Knowing When to Pull the Plug

**Barry M. Staw and
Jerry Ross**

Last year you authorized the expenditure of $500,000 for what you thought was a promising new project for the company. So far, the results have been disappointing. The people running the project say that with an additional $300,000 they can turn things around. Without extra funding, they cry, there is little hope. Do you spend the extra money and risk further losses, or do you cut off the project and accept the half-million-dollar write-off?

Managers face such quandaries daily. They range from developing and placing employees to choosing plant sites and making important strategic moves. Additional investment could either remedy the situation or lead to greater loss. In many situations, a decision to persevere only escalates the risks, and good management consists of knowing when to pull the plug.

These escalation situations are trouble. Most of us can think of times when we should have bailed out of a course of action. The Lockheed L 1011 fiasco and the Washington Public Supply System debacle (commonly referred to as WHOOPS) are spectacular examples of organizational failure to do so. Decisions to persist with these crippled ventures caused enormous losses.

Of course, all managers will make some mistakes and stick with some decisions longer than they ought to. Recent research has shown, however, that the tendency to pursue a failing course of action is not a random thing. Indeed, at times some managers, and even entire organizations, seem almost programmed to follow a dying cause.[1]

189

What leads executives to act so foolishly? Are they people who should never have been selected for responsible positions? Are these organizations simply inept? Or are they generally competent managers and companies that find themselves drawn into decisional quicksand, with many forces driving them deeper? Though we think this last description is probably the right one, we don't think the tendency is uncheckable. Managers and organizations that often fall into escalation traps can take steps to avoid them.

Why Projects Go out of Control

As a start to understanding why people get locked into losing courses of action, let's look first at what a purely rational decision-making approach would be. Consider, for example, the decision to pursue or scuttle an R&D or a marketing project. On the basis of future prospects, you'd have made the initial decision to pursue the project, and enough time would have passed to see how things were going. Ideally, you'd then reassess the situation and decide on future action. If you were following a fully rational approach, whatever losses might have occurred before this decision point would be irrelevant for your reassessment. With a cold, clear eye, you'd view the prospects for the future as well as your available options. Would the company be better off if it got out, continued with the project, or decided to invest more resources in it? You'd treat any previous expenses or losses as sunk costs, things that had happened in the past, not to be considered when you viewed the future.

In theory, pure rationality is great, but how many managers and organizations actually follow it? Not many. Instead, several factors encourage decision makers to become locked into losing courses of action.

THE PROJECT ITSELF

The first set of factors has to do with the project itself. "Is the project not doing well because we omitted an important factor from our calculations, or are we simply experiencing the downside of problems that we knew could occur?" "Are the problems temporary [bad weather or a soon-to-be-settled supplier strike] or more permanent [a steep downturn in demand]?" Expected or short-term problems are likely to encourage you to continue a project. You may even view them as necessary costs or investments for achieving large, long-term gains. If you expect problems to arise, when they do, they may convince you that things are going as planned.

A project's salvage value and closing costs can also impede withdrawal. An executive could simply terminate an ineffective advertising campaign in midstream, but stopping work on a half-completed facility is another story. A project that has very little salvage value and high closing costs—payments to terminated employees, penalties for breached contracts, and losses from the closing of facilities—will be much more difficult to abandon than a project in which expenditures are recoverable and exit is easy. It's understandable why so many financially questionable construction projects are pursued beyond what seems to be a rational point of withdrawal.[2]

Consider the Deep Tunnel project in Chicago, a plan to make a major addition to the city's sewer system that will eventually improve its capacity to handle major storms. Although the project has absorbed millions of dollars, it won't deliver any benefits until the entire new system is completed. Unfortunately, as each year passes, the expected date of completion recedes into the future while the bill for work to be finished grows exponentially. Of course, no one would have advocated the project if the true costs had been known at the outset. Yet, once begun, few have argued to kill the project.

The problem is that the project was structured in ways that ensured commitment. First, the project managers viewed each setback as a temporary situation that was correctable over time with more money. Second, they perceived all moneys spent as investments toward a large payoff they'd reap when the project was complete. Third, expenditures were irretrievable: the laid pipe in the ground has no value unless the entire project is completed, and it would probably cost more to take the pipe out of the ground than it's worth. Thus, like many other large construction and R&D projects, investors in the Deep Tunnel have been trapped in the course of action. Even though what they receive in the end may not measure up to the cost of attaining it, they have to hang on until the end if they hope to recoup any of their investment.

MANAGERS' MOTIVATIONS

Most of the factors concerning projects that discourage hanging on are evident to managers. They may not fully factor closing costs and salvage value into their initial decisions to pursue certain courses of action (since new ventures are supposed to succeed rather than fail), but when deciding whether to continue a project or not, executives are usually aware of these factors. Less obvious to managers, however, are the psychological factors that influence the way information about courses of action are gathered, interpreted, and acted on.

We are all familiar with the idea that people tend to repeat behavior if they are rewarded and to stop it if they are punished. According to the theory of reinforcement, managers will withdraw from a course of action in the face of bad news. This interpretation, however, ignores people's history of rewards. Managers have often been rewarded for ignoring short-run disaster, for sticking it out through tough times. Successful executives—people whose decisions have turned out to be winners even when the outlook had appeared grim—are particularly susceptible. It's tough for managers with good track records to recognize that a certain course isn't a satisfactory risk, that things aren't once again going to turn their way.

Reinforcement theory also tells us that when people receive rewards intermittently (as from slot machines), they can become quite persistent. If a decline in rewards has been slow and irregular, a person can go on and on even after the rewards have disappeared. Unfortunately, many business situations that escalate to disaster involve precisely this type of reinforcement pattern. Sales may fall slowly in fits and starts, all the while offering enough hope that things will eventually return to normal. The hope makes it difficult to see that the market may have changed in fundamental ways. Revenues that slowly sour or costs that creep upward are just the kind of pattern that can cause managers to hang on beyond an economically rational point.

Research has also shown other reasons that executives fail to recognize when a project is beyond hope. People have an almost uncanny ability to see only what accords with their beliefs. Much like sports fans who concentrate on their own team's great plays and the other team's fouls, managers tend to see only what confirms their preferences. For example, an executive who is convinced that a project will be profitable will probably slant estimates of sales and costs to support the view. If the facts challenge this opinion, the manager may work hard to find reasons to discredit the source of information or the quality of the data. And if the data are ambiguous, the manager may seize on just those facts that support the opinion. Thus information biasing can be a major roadblock to sensible withdrawal from losing courses of action.

In addition to the effects of rewards and biased information, a third psychological mechanism may be at work. Sometimes even when managers recognize that they have suffered losses, they may choose to invest further resources in a project rather than accept failure. What may be fostering escalation in these cases is a need for self-justification. Managers may interpret bad news about a project as a personal failure. And, like most of us who are protective of our self-esteem, managers may hang on or even invest further resources to "prove" the project a success.

A number of experiments have verified this effect of self-justification. Those who are responsible for previous losses, for example, have generally been found to view projects more positively and to be more likely to commit additional resources to them than are people who have taken over projects in midstream. Managers who are not responsible for previous losses are less likely to "throw good money after bad" since they have less reason to justify previous mistakes.[3]

Reinforcement, information biasing, and self-justification—three psychological factors that we're all subject to—can keep us committed to projects or actions we have started. Most managerial decisions, however, involve some additional factors that come into play when other people are around to observe our actions. These are social determinants.

SOCIAL PRESSURES

Managers may persist in a project not only because they don't want to admit error to themselves but also because they don't wish to expose their mistakes to others. No one wants to appear incompetent. Though persistence may be irrational from the organization's point of view, from the point of view of the beleaguered manager seeking to justify past behavior, it can be quite understandable. When a person's fate is tied to demands for performance and when accepting failure means loss of power or loss of a job, hanging on in the face of losses makes sense. Research has shown, for example, that job insecurity and lack of managerial support only heighten the need for external justification.[4] Thus when a manager becomes closely identified with a project ("that's Jim's baby"), he can be essentially forced to defend the venture despite mounting losses and doubts about its feasibility.

Beyond the personal risks of accepting losses, our ideas of how a leader should act can also foster foolish persistence. Culturally, we associate persistence—"staying the course," "sticking to your guns," and "weathering the storm"—with strong leadership. Persistence that happens to turn out successfully is especially rewarded. For example, when we think about the people who have become heroes in business and politics (Iacocca and Churchill, for examples), we see leaders who have faced difficult and apparently failing situations but who have hung tough until they were successful. If people see persistence as a sign of leadership and withdrawal as a sign of weakness, why would they expect managers to back off from losing courses of action? Recent research demonstrates that even though it may not add to the welfare of the organization, persistence does make a manager look like a leader.[5]

In short, the need to justify one's actions to others and to appear strong as a leader can combine with the three psychological factors to push managers into staying with a decision too long. This combination of forces does not, however, account for all debacles in which organizations suffer enormous losses through excessive commitment. In many of these cases structural factors also play a role.

ORGANIZATIONAL PUSHES AND PULLS

Probably the simplest element impeding withdrawal from losing projects is administrative inertia. Just as individuals do not always act on their beliefs, organizations do not always base their practices on their preferences. All the rules, procedures, and routines of an organization as well as the sheer trouble it takes for managers to give up day-to-day activities in favor of a serious operational disruption can cause administrative inertia. Dropping a line of business may mean changing corporate layoff policies, and moving people to other projects may violate seniority and hiring procedures. Sometimes it's just easier not to rock the boat.

Beyond such simple inertia, the politics of a situation can prevent a bailout. British Columbia's decision to stage the world's fair Expo '86 is one of the most recent public examples of the power of political forces to sustain a costly course of action. Expo '86 was supposed to operate close to the financial break-even point. But as plans for the fair got under way, the expected losses burgeoned. At first, the planners tried to minimize the financial hazards by providing heartening but biased estimates of revenues and costs. When they finally accepted the more dire financial projections, however, and even the director recommended cancellation, the planners still went ahead with the fair. Politically it was too late: the fortunes of too many businesses in the province were tied to Expo, it was popular with the voters, and the future of the premier and his political party were aligned with it. The province created a lottery to cope with the expected $300 million deficit, and the fair opened as scheduled.

Though the Expo example comes from the public sector, political force may also sustain costly business projects. As a venture withers, not only those directly involved with it may work to maintain it, but other interdependent or politically aligned units may support it as well. If the project's advocates sit on governing bodies or budget committees, efforts to stop it will meet further resistance. If a review finally does occur, the estimates of the costs and benefits of continuing the venture will very likely be biased.

On occasion, support for a project can go even deeper than administrative inertia and politics. When a project such as a long-standing line of business is closely identified with a company, to consider its discontinuation is to consider killing the very purpose of the company. (Imagine Hershey without chocolate bars or Kimberly-Clark without Kleenex.) A project or a division can become institutionalized in an organization.

Consider the plight of Lockheed with its L 1011 Tri-Star Jet program. Although every outside analysis of the program found the venture unlikely to earn a profit, Lockheed persisted with it for more than a decade and accumulated enormous losses. The problem was not ending the project per se but what it symbolized. The L 1011 was Lockheed's major entry in the commercial aviation market (in which it had been a pioneer), and Lockheed shrank from being identified as simply a defense contractor.

Pan American World Airways has recently gone through a similar institutional process. More than most airlines, Pan Am suffered huge losses after deregulation of the industry; it was even in danger of not meeting its debt obligations. Although the prospects for large profits in the airline industry were dim, Pan Am chose to sell off most of its other more profitable assets—first the Pan Am building in New York and then the Intercontinental Hotels Corporation—so as to remain in its core business. Finally, as losses continued, Pan Am sold its valuable Pacific routes to United Air Lines. Following these divestitures, the company was left with only U.S. and international routes in corridors where competition is heavy. Apparently, management didn't seriously consider the possibility of selling or closing the airline and keeping most of the other profitable subsidiaries. Pan Am is, after all, in the airline and not the real estate or hotel business.

Not all the forces we've described are relevant to every case, and not all are of equal influence in the situations where they operate. In many instances, commitment to a course of action builds slowly. Psychological and social forces come into play first, and only later does the structure make its impact. And, in a few cases, because the rational point of withdrawal has long passed, even the economic aspects of a project can cry out for continuation.

Still, some executives do manage to get themselves and entire organizations out of escalating situations. There *are* solutions.

Steps Executives Can Take Themselves

Executives can do many things to prevent becoming overcommitted to a course of action. Some of these solutions they can take care of on their own. Others involve getting the organization to do things differently. Let's look first at the remedies that executives themselves can apply.

RECOGNIZE OVERCOMMITMENT

The most important thing for managers to realize is that they may be biased toward escalation. For all the reasons we have mentioned, executives may delude themselves into thinking that a project will pull through—that success is around the corner. Recognizing overcommitment is, however, easier to preach than to practice. It usually takes enthusiasm, effort, and even passion to get projects off the ground and running in bureaucratic organizations. The organization depends on these responses for vitality. Consequently, the line between an optimistic, can-do attitude and overcommitment is very thin and often difficult to distinguish.

SEE ESCALATION FOR WHAT IT IS.   How, then, can managers know whether they have crossed the threshold between the determination to get things done and overcommitment? Although the distinction is often subtle, they can clarify matters by asking themselves the following questions:

1. Do I have trouble defining what would constitute failure for this project or decision? Is my definition of failure ambiguous, or does it shift as the project evolves?

2. Would failure on this project radically change the way I think of myself as a manager or as a person? Have I bet the ranch on this venture for my career or for my own satisfaction?

3. Do I have trouble hearing other people's concerns about the project, and do I sometimes evaluate others' competence on the basis of their support for the project?

4. Do I generally evaluate how various events and actions will affect the project before I think about how they'll affect other areas of the organization or the company as a whole?

5. Do I sometimes feel that if this project ends, there will be no tomorrow?

If a manager has answered yes to one or more of these questions, the person is probably overcommitted to a project.

BACK OFF. Just knowing that one is under the sway of escalation can help. But knowing is not enough. It is also necessary to take some steps to avoid overcommitment. One way is to schedule regular times to step back and look at a project from an outsider's perspective. A good question to ask oneself at these times is, "If I took over this job for the first time today and found this project going on, would I support it or get rid of it?" Managers could take their cues from bankers. When they take over others' portfolios, bankers usually try to clean up any troubled loans since they want to maximize the future returns associated with their own loan activity. Managers can also encourage their subordinates to reevaluate decisions. Most critical here is establishing a climate in which, regardless of whether the data are supportive or critical of the ongoing project, people convey accurate information. Just stating a "nothing but the truth" policy, however, is usually not enough to change the pattern of information reporting. The messenger with extremely critical but important information needs an explicit reward.

One forum for getting objective and candid feedback is a variant of the currently popular quality circle. Managers could regularly convene key staff members for "decision circles," in which fellow employees would offer honest evaluations of the hurdles a project faces and its prospects. Managers from other departments or sections might also attend or even chair such sessions to ensure an objective look at the problems. Managers might also hold regular "exchanges of perspective" in which colleagues could help each other see the truth about their operations.

CHANGE THE ORGANIZATION

Though it is possible to come up with an array of decision aids to help managers gain an objective perspective about the projects they run, one could argue that the problem of escalation is larger than any one person, that it's organizational in scope. Unfortunately, such a pessimistic view is at least partially correct. Much of what causes escalation is in the nature of organizations, not people.

If organizational action is called for, what can the system do to minimize escalation?

TURN OVER ADMINISTRATORS. One way to reduce the commitment to a losing course of action is to replace those associated with the original policy or project. If overcommitment stems from psychological and social forces facing the originators of the action, then their removal eliminates some of the sources of commitment.

Turning over project managers can of course be both disruptive and costly. Moreover, because people who were once associated with the discontinued venture may still be committed to it, management may find it difficult to draw the appropriate line for making a purge. Nonetheless, to make a clean break with the past, many organizations do make occasional personnel sweeps, sometimes more for their symbolic value than because of any real differences in decision making.

Still, we don't recommend turnover as the way to make changes. Like treating the disease by killing the patient, taking committed decision makers off a project may produce nothing but a demoralized staff and disaffected managers hesitant to try again.

SEPARATE DECISION MAKERS. One technique for reducing commitment that is far less drastic than turnover is to separate initial from subsequent decisions concerning a course of action. In some banks, for example, a "workout group" handles problem loans rather than the people who originally funded and serviced the loans.

The idea is not only that specialists should be involved in recouping bank funds but also that these officers are able to handle the loans in a more objective way than those who made the first decisions about the accounts.[6] Industrial companies could also make use of such procedures. They could separate funding from new-product-development decisions and hiring from promotion decisions. They could keep deliberations on whether to discontinue lines of business apart from day-to-day management decisions.

REDUCE THE RISK OF FAILURE. Another way to reduce commitment is to lessen the risk of failure. Because project failure can spell the end to an otherwise promising career, an administrator may be forced to defend a losing course of action. In a no-win dilemma, the trapped manager may think, "Things look bleak now, but there's no point in my suggesting that the company withdraw. If the project doesn't succeed, I have no future here anyway."

In some companies, management has reduced the costs of failure by providing rationalizations of losing courses of action and excuses for their managers. People are told that the losses are beyond anyone's control or that the fault lies with more general economic conditions, government regulation, or foreign competition. Although this route takes managers off the hook, it doesn't help them see a losing course for what it is or how they may avoid making the mistakes again.

Most companies do not want to take the pressure off their managers to perform as winners. Yet because a strong fear of failure can cause overcommitment, management is better off setting only a moderate cost for failure, something to avoid but not to fear intensely. A large computer company, for example, puts managers who have made big mistakes in a "penalty box." It makes them ineligible for major assignments for up to a year. After the penalty period, the managers are restored to full status in the organization and are again eligible to run major projects. Organizations trying to cope with escalation situations may find such a compromise between support for failure and demand for competence helpful.

IMPROVE THE INFORMATION SYSTEM. Several laboratory experiments have shown that people will withdraw from escalating situations when they see the high costs of persisting.[7] The presentation of such negative data is more difficult in organizations, however. Because no one wants to be the conveyer of bad news, information is filtered as it goes up the hierarchy. Furthermore, because those intimately involved with a project are not likely to distribute unflattering and less-than-optimistic forecasts, information is also biased at the source.

What, then, can organizations do to improve their information report? The most common solution is to increase their use of outside experts and consultants. The problem with consultants, however, is that they are no more likely to hear the truth than anyone else in the organization, and they also may not find it easy to tell management what it doesn't want to hear.

A better solution is to try to improve the honesty of reporting throughout the organization. By rewarding process as highly as product, managers can encourage candid reporting. The purpose of rewarding managers for the way a process is carried out is to make them attend as much to the quality of analysis and decision making as to the final results. Instead of acting as champions who inflate the prospects of their own projects and minimize their risks, managers offered process rewards are motivated to recognize problems and deal with them.

At the outset of projects, companies should encourage the creation of fail-safe options, ways to segment projects into small, achievable parts, and analyses of the costs of withdrawal. Later in the life of projects, companies should reward honest recognition of problems and clear examination of the alternatives, including withdrawal.

This kind of reward system is quite different from the usual practice of giving people recognition for success on their projects and punishing them for failure on their undertakings. Yet it is a system that should reduce many of the forces for escalation.

Boosting Experimentation

As we noted earlier in our discussion, an entire organization can be so caught up in supporting a project—especially an institutionalized one—that it ignores the cost of persistence.

Rather than trying to discredit an institutionalized project on economic grounds, a good strategy for withdrawal from it is to reduce its links with the central purposes of the organization. A useful tactic is to label the project peripheral or experimental so that managers can treat it on its own merits rather than as a symbol of the organization's central goal or mission.

Ideally, managers should consider all ventures imperfect and subject to question in an "experimenting organization."[8] Every program should be subject to regular reconsideration (à la zero-based budgeting), and every line of business should be for sale at the right price. In such an experimenting organization, projects wouldn't become institutionalized to the point where management couldn't judge them on their own costs and benefits. And because managers in such a system would be judged as much for recognition of problems facing their units and how they cope with them as for success and failure, experimenting organizations should be extremely flexible. When a market or a technology changes, the experimenting organization would not simply try to patch up the old product or plant but would be quick to see when it is best to pull the plug and start anew.

Notes

1. For more complete reviews of escalation research, see Barry M. Staw and Jerry Ross, "Understanding Escalation Situations: Antecedents, Prototypes, and Solutions," in *Research in Organizational Behavior*, ed. L. L. Cummings and Barry M. Staw (Greenwich, Conn.: JAI Press, 1987); and Joel Brockner and Jeffrey Z. Rubin, *Entrapment in Escalating Conflicts* (New York: Springer-Verlag, 1985).

2. See Gregory B. Northcraft and Gerrit Wolf, "Dollars, Sense, and Sunk Costs: A Lifecycle Model of Resource Allocation," *Academy of Management Review*, April 1984, p. 22.

3. For experiment results, see Barry M. Staw, "Knee-deep in the Big Muddy: A Study of Escalating Commitment to a Chosen Course of Action," in *Organizational Behavior and Human Performance*, June 1976, p. 27; Alan Tegar, *Too Much Invested to Quit* (New York: Pergamon Press, 1980); and Max H. Bazerman, R. I. Beekum, and F. David Schoorman, "Performance Evaluation in a Dynamic Context: A Laboratory Study of the Impact of Prior Commitment to the Ratee," *Journal of Applied Psychology*, December 1982, p. 873.

4. Frederick V. Fox and Barry M. Staw, "The Trapped Administrator: The Effects of Job Insecurity and Policy Resistance upon Commitment to a Course of Action," *Administrative Science Quarterly*, September 1979, p. 449.

5. Barry M. Staw and Jerry Ross, "Commitment in an Experimenting Society: An Experiment on the Attribution of Leadership from Ad-

ministrative Scenarios," *Journal of Applied Psychology,* June 1980, p. 249.

6. See Roy J. Lewicki, "Bad Loan Psychology: Entrapment and Commitment in Financial Lending," Graduate School of Business Administration Working Paper No. 80–25 (Durham, N.C.: Duke University, 1980).

7. Bruce E. McCain, "Continuing Investment Under Conditions of Failure: A Laboratory Study of the Limits to Escalation," *Journal of Applied Psychology,* May 1986, p. 280; and Edward G. Conlon and Gerrit Wolf, "The Moderating Effects of Strategy, Visibility, and Involvement on Allocation Behavior: An Extension of Staw's Escalation Paradigm," *Organizational Behavior and Human Performance,* October 1980, p. 172.

8. Donald T. Campbell, "Reforms as Experiments," *American Psychologist,* April 1969, p. 409.

PART
IV

Planning and Controlling

1
Essential Elements of Project Financing

Larry Wynant

In recent years numerous industrial projects have been undertaken around the world that have consumed enormous amounts of capital. Rapid inflation, novel technological characteristics, and (often) a remote location have combined to require sums that tax the financial capacity of even the largest corporations.

Four years ago a survey of ongoing nuclear power, mining, and natural resource projects found more than 200 with anticipated capital costs exceeding $500 million.[1] Since then inflation has, of course, accelerated sharply. Moreover, the developmental nature and foreign location of many of these ventures involve such enormous monetary risks that the outcome of a project has a tremendous impact on the sponsoring company.

The companies and their investment bankers have devoted considerable ingenuity to designing ownership structures and financing packages that cope with these capital demands and risk pressures. Joint venture arrangements and government support for projects are two avenues that they have followed.

At a time when U.S. business is already constrained by high leverage ratios and high interest rates, the prospect of further inflation and stepped-up spending requirements influences the capital-intensive company to seek imaginative ways of obtaining funding. My research (see Appendix) suggests that project financing can be a very effective vehicle for enlarging the amount of debt available to a new undertaking as well as for managing the sponsor's exposure to the associated risks.

This technique is usually applied to extremely large natural resource and energy investments costing hundreds of millions of dollars. The same strategy, however, can be useful in cases where capital needs are manageable but risks are great. The transportation, power, chemicals, and agribusiness sectors in particular have used project financing for all sizes of investments.

It is easy to see why. Exhibit I indirectly traces the investment required for a unit of capacity in several capital-intensive industries by measuring assets to revenues during the 1955–1975 period. Metal mining and primary metals have been especially pressured by rising capacity costs.

For many companies in these industries faced with the necessity of replacing or updating plant, debt financing naturally has been the main recourse. Exhibit II illustrates the increased reliance on leverage over the past two decades.

Capital needs could mushroom in the near future; many U.S. corporations will have to search for new funding to cover their needs for strategically and economically attractive investments. A counter-response to the warnings ten years ago of a capital crunch for the 1975–1985 decade argued that demand and supply mechanisms in the capital markets and innovative financing techniques would avert a crisis. In my opinion, project financing—a major innovation of the recent past—offers considerable promise for meeting these challenges.

The definitions of this approach run the gamut, depending on the advantage or objective that the financing package is designed to achieve. The following summary, however, captures the basic elements: project financing is a financing of a major independent capital investment that the sponsoring company has segregated from its assets and general purpose obligations. The economic prospects of the project, combined with commitments from the sponsor and third parties, provide the support for extensive borrowings carrying limited financial recourse to the parent company.

Several characteristics distinguish project financing from traditional arrangements:

The undertaking is established as a separate entity and relies heavily on leverage, generally for 65% to 75% of its capital needs.

The borrowing is linked directly to the assets and cash flow potential of the venture.

Exhibit I. Ratios of Total Assets to Total Sales in Selected Industries, 1955–1975

	1955	1960	1966	1971	1975
Manufacturing					
Chemicals	.85	.90	.85	.89	.85
Machinery	.75	.79	.74	1.02	1.00
Paper and allied products	.81	.88	.89	.95	.83
Petroleum refining	.95	1.06	1.07	1.09	*
Primary metals	.78	.98	.88	1.20	1.01
Rubber and plastic products	.58	.66	.71	.75	.72
Mining					
Metal mining	1.45	1.96	1.48	2.32	2.20
Crude petroleum and natural gas	1.39	1.62	1.29	1.21	*
Agriculture, forestry, and fishing	1.01	.92	.88	.82	.79
Construction	.47	.47	.47	.51	.54

*Ratios are unavailable because of changes in industry definition.
Source: Internal Revenue Service, *Statistics of Income, Corporation Income Tax Returns* (for the particular years).

Exhibit II.   *Use of Leverage in Selected Manufacturing Industries, 1960–1978*
(Ratio of short- and long-term debt to stockholders' equity)

	1960	1965	1970	1975	1978
All manufacturing	.25	.28	.45	.42	.41
Chemicals	.23	.32	.41	.43	.46
Machinery	.27	.28	.45	.39	.37
Paper and allied products	.25	.34	.59	.56	.53
Petroleum refining*	.19	.19	.29	.19	.27
Primary metals	.24	.29	.52	.49	.56
Rubber and plastic products	.32	.38	.66	.53	.55

*Ratios are not strictly comparable because of changes in industry definition.
Source: Federal Trade Commission, *Quarterly Financial Report for Manufacturing and Trade Corporations* (for the particular years).

Commitments by third parties (suppliers, customers, and government agencies) and the sponsor make up important elements of the credit support.

The sponsor's guarantees to lenders usually do not cover all the risks involved.

The debt of the project is differentiated, at least for balance-sheet purposes, from the parent company's direct obligations.

Structuring the Venture

Tailoring this kind of enterprise requires a trade-off between the sponsor's desired risk exposure and the economics of the venture, including commitments by the sponsor and other parties to satisfy lenders' concerns that it can support a wide base of debt financing. Accomplishing this balance for projects that involve large front-end investments and great marketing, technology, and political uncertainties demands considerable time, cost negotiations, and financial expertise.

The extent of financial engineering needed calls for the services of an experienced adviser. Many of the larger U.S. commercial and investment banks have established project financing departments and participate regularly in lending syndicates. A handful of the largest international commercial banks and an equally small number of investment houses have gained dominance as advisers in extremely large and complex project undertakings.

No one financing package, of course, would suit the needs of all projects. Each new development carries unique risks and capital needs and will have access to different funding sources. However, negotiating an underwriting of any project venture demands the corporate financial staff's attention to these key elements of the task:

1. Assessment of the start-up and operating risks and the range and likelihood of negative consequences.
2. Identification of the major lending sources and the terms for obtaining funds.
3. Analysis of the opportunities for reducing or laying off the risks.
4. Achieving the leverage targets through special fund sources and support arrangements.
5. Structuring of the ownership and credit arrangements to allow flexibility for future financing.

ASSESSMENT OF THE RISKS

Each player in a major project—sponsor, lending institution, government agency, customer for the output, and host government in the case of a foreign venture—will view its prospects and characteristics with different objectives and considerations. Consequently, the negotiations necessary to design the financing package are complex and lengthy.

The initial task confronting the financial officer of the parent company, of course, is to investigate the feasibility of underwriting the investment on a project basis. This would call for creation of a separate company with clearly delineated operating and financial prospects: estimated capital requirements, anticipated output levels, technology or production requirements, raw materials sources, expected customers and future market conditions, and the structural and operating relationships between the project and the parent.

Designing a financing package that reduces the sponsor's risk exposure and presents the lenders with a strong proposal is of primary importance. With the aid of computer simulation to estimate the impact of such variables as market prices and operating costs on profitability and return on investment, the corporate financial staff can get an idea of the potential risks:

START-UP COST OVERRUNS.   The long start-up period for a major venture (sometimes ten years in an exploration project) obviously adds to the potential for serious underestimation of costs. Many recent projects have entailed capital expenditures as high as 200% of original estimates.

Inflation, inaccurate engineering and design studies, and large operating deficits during the start-up phase are the usual reasons cited. All three of these underlay the problems of one company that had arranged $120 million of financing for an Indonesian copper mining development requiring inland construction in a remote mountainous region and a novel pipeline system for carrying the ore in slurry to the coast. By completion time three years later, modification of the site had pushed costs to more than $200 million.

UNEXPECTEDLY HIGH OPERATING COSTS.   Incorrect estimates of operating costs can result from many factors: inaccurate assessment of the production or recovery process, poor engineering to meet product quality and quantity specifications, low productivity of foreign labor, unexpectedly high equipment replacement, inflation or unexpected price hikes for certain production components, and changes in parity of currencies for international projects.

The sponsors of a joint nickel-mining venture in Australia in the mid-1970s, for example, had negotiated long-term sales contracts in U.S. dollars. Operating expenses began climbing dramatically as the Australian dollar was revalued. The production process used oil as a fuel source, and the price of that commodity soared. The combination of cost pressures caused the sponsors to eventually write off their equity investment in the project.

VOLATILE MARKET CONDITIONS.   A venture producing a commodity product is likely to encounter changing market prices over its expected life. Therefore, an estimate of future prices at the planning stage is subject to considerable error.

IN FOREIGN VENTURES, HIGH POLITICAL RISKS.   The political uncertainties surrounding foreign projects have become very serious during the past decade as developing countries and industrialized nations alike have adopted a more hostile posture toward foreign investments. Instances of outright expropriation by developing nations, such as Peru, Chile, and Cuba, as well as industrialized countries, such as Canada's nationalization of the potash industry in the mid-1970s, have been well publicized. But indirect actions by host governments—including foreign exchange restrictions, currency inconvertibility, increases in local taxes or royalties, demands for equity participation—can destroy or at least impair the economic attractiveness of a project.

Executives of the companies I studied all related incidents of intervention by foreign governments. One case involved increased royalties imposed on the project's output; in another, a sudden change in permitted depletion allowances resulted in a tax levy on past income of more than $25 million.

IDENTIFICATION OF LOAN SOURCES

Depending on the nature and location of the undertaking, potential sources for financing include export credits, international financing agencies, private lenders, and customers.

During the past two decades, many of the industrialized nations have established export credit and loan insurance programs. In the

United States, the Export-Import Bank (Ex-Im) grants loan financing and gives guarantees to stimulate the exports of U.S. manufacturers, while the Overseas Private Investment Corporation (OPIC) provides insurance against risks of expropriation, currency inconvertibility, and war damage, as well as strictly business risks, for projects in some 90 developing nations. Similar funding and insurance can be obtained from other government agencies, such as the Export Insurance Division in Japan and the Export Credit Guarantee Department in Great Britain.

Theoretically, all the OECD countries will match terms and rates offered by their export credit agencies. But the agencies of some industrialized countries, particularly France, Britain, and Japan, have offered more competitive rates through "mixed" credits that combine concessionary aid lending with normal, market-related rates. Ex-Im has recently adopted a more aggressive posture by matching competing rates and offering more financing on an ad hoc basis and by pushing for fuller export financing agreements with other governments.

The terms for and costs of export financing and insurance are generally very attractive. Loans are usually provided with a long maturity on a fixed-price basis at rates somewhat better than free market conditions would permit. Similarly, private lenders are granted low-cost insurance protection.

Other politically sponsored funding sources available for industrial projects are the World Bank and regional lending organizations such as the Inter-American Development Bank and the Asian Development Bank. These entities generally emphasize development projects in Third World countries and may offer certain advantages in rates and loan maturities.

Loans from commercial banks are available through their participation in export credit programs as well as on the strength of the project's repayment capacity. Inasmuch as any loan proposal to a lending institution must meet the tests of a normal credit risk, the financial executive of the sponsoring company will be obliged to ascertain the costs involved as well as the level and types of risks that are acceptable to the lending groups.

Project financing was an outgrowth of the expansionary mood that pervaded the banking industry in the late 1960s and early 1970s. In their eagerness to get into an exciting new area and secure a position in international lending, bankers took on many project loans without fully recognizing the risks in nonrecourse or limited-recourse arrangements.

Many loans were granted that lacked, for example, completion agreements by the parent companies or assessments by the lenders of the sponsors' capacity or willingness to produce more equity if necessary. The loan agreements for a $600 million project in Peru in the early 1970s, for instance, were silent as to stockholders' responsibilities for cost overruns of more than $20 million. The ultimate project costs exceeded $725 million, which forced the lending group to renegotiate its financial support.

Borrowers no longer have such freedom. Problem projects, rampant inflation, and concerns about the risks of foreign loans—not to mention the cost overruns—have caused the banking industry to insist on much tighter agreements and stronger loan support from sponsors. The completion agreement for a recent $100 million Wyoming coal project committed the owners to meet volume and cost specifications for a minimum period of continuous operation and to provide all additional equity needed for completion of the undertaking.

The large international banks, however, still remain prepared to assume the political risks for foreign projects. In a venture abroad nowadays, the political climate often presents the most serious hazards.

Customer credits should also be explored as a source of loans. U.S. utility companies, for example, increasingly subsidize exploration and development through advance payments to oil companies in return for secured sources of gas or petroleum. The market for the output of the project may be tight enough to permit the sponsors to bargain for low-cost financing from customers. In nickel, copper, and other metals, market conditions have obliged Japanese and West German companies to seek long-term sources of supply. For many new projects the companies were willing to provide financing directly or solicit support from their government funding agencies.

To obtain the most favorable deal, the financial executive and financing specialist must search out all lending sources. As one financial vice president said: "It's essential that the financial officer know the credit market thoroughly and design the financing to fit existing demand and supply conditions. It's important to know lenders around the world—their preferences, needs, and idiosyncrasies—and what one lender is prepared to do that others won't."

His company had engineered two successful overseas financings, each tailored to take advantage of the opportunities at the time. In one, the company obtained credit from U.S. commercial banks anxious to get involved in international business of this sort. In the other, the company was able to tap local banks because the host government gave incentives to them in order to aid industrial development in outlying regions of the country.

REDUCING THE RISKS

As I have indicated, the growing popularity of project financing is in great part a consequence of cost escalations that surpass normal corporate resources. But even in the case of a small venture, or in the absence of capital restraints in underwriting a large venture, the project may involve risks that are unacceptable to the parent company.

Linking the financing to the fortunes of the project, however, can permit transfer of some hazards to other parties. In the case of foreign developments, for instance, credit and insurance programs offered by the industrialized nations provide nonrecourse financing and transfer some of the commercial and political risks to the funding agencies.

If demand and supply conditions for the eventual output are favorable, the sponsor can negotiate with customers to provide debt financing or absorb greater price risks in return for an assured future supply. Floor prices and price escalation clauses enable the sponsor to shift the consequences of price uncertainties to the project's "offtakers." Direct financial participation by customers reduces the other major element of market risk—the possibility that the sales agreements will not be honored.

During the past decade, two major foreign mining developments by one U.S. company received the go-ahead largely because (1) the governments involved were ready to provide export credit financing or loan guarantees to ensure raw materials sources for domestic needs and (2) the smelters and metal processors wanted to lock in supplies. These projects represented roughly 70% of the company's total assets, so it could not finance them alone.

The willingness of the large international banks to assume political risk is a reflection of their diversified loan portfolios, through which they can spread the hazards of foreign projects. (Of course, the banks charge risk premiums on these loans.) Furthermore, an institution's position and influence as a large international banker may cause the host government to think twice about expropriation or other actions that would jeopardize the project's success, thereby alienating an important segment of the credit market.

The companies whose executives I interviewed had employed a number of measures to minimize the political risks for large foreign ventures. Among these measures were agreements with lenders to carry the risks, purchase of political risk insurance for the equity investment, and formation of large lending consortia to include institutions from countries that were either trading partners or major creditors of the host governments.

This type of strategy unfolded in 1976 when Peru sought a $300 million balance-of-payments loan from a syndicate of U.S. money center banks. They granted the loan on condition of satisfaction of two matters concerning U.S. customers of the banks—namely, a back-tax dispute with Southern Peru Copper Co. (owned by AMAX Inc.) and compensation for Peru's expropriation in 1975 of Marcona Mining Co. (a joint venture of Cyprus Mines and Newmont Mining Corp.).

ACHIEVING THE LEVERAGE TARGET

A project financing typically obtains debt funding equivalent to 65% to 75% of total capital needs. To procure such extensive support, the financial officer has to structure the agreements (1) to satisfy the demands of private lenders who are only prepared to assume normal credit risks and (2) to lay off any additional risks to partners, customers, or government institutions.

A study of 17 completed financings for new mines and related developments found that more than half had serious problems and could not generate sufficient cash flow to cover debt servicing.[2] Only one project, however, resulted in a loss to lenders. All of these projects were highly leveraged, yet they had satisfied the banks' requirements of being within the boundaries of normal credit risks.

The lenders must be provided with complete, detailed estimates of the project's risks and return potential, including feasibility studies, engineering reports, and particulars of commitments by the contractors, suppliers, and customers. In a loan to the sponsoring company, the lenders are much less concerned with the economic prospects of the particular investment than with the parent's creditworthiness and ability to meet debt obligations.

A project financing proposal forces lenders to revise their assessment of the parent's debt-service capacity to include the forecasted cash flow for the undertaking. Investment bankers use the term "lenders' psychology" to suggest that lending institutions are locked in by traditional debt-equity ratios in the particular industry. By setting up the project as a separate borrowing entity, however, the sponsor can better demonstrate its prospects and debt-servicing capacity.

In trying to maximize borrowing capacity, one financial vice president has pursued a "sum of the parts is greater than the whole" strategy. On a project basis the company had financed two overseas developments totaling $400 million and a domestic expansion program of roughly the same size.

On the strength of the projects, management had succeeded in making risk-sharing arrangements with major banks and, in the case of the foreign investments, similar arrangements with customers. The executive was convinced that the direct and indirect borrowings, equivalent to about 85% of the total investment, greatly exceeded the level of debt financing that the rating agencies or major lenders would have considered reasonable if financed by the parent. The company's debt ratio at the time averaged about 30%.

PRESERVING FINANCIAL FLEXIBILITY

Corporate financial officers aim to achieve a balance between the company's risk exposure and the amount of project leverage that they can negotiate—while retaining the parent company's financial flexibility. Top management must decide the level of commitment the company can afford to undertake as well as the form of that commitment.

The aspect of project financing that has received the greatest promotion is the ability of the proposal to raise funds solely on its own merits, without parent company guarantees. Such instances, however, are rare. Two of them, both undertaken by Freeport Minerals in the late 1960s, were a $120 million copper project in Indonesia and a $305 million nickel mine and processing plant in Australia. The initial equity investment in each case amounted to less than 25%, and the loans were totally nonrecourse to Freeport. However, full credit support had been offered by Ex-Im and OPIC to the U.S. lenders in the Indonesian project, and a considerable amount of purchasing financing had been used for both ventures.

The sponsors are usually required to provide *some* form of credit support. The level of support may, however, amount to only limited guarantees. Lenders view with alarm the prospect of a project unfinished due to engineering or technical problems or a large cost overrun. Hence bankers generally ask the owners beforehand to sign an agreement stipulating tests of physical and/or economic completion. After the completion provisions are met, the project loans become nonrecourse, thereby returning autonomy to the sponsor in financing any new projects.

High-risk ventures can normally get credit only if the parent gives general guarantees to the lenders. Full guarantees show up as direct liabilities on the sponsor's balance sheet.

But a host of financing arrangements have emerged that provide indirect credit. Long-term purchase commitments, a very common medium, commit sponsors to payments sufficient to service the debt. "Take or pay" contracts are often used to support the borrowing. A recent coal project of roughly $100 million was financed off the balance sheet on the strength of such a contract with a utility. For the promise of an assured supply, the customer agreed to pay, even in the absence of output, enough to cover interest and principal payments.

Other examples of indirect credits are cost-sharing arrangements, where sponsors are obliged to provide their pro rata shares of all costs including debt-service payments and parent indirect guarantees, such as working capital maintenance clauses.

The nature of the sponsor's loan support can critically affect its flexibility for two reasons:

1. A limited-recourse arrangement can free up the parent's borrowing capacity for future expansion. A completion agreement, as opposed to a full guarantee of the project loans, enables the sponsor to piggyback its credit from project to project. Therefore, the financial officer should try to negotiate a minimum credit support in terms of the types of risks covered and the length of the guarantee period.

2. The manner in which the project loans are reported in financial statements can affect the parent's borrowing strength. The off-balance-sheet treatment of most project loans is promoted as a great benefit, although the advantage has not reduced over time. In the wake of recent changes in lease accounting to permit fuller disclosure of underlying financial obligations, the balance-sheet treatment of indirect liabilities is receiving more attention from the SEC and accounting bodies.

Even so, the indirect nature of typical sponsor guarantees, joint ownerships, and (often) a foreign location are factors that still permit a project loan to be unconsolidated or reported on the parent's balance sheet under a caption other than long-term debt—usually in a footnote. Suppose that a U.S. manufacturer has established many of its affiliated ventures as separate borrowing entities, backed by completion agreements. Viewing its completion guarantees simply as part of doing normal business, the company might not report them as contingent liabilities in its financial statements.

The rating agencies tend to look on off-balance-sheet obligations more favorably than direct debt. One investment banker I talked to employed this rule of thumb: the rating agencies generally ignore an off-balance-sheet financing unless the obligations amount to more than 5% to 10% of the parent's assets. Moreover, project financings typically fall outside the debt restrictions in loan indentures.

To test whether the benefits from such maneuvering are real or illusory, I sent 140 mail questionnaires to the largest commercial banks and life insurance companies as well as to pension and mutual fund managers and security analysts at the major investment houses. The responses suggest that for most institutions, indirect liabilities are not formally or at least not fully included in their analysis of a company's financial position.

Exhibit III summarizes the evaluation procedures used by analysts for some off-balance-sheet financing techniques. For the most familiar indirect liability—leases—the bulk of the respondents had developed formal evaluation techniques such as equating leases with debt for calculating balance-sheet ratios or estimating the company's fixed-charge coverage. However, contingency guarantees and long-term purchase commitments, which are less-understood liabilities, are either ignored because of inadequate disclosure or treated informally as a separate factor.

It is dangerous to conclude that informal procedures are ineffective. But a likely tendency by the respondents to indicate what they felt was the desired answer, regardless of the practices actually employed, and analysis of their added written responses suggest that an informal procedure may really mean that the liability escapes adequate recognition.

Close to 90% of the survey group expressed belief that leasing, purchase agreements, contingency guarantees and other special financing arrangements enhance a company's borrowing capacity. The respondents offered balance-sheet treatment as the most popular explanation. The group also noted that the typical obligations

Exhibit III.   Lenders' and Analysts' Evaluation of Off-Balance-Sheet Obligations

Method of evaluation	Percent of respondents indicating treatment for:		
	Leases	Contingency guarantees	Long-term service of purchase commitments
1. Treated as a separate factor to be weighed in the credit evaluation	11%	34%	—
2. Impact of the contract on future operations assessed	—	—	51%
3. Included as a form of debt in balance-sheet ratios	15	30	21
4. Required payments included in calculating fixed-charge coverage ratios	14	—	—
5. Both no. 3 and no. 4	53	—	—
6. Generally ignored	4	—	—
7. Given minor consideration because guarantee is limited	—	4	—
8. Given minor consideration because of inadequate information	—	30	36
9. Not specified	3	2	2

in a project financing are seldom controlled by private or public loan agreements. (Answers to industry-specific questions, such as those concerning production-payment financing, confirm the general results shown in Exhibit III.)

Financing Costs

In addition to risk-reduction and borrowing-capacity advantages, project financing can serve other ends. Tax considerations and concerns over common liabilities in a joint venture arrangement can make a strong case for this kind of structure in many situations.

The benefits obviously are not without cost. Most large ventures involve multiple lending groups and undertakings by numerous parties, and the additional management, legal, and syndication activities translate into high front-end fees. A range of .5% to 1.5% on a deal of a couple of hundred million dollars is normal. To an extent the charge depends on the amount of work that the commercial or investment bank has to put into the financing. Also, of course, a smaller company will be obliged to lay out a higher percentage than, say, a prime rate borrower.

The process of spreading risks to produce a limited-recourse financing may also entail significant costs, depending on which parties are asked to shoulder the risks. Private lenders are generally unwilling to assume equity positions and, in the case of a foreign venture, the political risk premium or project loan usually equals the rate differential charged the particular country. But since commercial banks have a comparative advantage in assuming risks abroad, the expected returns from the undertaking (net of interest charges) will actually increase in the case of project financing.

Projects can also obtain funding or risk insurance from government agencies at favorable rates. As to securing financial commitments from customers, if demand and supply conditions are unfavorable, customer participation may require substantial price concessions.

Most of the financings undertaken by the companies included in my study involved an overall loan premium of one to two percentage points above the parent company's borrowing rate. However, these premiums were minor considering the high leverage and minimal recourse in the agreements.

But project financing is not always a cheap form of financing; many proposals have been abandoned or ultimately underwritten conventionally because the costs of project financing became prohibitive. One copper producer, for example, opted to underwrite a $200 million domestic refinery itself, despite the massive capital requirements. The project was to be integrated so closely into the company's operations that a limited-recourse financing would have provided few benefits. If difficulties had arisen, the company would have been forced to bail out the refinery anyway. As the financial vice president explained later, "Since the financing would use up our overall credit capacity, why not do it in the simplest and least costly fashion?"

Future Financing Needs

While the capital shortage widely heralded a few years ago has not materialized, the needs of U.S. industry for larger infusions of capital are nevertheless enormous. As economists and other members of the financial community have pointed out, the level of spending on plant and equipment has fallen considerably behind that of other large industrialized nations.[3] How much funding is needed depends, of course, on how rapidly business pushes ahead with an overhaul of its basic plant and how inflation affects the costs of new or replaced capacity.

In addition, companies are facing project costs that tax their financial capacities on a scale basis or because of the high risks involved—or both. A complicating element is the fact that many corporations, handicapped by an already high level of debt financing, will be forced to seek outside funding. So in many cases project financing is a feasible strategy.

The nature of project financing will continue to evolve as structuring techniques are further developed in response to new capital projects and changing moods in the financial community. For the foreseeable future, however, loan proposals that do not protect institutional lenders through provision for substantial recourse to either the parent companies or other third parties will not meet with much success. Nevertheless, project financing remains a highly effective strategy for sharing risks and increasing the debt-financing capacity of the venture.

Appendix

Research Procedure

My conclusions grew from a close study of the experiences of investment houses and major companies that have used project financing structures. I conducted field interviews with specialists at the American and Canadian commercial and investment banks that are widely acknowledged to be leaders in this field.

Through a mail questionnaire sent to 140 commercial banks, life insurance companies, money managers, and investment firms, I investigated the attitudes of financial institutions toward project loans. In addition, I explored in depth the motives and financial strategies behind roughly a dozen domestic and foreign projects, initiated from 1967 to 1976, that had employed this type of funding. The bulk of the cases chosen were mineral exploration ventures simply because escalating capital demands for such undertakings have forced this industry to innovate with the project financing technique.

Notes

1. *The Banker,* January 1976, p. 77.
2. Grover R. Castle, "Project Financing—Guidelines for the Commercial Banker," *Journal of Commercial Bank Lending,* April 1975, p. 14.
3. See, for example, George E. Cruikshank, "Capital Shortage May Shortchange Development," *Nation's Business,* April 1979, p. 84.

2
New Projects:
Beware of False Economies

David Davis

The new plant has had a 100% cost overrun and an eight-month completion delay, and now, six months after start-up, it runs at less than half the capacity planned in the original design. The work force is disgruntled after a series of production crises, the customers are increasingly impatient, the original project manager has been fired, and the plant manager is feeling shaky.

Such a situation, unfortunately, describes the fate of many new projects in recent years. Capital expenditure overruns and poor performance are symptoms of a widespread disease affecting pioneer projects. Research reports on new projects verify the general impression that estimates of their performance, timetables, and costs are extraordinarily accident-prone, particularly when they involve new technology. In Britain the disease has a name, the "Concorde syndrome," honoring the airplane project that overran its estimated budget by several thousand percent. The name may differ elsewhere, but the phenomenon is the same. In the United States nuclear power plant overruns are highly publicized. Rarely anywhere does a new project, especially a high-tech undertaking, come on line on time, on budget, and up to scratch.

A Rand Corporation study on pioneer process plants chronicles this problem.[1] Although the Rand study focuses on pioneer technologies only in the energy industry, it serves as a useful indication of pioneer plants' lackluster performance because of poor design. The data show, for instance, that the first estimates of the construction cost of pioneer process plants are typically less than half the eventual cost and many are in the range of only one-third. Very few are accurate to within 20%.

The Rand report demonstrates unequivocally that the errors in cost estimates for new plants were dramatically greater when the estimates were based on vague rather than detailed design specifications. When the estimates were generated on the basis of R&D data, the average project eventually overran its budget by more than 100%. As one might expect, as the level of project definition and the quantity of engineering data increase, the overrun declines to about 10% at a fully costed design stage. Attempts to save time and money on initial planning and definition, because of haste or lack of an adequately sized design department, or insufficient funds, are always disastrous.

PIMS data corroborate the results of this Rand report.[2] These findings derive from a study of a large number of start-up ventures involving many companies in a diverse set of industries. Since the PIMS information shows the performance of new projects in terms of achieved market share versus plan, rather than production volume versus design capacity, the findings are not perfectly comparable with those of the Rand study. Volume and market share, however, and design output and plan are sufficiently analogous to indicate a high degree of corroboration.

The PIMS studies forcefully show that the single-industry Rand data are not unique to energy endeavors but apply equally to other industries. Their data show that the typical new project falls a long way short of plan; more than 80% of the projects investigated failed to achieve estimated market share.

The internal responses to the news that expenditures are getting out of control are also remarkably similar. Managers are creatures of habit, and they almost always panic when cost overruns mount. Their fright is understandable since overruns of new projects, especially those involving new technology, often double or triple original estimates, run into many millions of dollars, and can irrevocably damage the careers of those responsible.

In panic, project managers desperately search for budget items to cut. This coping response is effective for a small overrun—say one of 25%—but doesn't work for a large overrun where there isn't enough slack to realize the necessary economies. What the organization faces in such circumstances is not an overrun but a gross original underestimate. No amount of after-the-fact savings can bring the project within its hopelessly unrealistic budget.

Project managers, nevertheless, attempt to solve the problem by making cuts. In general, they rarely perceive hardware cuts—buildings, materials, equipment—as feasible. Rather, they see as the easiest areas to cut those with the least obvious benefits—managerial and design overhead, process control software, equipment quality assurance programs, and test procedures. Ironically, these are the very areas whose costs are often underestimated in the first place.

The favorite candidates for cuts tend to be all those areas that are poorly understood, such as systems and software, quality assurance, and test programs. Project managers often view instrumentation as peripheral to the main process and trim it back, thus changing the operation from a controlled exercise to a gamble. Such gambles rarely pay off: lack of instrumentation at a critical moment can stop a factory. Intangible systems gone wrong can have very tangible results.

How Serious Is the Overrun?

How can management spot a serious overrun in its early stages? Managers cannot, of course, relax budget guidelines every time a project overruns nor can they precipitate a lengthy investigation at every turn of new project development. Just because a project doesn't involve high technology doesn't mean it's safe either; high-tech industries are not the only ones that suffer this problem.

Most capital-intensive investments are high risk because the exit barriers and the high investment levels make it extraordinarily difficult to achieve the profits necessary to earn the requisite return. The expected average ROI for start-up ventures is near zero in the first five years, and ROIs are often negative for the first three or four years. Capital-intensive projects create pressures both on costing and on the effective functioning of the new project after it starts up.

A complex new venture creates many problems for a company. Complex in this context does not necessarily mean high technology—although it often does—for complexity is very much in the eye of the beholder. What is complex for one company may not be for another, because of differences in size, experience, and type of industry. Newness is a good yardstick. If your company is contemplating a major investment project that involves a new technology, market, or a size new to the company, serious overruns are a real possibility.

When an overrun threatens, the questions to ask are simple:

In your industry, does the project involve pioneer technology?

If the technology is not pioneer, is it new to your company? Has any of your project managers implemented this type of project before?

Is the project much bigger than any your company has handled before?

Was the project costed before the design was completed?

In regard to the last question, the Rand study showed that a surprisingly large number of pioneer projects have their budgets agreed on before completion of the final design. No doubt this practice is partly the result of the planning timetables of large organizations. Detailed design is an expensive process that is often delayed until management and the board of directors approve the project. The Rand study demonstrates unequivocally that the sketchier the design at budget approval time, the larger the overrun.

What often happens in preliminary design is a frugal approach is taken that turns out to be penny-wise but pound-foolish. A feasibility study, based on inadequate detail, forms the basis of the proposal sent to the board of directors. Project managers base cost estimates on guesses and don't attempt to test the validity of their appraisals by drawing up detailed specifications and asking for bids. In the case of a new-to-company project, a feasibility study often simply takes the cost of a similar plant or process used elsewhere and adds an inflation factor. It does not, for example, study compatibility of the preliminary design with local materials or the environment.

Although a company by this procedure may save the expense of a full design at an early stage of a proposal—and therefore expenses on proposals that never get off the ground—the ramifications of committing capital to a project on the basis of a sketchy feasibility study are enormous.

If, as a manager, you find that a project your company is developing has gone well beyond its estimates and the answer to any of the three questions on its newness is yes, it is probable that you have a serious overrun. If the answer to question four concerning the use of a feasibility study is also yes, then it is highly likely that you have a serious overrun arising from incorrect estimates.

What to Do

An overrun usually puts lower and middle managers in an inescapable box because they don't have the necessary decision-making powers. In most cases, only senior executives are in a position to take action.

Although the usual routine of "retrench, retrieve, revise, and review" is useful in dealing with overruns, management should instigate the following procedures when the problem is serious.

VERIFY THE NATURE OF THE PROBLEM

Senior managers' most important task in dealing with a budget-breaking project—and indeed with any project—is creating a corporate environment that encourages honest and frank disclosure. Everyone concerned with the project must be prepared to recognize and announce serious snags when they become evident. This can be difficult, especially when the first sign of failure precipitates a search for a scapegoat. Only senior management can set the tone for an environment of openness essential for the recovery of a project taking the wrong road.

The ways in which senior executives choose to discourage cover-ups and recriminations depend on their management styles. Some companies accept errors of judgment as the inevitable consequence of high-risk activity; top officers do not react to bad decisions in a punitive manner so long as the perpetrators deal with their mistakes promptly and do not repeat them. In such a regime, concealment of a problem is the cardinal sin that is punished harshly.

Another company's approach might resemble the "no surprises" management style at ITT under Harold Geneen, who insisted on early quantitative analysis in excruciating detail and on follow-up thoroughness on a scale rarely seen elsewhere. This kind of tough, unforgiving management style with its insistence on extreme detail can work only if project managers either get it right the first time or react with utmost honesty when a project starts to slip.

Other managers keep new ventures under control through powerful operations audit departments that check major projects thoroughly at each stage, beginning with the first budgets. The control mechanism a company chooses to oversee new projects should, of course, fit its corporate structure and management methods.

However it goes about it, a company should develop the means to identify early on whether an overrun is a major or a minor problem. Most disasters start as a series of 10% slippages, so it is essential to have access to the data necessary to judge the nature of these failures to meet estimate deadlines. The standard technique of increasing the budget pressure has at least a chance of curbing bona fide 10% overruns. Serious overruns require more drastic measures, and the sooner these are taken, the better.

REENGINEER THE PROJECT

Since the cause of most serious overruns is an inadequate initial design, an important step in dealing with the problem is to reengineer the project as comprehensively as possible.

What management hopes to accomplish by reengineering is the identification and rectification of errors that resulted from proceeding with the project on the basis of a skimpy feasibility study with many unknowns and inaccurate estimates.

Company X provides a good example of the need for realistic, in-depth initial costing. This young company in a high-technology industry embarked on a large program involving two capital-intensive projects with complex technology and a high level of computer control. One project, completed at the end of 1981, was a classic case of a unit overrun that came on stream some 100% over estimate. Competitive considerations led to the initiation of another project before the first, disastrous project was operational.

With only a few differences in personnel, the same management group was responsible for both ventures. Each project involved a technology that was new to the management group and that had a history of difficulty in start-ups elsewhere. The company planned to link the computer controls for the two projects, but each was to have its own hardware and software.

Project 1 was costed before the design was completed, which was a particularly bad error because the technology was new. As a result its costing was hopelessly wrong. Parts of the budget overran from the very first day, sometimes by several hundred percent. This put intense pressure on costs throughout the development of the project, which in turn impaired Project 1's functioning after start-up.

In contrast, Project 2 was conceived and implemented in calmer circumstances. The top managers realized intuitively (although they were not talking about it) that something was dramatically wrong with how Project 1 was being handled, so they strengthened the management group by adding a planner experienced in the relationship between design and budget.

Before submitting the costing for Project 2 to the board of directors for approval, the group undertook a $250,000 full design through to quotations. Subsequently, although pressures on costs arose during development, these were far less frenetic than in the case of Project 1.

The effect of the different approaches to costing on the operational effectiveness of the projects was dramatic. Project 2 reached 90% of design output in 3 months or less, whereas Project 1 had reached only 60% of design output at the end of 24 months.

The statistical significance of the difference in performance of the two projects is shown in Exhibit I, which compares the performance

Exhibit I. *Performance of Two Major Projects against Rand Report Data*

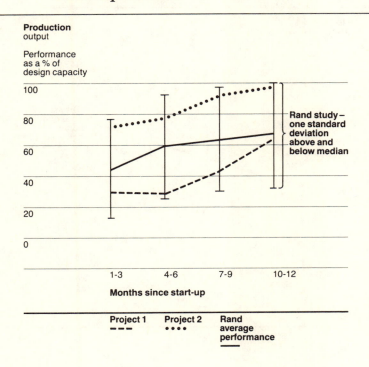

of Project 1 and Project 2 with the average performance (as a percentage of design capacity) of the pioneer process plants in the Rand report. In terms of the Rand average, during the first year of operations, Project 1's performance fell 20% below the average of pioneer plants, and Project 2's performance, for the most part, was 20% above average.

Although the Rand study covered a single industry only, the PIMS data show that the operational effectiveness of new projects, measured by market penetration, is considerably less than plan irrespective of industry for many years of the project life (see Exhibit II).

Exhibit II. Market Penetration, Planned vs. Actual

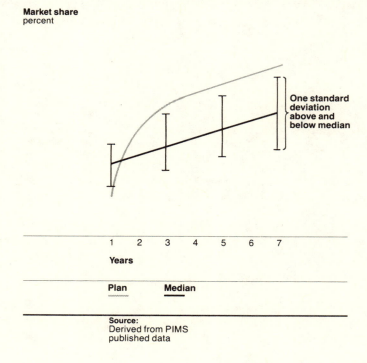

Market share
percent

One standard deviation above and below median

1 2 3 4 5 6 7

Years

Plan   Median

Source:
Derived from PIMS
published data

IDENTIFY UNDERESTIMATED AREAS

An engineering review enables management to spot areas where ignorance governs decisions. Such areas always exist with new projects, although the people connected with their development rarely admit it. Almost without exception, the costs in these areas are underestimated, and they are first in line for cutting at budget review.

One area reasonably representative of poor understanding in many complex modern plants is process control programming. It is used as an example several times in this article since it highlights so well both the causes and effects of designer and managerial ignorance. Companies going into ventures in which they are inexperienced are apt to be unaware of the cost and importance of adequate programming. They tend to neglect, or even ignore, the need for:

INTENSIVE CONTINGENCY PROGRAMMING AND INTERACTION CHECKING. It is very straightforward—and inexpensive—to program for a linear series of events, but much more difficult—and expensive—to plan for the possible interactions in a modern factory.

Projects with inadequate contingency programs can end up in a lot of trouble, especially with interactions based on automatic controls. Most automatically controlled factories have systems able to operate within microseconds of each other that can overwhelm other systems and subsystems in the plant. A project must have built-in contingency programs that guard against these and other interactions.

An example of what automatic controls can do that caught the popular imagination was the tiny fail-safe device in the Sir Adam Beck power station at Niagara Falls that tripped out on a cold November night in 1965 and, in 2.7 seconds, blacked out virtually the whole northeast United States and Canada.

AN INTENSIVE "HUMAN PROGRAMMING" EFFORT. It is hard enough to plan for a multiplicity of mechanical and electronic interactions without taking human responses into account. Nevertheless, new projects need systems that are robust in the face of the full scope of human reactions, ranging from the late-night languor of the back shift to the panic that occurs when the console unexpectedly lights up. The accident at Three Mile Island demonstrated this need in a macabre way.

As a rule of thumb, to have a reasonable probability of success, a process control program must cover more than 95% of all possible events.

A THOROUGH SERIES OF PROCESS SIMULATION TESTS.   Mistakes are inevitable in the design and development of new projects—particularly in high-tech projects—given the complexity of the systems involved. Process simulation tests can identify likely mistakes, but devising tests that deal with human, mechanical, and electronic interactions in the context of an incomplete project is difficult as well as time-consuming and costly.

Moreover, not all the failures will be found at the testing stage. It is necessary, therefore, that programming be designed in a manner that will permit diagnosis of potential and actual problems once the project is up and running.

Company X's Project 1 took a linear-logic approach, whereas Project 2 had built-in contingency programs to take complex interactions into account. Although it is impossible to quantify all the costs of delays and malfunctions, control system failures after start-up in Project 1 cost the equivalent in lost earnings of between six months' and one year's production. At a 15% discount rate, assuming that tax has minimal effect, losing one year's production at the beginning of a project's life is the same as adding 15% to the project cost. To put it another way, assuming a ten-year project life, a 20% residual value, and a high sales-investment ratio of 3 to 1, these delays are equivalent to a 1% cut in sales revenue over the life of a project. At a more usual new project sales-investment ratio of 1 to 1, the effect is the same as a sales revenue reduction of 3% for the project life (see Exhibit III).

These monetary losses do not take into account the effects on the company of disappointed customers, an atmosphere of failure in both the work force and management, a poor reputation in the industry and with competitors, and lack of enthusiasm on the part of investors.

AVOID FALSE SOLUTIONS

The typical response to an overrun is to cut costs wherever this seems possible. But this reaction can create, in the end, an even greater disaster if the overrun is caused by inadequate original costing in areas subsequently further starved of funds. In a des-

Exhibit III. Price Effect Equivalent for a One-Year Delay in Start-up

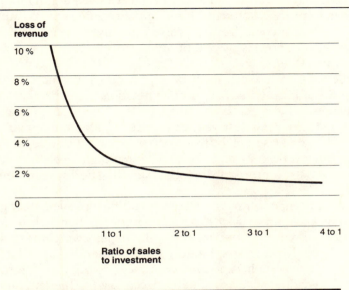

perate gamble to keep a project alive, managers can cripple a venture.

To carry on with the example of process control programming, cutting back on software investment is often seen as a good way to cheesepare project costs. The cause for this increasingly common harmful decision is the difficulty many managers have in assessing the value of intangible budget items. Like other factors critical to the cost, performance, and profit of new projects, software has several characteristics that attract budget cutters:

It is intangible.

Its importance is not easily quantified.

Project engineers and managers often understand poorly its use and value.

Managers perceive it to be expensive.

Moreover, cutting software investment during development of a project can have high leverage on its eventual operational effectiveness.

As we have seen, Company X's two projects provided some hard data on the effect of cutting back on software investment, as well as represented extremes of method. Project 1 used a minimum-cost approach to process software, limiting the planned expenditures to 19% of hardware cost; Project 2 raised the investment to 43%. The difference, therefore, was one of attitude to software as shown in expenditure level.

The level of software costs of both projects in the end were identical—45% of hardware costs. But as noted earlier, the operational effectiveness of Project 2 was much better than that of Project 1, especially during the first year of operation. This functional superiority did not arise solely from better software development, of course. But managers should recognize that high levels of software effectiveness are a prerequisite for outstanding performance by new projects.

Managers cannot blithely carry on spending money on intangibles in a badly overrun project. The characteristics that led to the selection of software for budget cuts—the expensive, poorly quantified, and poorly understood nature of the material—are shared by many other areas such as quality assurance programs, test routines, and training. But these are usually necessary for the viability of a project and cutting them out or cheeseparing their costs is not the answer to an overrun. Like software, these aspects of a project have high leverage on its eventual effectiveness.

The effect of software cuts during the development of Project 1 was that some 1% of total project costs were deferred, but not saved, at an eventual extra cost to the project in excess of 10% of total costs. In this case, a deferral of a few hundred thousand dollars resulted in further costs of many millions of dollars.

RECOST THE ENTIRE PROJECT

Rather than make irrational budget cuts of intangible items, what managers should do, once reengineering and a new design are complete, is to recost the new project on the basis of the latest design and review the market position for the project's products. Now it will be possible to make more accurate forecasts of external variables.

The reengineering exercise should have entailed a detailed design review, or even redesign, and should have included a thorough operational analysis that highlighted all doubtful or poorly understood areas. The objective study of the project must now take a hard look at costs. What will be necessary is detailed costing of all changed areas and probably recosting of the whole project.

Cost estimates at this time will also reflect changes in prices of materials and labor arising not only from differences in supplier markets but also from the experience gained during the implementation of the original design in terms of amendments and alterations of specifications.

The recosting should take into account an unbiased review of profit potential for the project, including those areas shown by the PIMS study to be often poorly estimated—market share and overall volume of market, pricing of the product output, and marketing expenses.

The difficulty of abandoning a project after several million dollars have already been committed to it tends to prevent objective review and recosting. For this reason, ideally an independent management team—one not involved in the project's development—should do the recosting and, if possible, the entire review. When the technology involved is new to the company but already in use elsewhere, it is always worthwhile to try to bring in a strong, outside technical management team well-versed in the technology to undertake this study.

ABANDON IF NECESSARY

If the numbers do not hold up in the review and recosting, the company should abandon the project. The number of bad projects that make it to the operational stage serve as proof that their supporters often balk at this decision.

There are a number of reasons for irrational behavior at this critical point, including many things that senior management can do little about. Obsessive enthusiasm by project managers, fascination with novelty and technology, and the good, old-fashioned need to achieve are important driving forces in any project. Under most circumstances it would be inadvisable to suppress these motivators; channeling of enthusiasm must be done carefully.

It is a brave manager who recommends the abandonment of a project under his command after a commitment of $20 million. Project managers who believe that closing down a project will wreck their careers are tempted to carry on in the hope they will have a slight chance of saving their reputations. Both courses carry the risk of disaster for those responsible for a project, but one—abandonment—is often far better for the company.

Senior managers need to create an environment that rewards honesty and courage and provides for more decision making on the part of project managers. Companies must have an atmosphere that encourages projects to succeed, but executives must also allow them to fail.

Starting new projects is fraught with risk. Costs may escalate and operational capabilities may decline as a project develops and goes on stream. Inadequate early cost estimates and improper budgeting increase risks and often lead to enormous overruns. The usual response to burgeoning expenses—to tighten budgets in intangible areas—leads to false economies that can cripple the operational capabilities of a project and will probably not save money after all.

When an overrun becomes serious, the only sensible recourse is to rework the project from the ground up and, if necessary, either abandon or rebudget. Minor cost cutting to buy time is counterproductive. Although false economies involving programming and other "soft-cost" areas may generate confidence or complacency, they do not solve any problems.

Decisions to reengineer, recost, and perhaps give up are hard to make. It is essential that senior managers monitor what is happening with new projects and be prepared to shoulder the difficult decisions themselves.

Notes

1. Edward Merrow, Kenneth Phillips, and Christopher Myers, *Understanding Cost Growth and Performance Shortfalls in Pioneer Process Plants* (Santa Barbara, Calif.: Rand Corp., September 1981).

2. Data presented as "Findings on Start-up Ventures" at the PIMS Membership Conference, Boston, Mass., 1981.

3
The ABCs of the Critical Path Method

Ferdinand K. Levy, Gerald L. Thompson, and Jerome D. Wiest

Recently added to the growing assortment of quantitative tools for business decision making is the Critical Path Method—a powerful but basically simple technique for analyzing, planning, and scheduling large, complex projects. In essence, the tool provides a means of determining (1) which jobs or activities, of the many that comprise a project, are "critical" in their effect on total project time, and (2) how best to schedule all jobs in the project in order to meet a target date at minimum cost. Widely diverse kinds of projects lend themselves to analysis by CPM, as is suggested in the following list of applications:

The construction of a building (or a highway).

Planning and launching a new product.

A turnaround in an oil refinery (or other maintenance projects).

Installing and debugging a computer system.

Research and engineering design projects.

Scheduling ship construction and repairs.

The manufacture and assembly of a large generator (or other job-lot operations).

Missile countdown procedures.

AUTHORS' NOTE: The preparation of this article was supported by the Office of Naval Research and the Bureau of Ships through grants to the Graduate School of Industrial Administration, Carnegie Institute of Technology. A different version of this material appears as Chapter 20 in *Industrial Scheduling,* edited by J. F. Muth and G. L. Thompson (Englewood Cliffs, New Jersey: Prentice-Hall, Inc., 1963). The job list and project graph for the house-building example were developed by Peter R. Winters.

Each of these projects has several characteristics that are essential for analysis by CPM:

1. The project consists of a well-defined collection of jobs (or activities) which, when completed, mark the end of the project.
2. The jobs may be started and stopped independently of each other, within a given sequence. (This requirement eliminates continuous-flow process activities, such as oil refining, where "jobs" or operations necessarily follow one after another with essentially no slack.)
3. The jobs are ordered—that is, they must be performed in technological sequence. (For example, the foundation of a house must be constructed before the walls are erected.)

What Is the Method?

The concept of CPM is quite simple and may best be illustrated in terms of a project graph. The graph is not an essential part of CPM; computer programs have been written which permit necessary calculations to be made without reference to a graph. Nevertheless, the project graph is valuable as a means of depicting, visually and clearly, the complex of jobs in a project and their interrelations:

First of all, each job necessary for the completion of a project is listed with a unique identifying symbol (such as a letter or number), the time required to complete the job, and its immediate prerequisite jobs. For convenience in graphing, and as a check on certain kinds of data errors, the jobs may be arranged in "technological order," which means that no job appears on the list until all of its predecessors have been listed. Technological ordering is impossible if a cycle error exists in the job data (e.g., job *a* precedes *b*, *b* precedes *c*, and *c* precedes *a*).

Then each job is drawn on the graph as a circle, with its identifying symbol and time appearing within the circle. Sequence relationships are indicated by arrows connecting each circle (job) with its immediate successors, with the arrows pointing to the latter. For convenience, all circles with no predecessors are connected to a circle marked "Start"; likewise, all circles with no successors are connected to a circle marked "Finish." (The "Start" and "Finish" circles may be considered pseudo jobs of zero time length.)

Typically, the graph then depicts a number of different "arrow paths" from Start to Finish. The time required to traverse each path is the sum of the times associated with all jobs on the path. The critical path (or paths) is the longest path (in time) from Start to Finish; it indicates the minimum time necessary to complete the entire project.

This method of depicting a project graph differs in some respects from that used by James E. Kelley, Jr., and Morgan R. Walker, who, perhaps more than anyone else, were responsible for the initial development of CPM. (For an interesting account of its early history see their paper, "Critical-Path Planning and Scheduling."[1]) In the widely used Kelley-Walker form, a project graph is just the opposite of that described above: jobs are shown as arrows, and the arrows are connected by means of circles (or dots) that indicate sequence relationships. Thus all immediate predecessors of a given job connect to a circle at the tail of the job arrow, and all immediate successor jobs emanate from the circle at the head of the job arrow. In essence, then, a circle marks an event—the completion of all jobs leading into the circle. Since these jobs are the immediate prerequisites for all jobs leading out of the circle, they must all be completed before *any* of the succeeding jobs can begin.

In order to accurately portray all predecessor relationships, "dummy jobs" must often be added to the project graph in the Kelley-Walker form. The method described in this article avoids the necessity and complexity of dummy jobs, is easier to program for a computer, and also seems more straightforward in explanation and application.

In essence, the critical path is the bottleneck route. Only by finding ways to shorten jobs along the critical path can the overall project time be reduced; the time required to perform noncritical jobs is irrelevant from the viewpoint of total project time. The frequent (and costly) practice of "crashing" *all* jobs in a project in order to reduce total project time is thus unnecessary. Typically, only about 10% of the jobs in large projects are critical. (This figure will naturally vary from project to project.) Of course, if some way is found to shorten one or more of the critical jobs, then not only will the whole project time be shortened but the critical path itself may shift and some previously noncritical jobs may become critical.

Example: Building a House

A simple and familiar example should help to clarify the notion of critical path scheduling and the process of constructing a graph.

The project of building a house is readily analyzed by the CPM technique and is typical of a large class of similar applications. While a contractor might want a more detailed analysis, we will be satisfied here with the list of major jobs (together with the estimated time and the immediate predecessors for each job) shown in Exhibit I.

In that exhibit, the column "immediate predecessors" determines the sequence relationships of the jobs and enables us to draw the project graph, Exhibit II. Here, in each circle the letter before the comma identifies the job and the number after the comma indicates the job time.

Following the rule that a "legal" path must always move in the direction of the arrows, we could enumerate 22 unique paths from Start to Finish, with associate times ranging from a minimum of 14 days (path *a-b-c-r-v-w-x*) to a maximum of 34 days (path *a-b-c-d-j-k-l-n-t-s-x*). The latter is the critical path; it determines the overall project time and tells us which jobs are critical in their effect on this time. If the contractor wishes to complete the house in less than 34 days, it would be useless to shorten jobs not on the critical path. It may seem to him, for example, that the brickwork (*e*) delays progress, since work on a whole series of jobs (*p-q-v-w*) must wait until it is completed. But it would be fruitless to rush the completion of the brickwork, since it is not on the critical path and so is irrelevant in determining total project time.

SHORTENING THE CP

If the contractor were to use CPM techniques, he would examine the critical path for possible improvements. Perhaps he could assign more carpenters to job *d*, reducing it from four to two days. Then the critical path would change slightly, passing through jobs *f* and *g* instead of *d*. Notice that total project time would be reduced only one day, even though two days had been shaved off job *d*. Thus the contractor must watch for possible shifting of the critical path as he effects changes in critical jobs.

Shortening the critical path requires a consideration of both engineering problems and economic questions. Is it physically possible to shorten the time required by critical jobs (by assigning more men to the job, working overtime, using different equipment, and so on)? If so, would the costs of speedup be less than the savings resulting from the reduction in overall project time? CPM is a useful tool because it quickly focuses attention on those jobs that are critical

Exhibit I. Sequence and Time Requirements of Jobs

JOB NO.	DESCRIPTION	IMMEDIATE PREDECESSORS	NORMAL TIME (DAYS)
a	START		0
b	EXCAVATE AND POUR FOOTERS	a	4
c	POUR CONCRETE FOUNDATION	b	2
d	ERECT WOODEN FRAME INCLUDING ROUGH ROOF	c	4
e	LAY BRICKWORK	d	6
f	INSTALL BASEMENT DRAINS AND PLUMBING	c	1
g	POUR BASEMENT FLOOR	f	2
h	INSTALL ROUGH PLUMBING	f	3
i	INSTALL ROUGH WIRING	d	2
j	INSTALL HEATING AND VENTILATING	d,g	4
k	FASTEN PLASTER BOARD AND PLASTER (INCLUDING DRYING)	i,j,h	10
l	LAY FINISH FLOORING	k	3
m	INSTALL KITCHEN FIXTURES	l	1
n	INSTALL FINISH PLUMBING	l	2
o	FINISH CARPENTRY	l	3
p	FINISH ROOFING AND FLASHING	e	2
q	FASTEN GUTTERS AND DOWNSPOUTS	p	1
r	LAY STORM DRAINS FOR RAIN WATER	c	1
s	SAND AND VARNISH FLOORING	o,t	2
t	PAINT	m,n	3
u	FINISH ELECTRICAL WORK	t	1
v	FINISH GRADING	q,r	2
w	POUR WALKS AND COMPLETE LANDSCAPING	v	5
x	FINISH	s,u,w	0

Exhibit II. Project Graph

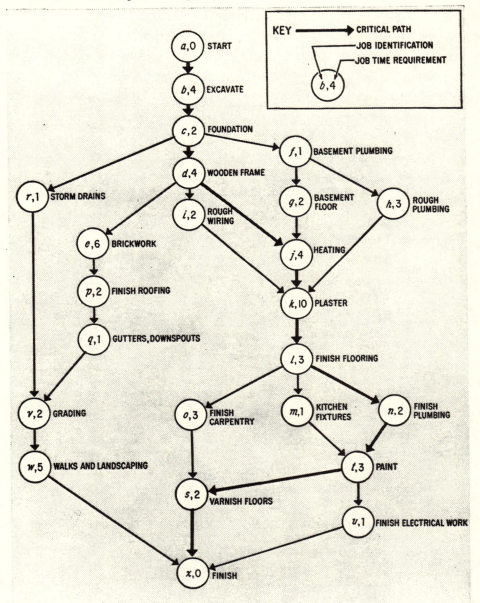

KEY ──────▶ CRITICAL PATH
           JOB IDENTIFICATION
           JOB TIME REQUIREMENT

$b,4$

$a,0$ START

$b,4$ EXCAVATE

$c,2$ FOUNDATION

$f,1$ BASEMENT PLUMBING

$d,4$ WOODEN FRAME

$r,1$ STORM DRAINS

$g,2$ BASEMENT FLOOR

$h,3$ ROUGH PLUMBING

$i,2$ ROUGH WIRING

$e,6$ BRICKWORK

$j,4$ HEATING

$p,2$ FINISH ROOFING

$k,10$ PLASTER

$q,1$ GUTTERS, DOWNSPOUTS

$l,3$ FINISH FLOORING

$v,2$ GRADING

$o,3$ FINISH CARPENTRY

$m,1$ KITCHEN FIXTURES

$n,2$ FINISH PLUMBING

$w,5$ WALKS AND LANDSCAPING

$t,3$ PAINT

$s,2$ VARNISH FLOORS

$u,1$ FINISH ELECTRICAL WORK

$x,0$ FINISH

to the project time, it provides an easy way to determine the effects of shortening various jobs in the project, and it enables the user to evaluate the costs of a "crash" program.

Two important applications of these features come to mind:

> Du Pont, a pioneer in the application of CPM to construction and maintenance projects, was concerned with the amount of downtime for maintenance at its Louisville works, which produces an intermediate product in the neoprene process. Analyzing the maintenance schedule by CPM, Du Pont engineers were able to cut downtime for maintenance from 125 to 93 hours. CPM pointed to further refinements that were expected to reduce total time to 78 hours. As a result, performance of the plant improved by about one million pounds in 1959, and the intermediate was no longer a bottleneck in the neoprene process.
>
> PERT (i.e., Program Evaluation Review Technique), a technique closely related to the critical path method, is widely credited with helping to shorten by two years the time originally estimated for completion of the engineering and development program for the Navy's Polaris missile. By pinpointing the longest paths through the vast maze of jobs necessary for completion of the missile design, PERT enabled the program managers to concentrate their efforts on those activities that vitally affected total project time.[2]

Even with our small house-building project, however, the process of enumerating and measuring the length of every path through the maze of jobs is tedious. A simple method of finding the critical path and, at the same time, developing useful information about each job is described next.

Critical Path Algorithm

If the start time or date for the project is given (we denote it by S), then there exists for each job an earliest starting time (ES), which is the earliest possible time that a job can begin, if all its predecessors are also started at their ES. And if the time to complete the job is t, we can define, analogously, its earliest finish time (EF) to be ES + t.

There is a simple way of computing ES and EF times using the project graph. It proceeds as follows:

1. Mark the value of S to the left and to the right of Start.

2. Consider any new unmarked job *all of whose predecessors have been marked,* and mark to the left of the new job the *largest* number marked to the right of any of its *immediate* predecessors. This number is its early start time.
3. Add to this number the job time and mark the result (EF time) to the right of the job.
4. Continue until Finish has been reached, then stop.

Thus, at the conclusion of this calculation the ES time for each job will appear to the left of the circle which identifies it, and the EF time will appear to the right of the circle. The number which appears to the right of the last job, Finish, is the early finish time (F) for the entire project.

To illustrate these calculations let us consider the following simple production process:

An assembly is to be made from two parts, A and B. Both parts must be turned on the lathe, and B must be polished while A need not be. The list of jobs to be performed, together with the predecessors of each job and the time in minutes to perform each job, is given in Exhibit III.

The project graph is shown in Exhibit IV. As previously, the letter identifying each job appears before the comma and its job time after the comma. Also shown on the graph are the ES and EF times for

Exhibit III. Data for Production Process

JOB NO.	DESCRIPTION	IMMEDIATE PREDECESSORS	NORMAL TIME (MINUTES)
a	START		0
b	GET MATERIALS FOR A	*a*	10
c	GET MATERIALS FOR B	*a*	20
d	TURN A ON LATHE	*b,c*	30
e	TURN B ON LATHE	*b,c*	20
f	POLISH B	*e*	40
g	ASSEMBLE A AND B	*d,f*	20
h	FINISH	*g*	0

each job, assuming that the start time, S, is *zero*. The ES time appears to the left of the circle representing a job, and the EF time appears to the right of the circle. Note that F = 100. The reader may wish to duplicate the diagram without these times and carry out the calculations for himself as a check on his understanding of the computation process described above.

LATEST START AND FINISH TIMES

Suppose now that we have a target time (T) for completing the project. T may have been originally expressed as a calendar date, e.g., October 1 or February 15. When is the latest time that the project can be started and finished?

In order to be feasible it is clear that T must be greater (later) than or equal to F, the early finish time for the project. Assuming this is so, we can define the concept of late finish (LF), or the latest time that a job can be finished, without delaying the total project beyond its target time (T). Similarly, late start (LS) is defined to be LF − t, where t is the job time.

These numbers are determined for each job in a manner similar to the previous calculations except that we work from the end of the project to its beginning. We proceed as follows:

1. Mark the value of T to the right and left of Finish.
2. Consider any new unmarked job *all of whose successors have been marked,* and mark to the right of the new job the *smallest* LS time marked to the left of any of its immediate successors.

    The logic of this is hard to explain in a few words, although apparent enough by inspection. It helps to remember that the smallest LS time of the successors of a given job, if translated into calendar times, would be the latest finish time of that job.
3. Subtract from this number the job time and mark the result to the left of the job.
4. Continue until Start has been reached, then stop.

    At the conclusion of this calculation the LF time for a job will appear to the right of the circle which identifies it, and the LS time for the job will appear to the left of the circle. The number appearing to the right of Start is the latest time that the entire project can be started and still finish at the target time T.

In Exhibit V we carry out these calculations for the example of Exhibit III. Here T = F = 100, and we separate early start and

Exhibit IV.   Calculation of Early Start and Early Finish Times for Each Job

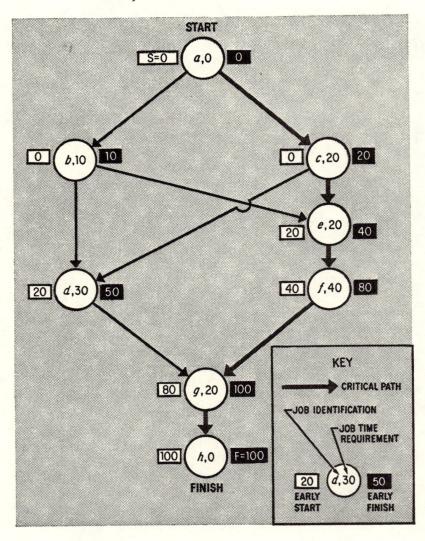

Exhibit V. Calculation of Late Start and Late Finish Times for Each Job

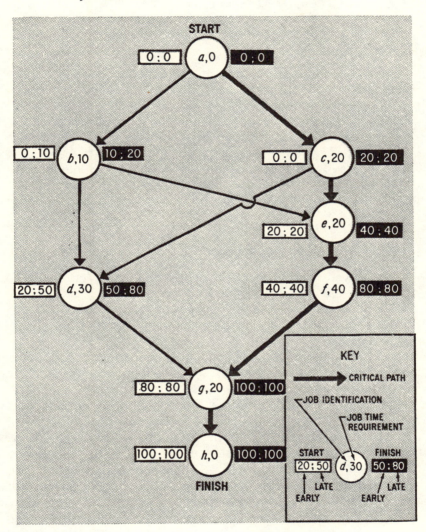

finish and late start and finish times by semicolons so that ES; LS appears to the left of the job and EF; LF to the right. Again the reader may wish to check these calculations.

Concept of Slack

Examination of Exhibit V reveals that some jobs have their early start equal to late start, while others do not. The difference between a job's early start and its late start (or between early finish and late finish) is called total slack (TS). Total slack represents the maximum amount of time a job may be delayed beyond its early start without necessarily delaying the project completion time.

We earlier defined critical jobs as those on the longest path through the project. That is, critical jobs *directly* affect the total project time. We can now relate the critical path to the concept of slack.

FINDING THE CRITICAL PATH

If the target date (T) equals the early finish date for the whole project (F), then all critical jobs will have *zero* total slack. There will be at least one path going from Start to Finish that includes critical jobs only, i.e., the *critical path*.

If T is greater (later) than F, then the critical jobs will have total slack equal to T minus F. This is a minimum value; since the critical path includes only critical jobs, it includes those with the smallest TS. All noncritical jobs will have *greater* total slack.

In Exhibit V, the critical path is shown by darkening the arrows connecting critical jobs. In this case there is just one critical path, and all critical jobs lie on it; however, in other cases there may be more than one critical path. Note that T = F; thus the critical jobs have zero total slack. Job *b* has TS = 10, and job *d* has TS = 30; either or both of these jobs could be delayed by these amounts of time without delaying the project.

Another kind of slack is worth mentioning. Free slack (FS) is the amount a job can be delayed without delaying the early start of any other job. A job with positive total slack may or may not also have free slack, but the latter never exceeds the former. For purposes of computation, the free slack of a job is defined as the difference between the job's EF time and the *earliest* of the ES times of all its immediate successors. Thus, in Exhibit V, job *b* has FS of 10, and job *d* has FS of 30. All other jobs have zero free slack.

SIGNIFICANCE OF SLACK

When a job has zero total slack, its scheduled start time is automatically fixed (that is, ES = LS); and to delay the calculated start time is to delay the whole project. Jobs with positive total slack, however, allow the scheduler some discretion in setting their start times. This flexibility can usefully be applied to smoothing work schedules. Peak loads that develop in a particular shop (or on a machine, or within an engineering design group, to cite other examples) may be relieved by shifting jobs on the peak days to their late starts. Slack allows this kind of juggling without affecting project time.[3]

Free slack can be used effectively at the operating level. For example, if a job has free slack, the foreman may be given some flexibility in deciding when to start the job. Even if he delays the start by an amount equal to (or less than) the free slack, the delay will not affect the start times or slack of succeeding jobs (which is not true of jobs that have no free slack). For an illustration of these notions, we return to our house-building example.

BACK TO THE CONTRACTOR

In Exhibit VI, we reproduce the diagram of house-building jobs, marking the ES and LS to the left, and the EF and LF to the right of each job (for example, "0;3" and "4;7" on either side of the *b*,4 circle). We assume that construction begins on day zero and must be completed by day 37. Total slack for each job is not marked, since it is evident as the difference between the pairs of numbers ES and LS or EF and LF. However, jobs that have positive free slack are so marked. There is one critical path, which is shown darkened in the diagram. All critical jobs on this path have total slack of three days.

Several observations can be drawn immediately from the diagram:

1. The contractor could postpone starting the house three days and still complete it on schedule, barring unforeseen difficulties (see the difference between early and late times at the Finish). This would

Exhibit VI.　Project Graph with Start and Finish Times

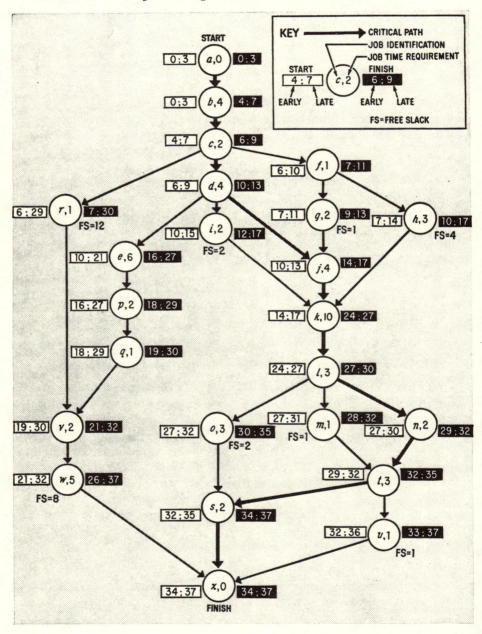

reduce the total slack of all jobs by three days, and hence reduce TS for critical jobs to zero.

2. Several jobs have free slack. Thus the contractor could delay the completion of *i* (rough wiring) by two days, *g* (the basement floor) by one day, *h* (rough plumbing) by four days, *r* (the storm drains) by 12 days, and so on—without affecting succeeding jobs.

3. The series of jobs *e* (brickwork), *p* (roofing), *q* (gutters), *v* (grading), and *w* (landscaping) have a comfortable amount of total slack (nine days). The contractor can use these and other slack jobs as "fill in" jobs for workers who become available when their skills are not needed for currently critical jobs. This is a simple application of workload smoothing: juggling the jobs with slack in order to reduce peak demands for certain skilled workers or machines.

If the contractor were to effect changes in one or more of the critical jobs, by contrast, the calculations would have to be performed again. This he can easily do; but in large projects with complex sequence relationships, hand calculations are considerably more difficult and liable to error. Computer programs have been developed, however, for calculating ES, LS, EF, LF, TS, and FS for each job in a project, given the set of immediate prerequisites and the job times for each job.[4]

Handling Data Errors

Information concerning job times and predecessor relationships is gathered, typically, by shop foremen, scheduling clerks, or others closely associated with a project. It is conceivable that several kinds of errors may occur in such job data:

1. The estimated job times may be in error.

2. The predecessor relationship may contain cycles: e.g., job *a* is a predecessor for *b*, *b* is a predecessor for *c*, and *c* is a predecessor for *a*.

3. The list of prerequisites for a job may include more than the immediate prerequisites; e.g., job *a* is a predecessor of *b*, *b* is a predecessor of *c*, and *a* and *b* both are predecessors of *c*.

4. Some predecessor relationships may be overlooked.

5. Some predecessor relationships may be listed that are spurious.

How can management deal with these problems? We shall examine each briefly in turn.

JOB TIMES.   An accurate estimate of total project time depends, of course, on accurate jobtime data. CPM eliminates the necessity (and expense) of careful time studies for *all* jobs. Instead the following procedure can be used:

- Given rough time estimates, construct a CPM graph of the project.
- Then those jobs that are on the critical path (together with jobs that have very small total slack, indicating that they are nearly critical) can be more closely checked, their times re-estimated, and another CPM graph constructed with the refined data.
- If the critical path has changed to include jobs still having rough time estimates, then the process is repeated.

In many projects studied, it has been found that only a small fraction of jobs are critical; so it is likely that refined time studies will be needed for relatively few jobs in a project in order to arrive at a reasonably accurate estimate of the total project time. CPM thus can be used to reduce the problem of Type 1 errors at a small total cost.

PREREQUISITES.   A computer algorithm has been developed to check for errors of Types 2 and 3 above. The algorithm (mentioned in note 4) systematically examines the set of prerequisites for each job and cancels from the set all but immediate predecessor jobs. When an error of Type 2 is present in the job data, the algorithm will signal a "cycle error" and print out the cycle in question.

WRONG OR MISSING FACTS.   Errors of Types 4 and 5 cannot be discovered by computer routines. Instead, manual checking (perhaps by a committee) is necessary to see that prerequisites are accurately reported.

Cost Calculations

The cost of carrying out a project can be readily calculated from the job data if the cost of doing each job is included in the data. If jobs are done by crews, and the speed with which the job is done depends on the crew size, then it is possible to shorten or lengthen the project time by adding or removing men from crews. Other means for compressing job times might also be found; but any speedup is likely to carry a price tag. Suppose that we assign to each job a "normal time" and a "crash time" and also calculate the associated costs necessary to carry the job in each time. If we want to shorten the project, we can assign some of the critical jobs to their crash time, and compute the corresponding direct cost. In this way it is possible to calculate the cost of completing the project in various total times, with the direct costs increasing as the overall time decreases.

Added to direct costs are certain overhead expenses which are usually allocated on the basis of total project time. Fixed costs per project thus decrease as project time is shortened. In ordinary circumstances a combination of fixed and direct costs as a function of total project time would probably fall into the pattern shown in Exhibit VII. The minimum total cost (point A) would likely fall to the left of the minimum point on the direct cost curve (point B)

Exhibit VII.   Typical Cost Pattern

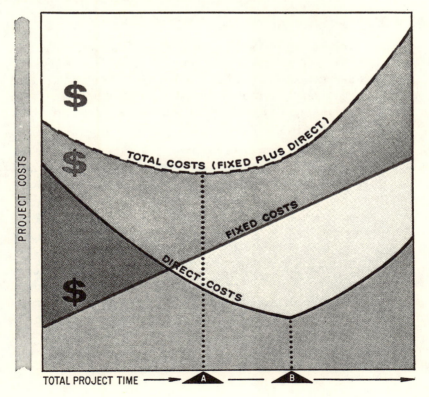

indicating that the optimum project time is somewhat shorter than an analysis of direct costs only would indicate.

Other economic factors, of course, can be included in the analysis. For example, pricing might be brought in:

> A large chemical company starts to build a plant for producing a new chemical. After the construction schedule and completion date are established, an important potential customer indicates a willingness to pay a premium price for the new chemical if it can be made available earlier than scheduled. The chemical producer applies techniques of CPM to its construction schedule and calculates the additional costs associated with "crash" completion of jobs on the critical path. With a plot of costs correlated with total project time, the producer is able to select a new completion date such that the increased costs are met by the additional revenue offered by the customer.

New Developments

Because of their great potential for applications, both CPM and PERT have received intensive development in the past few years. This effort is sparked, in part, because of the Air Force (and other governmental agency) requirements that contractors use these methods in planning and monitoring their work. Here are some illustrations of progress made:

> One of the present authors (Wiest) has developed extensions of the work-load smoothing algorithm. These extensions are the so-called SPAR (for Scheduling Program for Allocating Resources) programs for scheduling projects having limited resources.

> A contemporaneous development by C-E-I-R, Inc., has produced RAMPS (for Resource Allocation and Multi-Project Scheduling), which is similar but not identical.

> The most recent version of PERT, called PERT/COST, was developed by the armed services and various businesses for use on weapon-systems development projects contracted by the government. Essentially, PERT/COST adds the consideration of resource costs to the schedule produced by the PERT procedure. Indications of how smoothing can be accomplished are also made. Other recent versions are called PERT II, PERT III, PEP, PEPCO, and Super PERT.

Conclusion

For the manager of large projects, CPM is a powerful and flexible tool, indeed, for decision making:

- It is useful at various stages of project management, from initial planning or analyzing of alternative programs, to scheduling and controlling the jobs (activities) that comprise a project.
- It can be applied to a great variety of project types—from our house-building example to the vastly more complicated design project for the Polaris—and at various levels of planning—from scheduling jobs in a single shop, or shops in a plant, to scheduling plants within a corporation.
- In a simple and direct way it displays the interrelations in the complex of jobs that comprise a large project.
- It is easily explainable to the layman by means of the project graph. Data calculations for large projects, while tedious, are not difficult, and can readily be handled by a computer.
- It pinpoints attention to the small subset of jobs that are critical to project completion time, thus contributing to more accurate planning and more precise control.
- It enables the manager to quickly study the effects of "crash" programs and to anticipate potential bottlenecks that might result from shortening certain critical jobs.
- It leads to reasonable estimates of total project costs for various completion dates, which enable the manager to select an optimum schedule.

Because of the above characteristics of CPM—and especially its intuitive logic and graphic appeal—it is a decision-making tool which can find wide appreciation at all levels of management.[5] The project graph helps the foreman to understand the sequencing of jobs and the necessity of pushing those that are critical. For the manager concerned with day-to-day operations in all departments, CPM enables him to measure progress (or lack of it) against plans and to take appropriate action quickly when needed. And the underlying simplicity of CPM and its ability to focus attention on crucial problem areas of large projects make it an ideal tool for the top manager. On his shoulders falls the ultimate responsibility for overall planning and coordination of such projects in the light of company-wide objectives.

Notes

1. *Proceedings of the Eastern Joint Computer Conference,* Boston, December 1–3, 1959; see also James E. Kelley, Jr., "Critical-Path Planning and Scheduling: Mathematical Basis," *Operations Research,* May–June 1961, pp. 296–320.

2. See Robert W. Miller, "How to Plan and Control with PERT," HBR March–April 1962, p. 93.

3. For a method for smoothing operations in a job shop, based on CPM and the use of slack, see F. K. Levy, G. L. Thompson, and J. D. Wiest, "Multi-ship, Multi-Shop Production Smoothing Algorithm," *Naval Logistics Research Quarterly,* March 9, 1962.

4. An algorithm on which one such computer program is based is discussed by F. K. Levy, G. L. Thompson, and J. D. Wiest, in chapter 22, "Mathematical Basis of the Critical Path Method," *Industrial Scheduling* (see Authors' Note, p. 237).

5. See A. Charnes and W. W. Cooper, "A Network Interpretation and a Directed Sub-Dual Algorithm for Critical Path Scheduling," *Journal of Industrial Engineering,* July–August 1962, pp. 213–219.

4
How to Plan and Control
with PERT

Robert W. Miller

The last three years have seen the explosive growth of a new family of planning and control techniques adapted to the Space Age. Much of the development work has been done in the defense industry, but the construction, chemical, and other industries have played an important part in the story, too.

In this article we shall consider what is perhaps the best known of all of the new techniques, Program Evaluation Review Technique. In particular, we shall look at:

PERT's basic requirements, such as the presentation of tasks, events, and activities on a network in sequential form with time estimates.

Its advantages, including greatly improved control over complex development and production programs, and the capacity to distill large amounts of data in brief, orderly fashion.

Its limitations, as in situations where there is little interconnection between the different activities pursued.

Solutions for certain difficulties, e.g., the problem of relating time needed and job costs in the planning stage of a project.

Policies that top management might do well to adopt, such as taking steps to train, experiment with, and put into effect the new controls.

Leading Features

The new techniques have several distinguishing characteristics:

1. They give management the ability to plan the best possible use of resources to achieve a given goal, within overall time and cost limitations.

2. They enable executives to manage "one-of-a-kind" programs, as opposed to repetitive production situations. The importance of this kind of program in the national and world economy has become increasingly clear. Many observers have noted that the techniques of Frederick W. Taylor and Henry L. Gantt, introduced during the early part of the century for large-scale production operations, are inapplicable for a major share of the industrial effort of the 1960s— an era aptly characterized by Paul O. Gaddis as the "Age of Massive Engineering."[1]

3. They help management to handle the uncertainties involved in programs where no standard cost and time data of the Taylor-Gantt variety are available.

4. They utilize what is called "time network analysis" as a basic method of approach and as a foundation for determining manpower, material, and capital requirements.

CURRENT EFFORTS AND PROGRESS

A few examples may serve to indicate for top management the current status of the new techniques:

The Special Projects Office of the U.S. Navy, concerned with performance trends in the execution of large military development programs, introduced PERT on its Polaris Weapon Systems in 1958. Since that time, PERT has spread rapidly throughout the U.S. defense and space industry. Currently, almost every major government and military agency concerned with Space Age programs is utilizing the technique, as are large industrial contractors in the field. Small businesses wishing to participate in national defense programs will find it increasingly necessary to develop a PERT capability if they wish to be competitive in this field.

At about the same time the Navy was developing PERT, the DuPont company, concerned with the increasing costs and time required to bring new products from research to production, initiated a study which resulted in a similar technique known as CPM (Critical Path Method). The use of the Critical Path Method has spread quite widely, and is particularly concentrated in the construction industry.

A very considerable amount of research now is taking place on the "extensions" of PERT and CPM time-network analysis, into the areas of manpower, cost, and capital requirements. As an ultimate objective, "trade-off" relationships between time, cost, and product or equipment performance objectives are being sought. This research is being sponsored in two ways—directly by the military and privately by large companies. Anyone familiar with the current scene will be impressed by the amount of activity taking place in this field. For example, at least 40 different code names or acronyms representing variations of the new management controls have come to my attention.

Applications of the new techniques, beyond the original engineering-oriented programs for which they were developed, are increasing every day. The PERT approach is usefully introduced in such diverse situations as planning the economy of an underdeveloped nation or establishing the sequence and timing of actions to effect a complex merger.

What Is PERT?

Now let us turn to PERT in particular. What are its special characteristics and requirements?

The term is presently restricted to the area of time and, as promulgated by the Navy, has the following basic requirements:

1. All of the individual tasks to complete a given program must be visualized in a clear enough manner to be put down in a *network,* which is comprised of *events* and *activities.* An event represents a specified program accomplishment at a particular instant in time. An activity represents the time and resources which are necessary to progress from one event to the next. Emphasis is placed on defining events and activities with sufficient precision so that there is no difficulty in monitoring actual accomplishment as the program proceeds. Exhibit I shows a typical operating-level PERT network from the electronics industry.

2. Events and activities must be sequenced on the network under a highly logical set of ground rules which allow the determination of important critical and subcritical paths. These ground rules include the fact that no successor event can be considered completed until all of its predecessor events have been completed, and no "looping" is allowed, i.e., no successor event can have an activity dependency which leads back to a predecessor event.

3. Time estimates are made for each activity of the network on a three-way basis, i.e., optimistic, most likely, and pessimistic elapsed-time figures are estimated by the person or persons most familiar with the activity involved. The three time estimates are required as a

Exhibit I. Portion of a Typical Operating Network Superimposed on Total Network

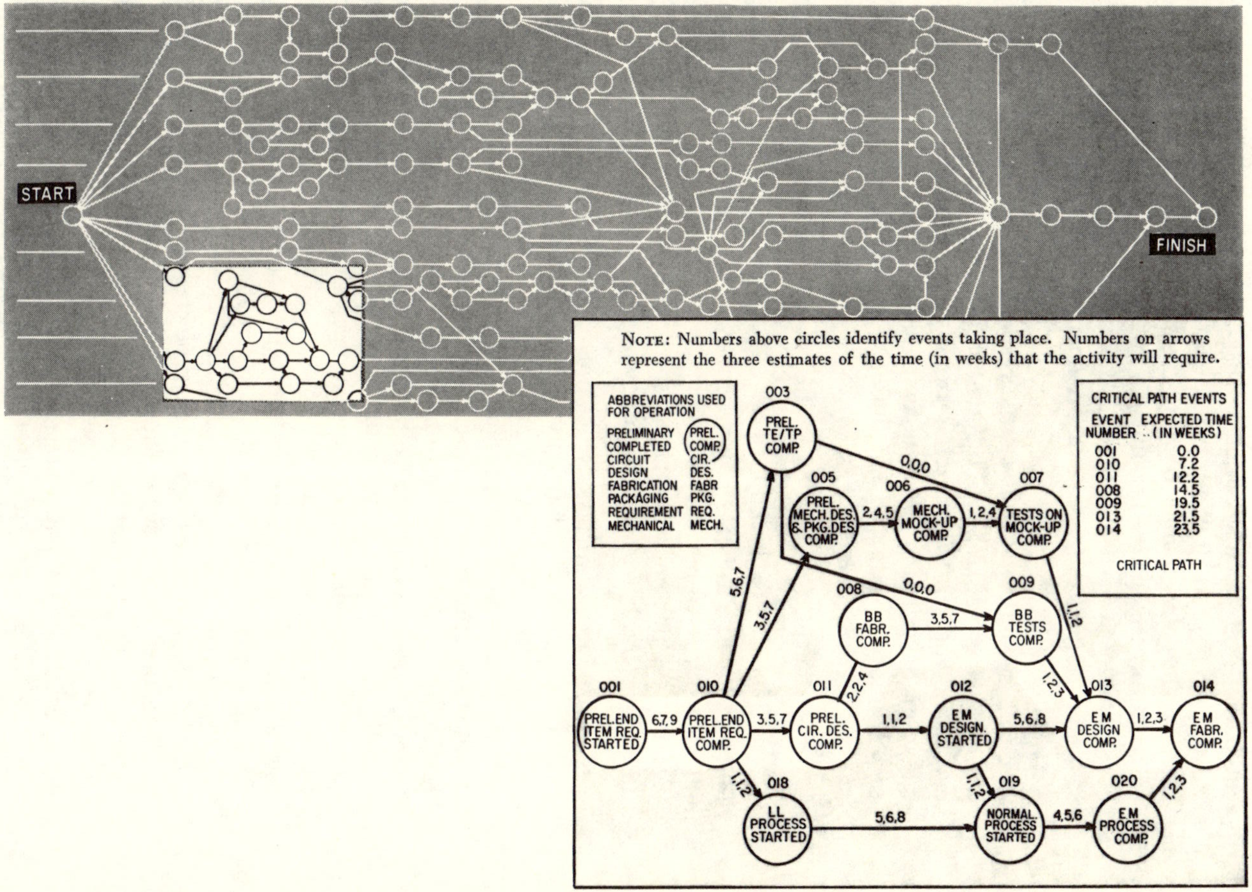

NOTE: Numbers above circles identify events taking place. Numbers on arrows represent the three estimates of the time (in weeks) that the activity will require.

gauge of the "measure of uncertainty" of the activity, and represent full recognition of the probabilistic nature of many of the tasks in development-oriented and nonstandard programs. It is important to note, however, that, for the purposes of computation and reporting, the three time estimates are reduced to a single expected time (t_e) and a statistical variance (σ^2).

4. Depending on the size and complexity of the network, computer routines are available to calculate the critical path through it. Computers can also calculate the amount of slack (viz., extra time available) for all events and activities not on the critical path. A negative slack condition can prevail when a calculated end date does not achieve a program date objective which has been established on a prior—and often arbitrary—basis.

TIME ESTIMATES

Interpretation of the concepts of optimistic, most likely, and pessimistic elapsed times has varied over the past few years. The definitions which, in my opinion, represent a useful consensus are as follows:

- *Optimistic*—An estimate of the *minimum* time an activity will take, a result which can be obtained only if unusual good luck is experienced and everything "goes right the first time."
- *Most likely*—An estimate of the *normal* time an activity will take, a result which would occur most often if the activity could be repeated a number of times under similar circumstances.
- *Pessimistic*—An estimate of the *maximum* time an activity will take, a result which can occur only if unusually bad luck is experienced. It should reflect the possibility of initial failure and fresh start, but should not be influenced by such factors as "catastrophic events"—strikes, fires, power failures, and so on—unless these hazards are inherent risks in the activity.

The averaging formulas by which the three time estimates are reduced to a single expected time (t_e), variance (σ^2), and standard deviation (σ) are shown in the Appendix. The approximations involved in these formulas are subject to some question, but they have been widely used and seem appropriate enough in view of the inherent lack of precision of estimating data. The variance data for an entire network make possible the determination of the *probability of meeting an established schedule date,* as shown in the Appendix.

CRITICAL PATH

In actual practice, the most important results of the calculations involved in PERT are the determination of the critical path and slack times for the network. Exhibit II contains data on the critical path and slack times for the sample network shown in Exhibit I (they are based on the method of calculation given in the Appendix). The data are shown in the form of a *slack order report* (lowest to highest slack), which is perhaps one of the most important output reports of PERT.

Other output reports, such as event order and calendar time order reports, are also available in the PERT system.

The actual utilization of PERT involves review and action by responsible managers, generally on a biweekly basis. Because time prediction and performance data are available from PERT in a "highly ordered" fashion (such as the slack order report), managers are given the opportunity to concentrate on the important critical path activities. The manager must determine valid means of shortening lead times along the critical path by applying new resources or additional funds, which are obtained from those activities that can "afford" it because of their slack condition. Alternatively, he can re-evaluate the sequencing of activities along the critical path. If necessary, those activities which were formerly connected in a series can be organized on a parallel or concurrent basis, with the associated trade-off risks involved. As a final, if rarely used, alternative, the manager may choose to change the scope of work of critical path activities in order to achieve a given schedule objective.

It should be pointed out that the PERT system requires constant updating and reanalysis; that is, the manager must recognize that the outlook for the completion of activities in a complex program is in a constant state of flux, and he must be continually concerned with problems of re-evaluation and reprograming.

BENEFITS GAINED

Perhaps the major advantage of PERT is that the kind of planning required to create a valid network represents a major contribution to the definition and ultimate successful control of a complex program. It may surprise some that network development and critical path analysis do, in fact, reveal interdependencies and problem areas which are either not obvious or not well defined by conventional planning methods. The creation of the network is a fairly

Exhibit II. **Slack Order Report**

	PERT SYSTEM		Airborne Computer — Slack Order Report			
Date **7/12/61**		Week **0.0**		Time in Weeks	Page **1**	
Event	T_E	T_L	T_L-T_E	T_s	P_r	
001	0.0	0.0	0			T_E = Expected event date
010	7.2	7.2	0			
011	12.2	12.2	0			T_L = Latest allowable event date
008	14.5	14.5	0			T_L-T_E = Event slack
009	19.5	19.5	0			T_s = Scheduled event date
013	21.5	21.5	0			
014	23.5	23.5	0	23.5	.50	P_r = Probability of achieving T_s date
020	20.6	21.5	+ .9			
019	15.6	16.5	+ .9			
012	14.4	15.3	+ .9			
018	9.4	10.3	+ .9			
007	18.2	20.3	+2.1			
006	16.0	18.1	+2.1			
005	13.2	14.3	+2.1			
003	14.2	19.5	+5.3			

demanding task, and is a sure-fire indicator of an organization's ability to visualize the number, kind, and sequence of activities needed to execute a complex program.

Another advantage of PERT, especially where there is a significant amount of uncertainty, is the three-way estimate. While introducing a complicating feature, this characteristic does give recognition to those realities of life which cause difficulties in most efforts at planning the future. The three-way estimate should result in a greater degree of honesty and accuracy in time forecasting; and, as a minimum, it allows the decision maker a better opportunity to evaluate the degree of uncertainty involved in a schedule—particularly along the critical path. If he is statistically sophisticated, he may even wish to examine the standard deviation and probability of accomplishment data, which were mentioned previously as features of PERT. (If there is a minimum of uncertainty in the minds of personnel estimating individual activity times, the single-time approach may, of course, be used, while retaining all the advantages of network analysis.)

And, finally, the common language feature of PERT allows a large amount of data to be presented in a highly ordered fashion. It can be said that PERT represents the advent of the management-by-exception principle in an area of planning and control where this principle had not existed with any real degree of validity. An additional benefit of the common language feature of PERT is the fact that many individuals in different locations or organizations can easily determine the specific relationship of their efforts to the total task requirements of a large program.

This particular benefit of PERT can represent a significant gain in the modern world of large-scale undertakings and complex organizational relationships.

Coping with Problems

A new and important development like PERT naturally is attended by a certain amount of confusion and doubt. PERT does indeed have its problems. However, they are not always what businessmen think they are, and often there is an effective way of coping with the restrictions. In any event, it is time to compare the situations in which PERT works best with situations in which real (or imagined) troubles occur.

UNCERTAIN ESTIMATES

One key question concerns the unknowns of time and resources that management frequently must contend with.

In PERT methodology an available set of resources including manpower and facilities is either known or must be assumed when making the time estimates. For example, it is good practice to make special notations directly on the network when some special condition (e.g., a 48-hour rather than a 40-hour week) is assumed. Experience has shown that when a well-thought-through network is developed in sufficient detail, the first activity time estimates made are as accurate as any, and these should not be changed unless a new application of resources or a trade-off in goals is specifically determined. A further caution is that the first time estimates should not be biased by some arbitrarily established schedule objective, or by the assumption that a particular activity does not appear to be on a critical path. Schedule biasing of this kind, while it obviously cannot be prevented, clearly atrophies some of the main benefits of the technique—although it is more quickly "discovered" with PERT than with any other method.

Because of the necessity for assumptions on manpower and resources, it is easiest to apply PERT in *project-structured* organizations, where the level of resources and available facilities are known to the estimator. PERT does not itself *explicitly* resolve the problem of multiprogram planning and control. But there is general recognition of this problem, and considerable effort is being devoted to a more complete approach to it. Meanwhile, in the case of common resource centers, it is generally necessary to undertake a loading analysis, making priority assumptions and using the resulting data on either a three-time or single-time basis for those portions of the network which are affected. It should be pointed out, however, that in terms of actual experience with PERT, the process of network development forces more problems of resource constraint or loading analysis into the open for resolution than do other planning methods.

Although PERT has been characterized as a new management control approach for R&D effort, it has perhaps been most usefully applied in those situations where there is a great deal of interconnection between the activities of a network, or where there are interface connections between different networks. Certainly, network development and critical path analysis are *not* too appropriate for the pure research project, where the capabilities of small numbers of individuals with highly specialized talents are being utilized at a "constant rate" and where their activities have no significant dependence on other elements of the organization.

JUSTIFYING THE COST

One of the most frequently raised objections to PERT is the cost of its implementation. A fundamental point to examine here is whether or not a currently established planning system is giving value commensurate with its cost—or perhaps more basic still, whether the system is used at all effectively to pinpoint and control problem areas. It is quite true that, by the very nature of its logical requirements for networking, the PERT approach calls for a higher degree of planning skill and a greater amount of detail than is the case with conventional methods. In addition, the degree of detail—or the "level of indenture," as it is called—is a function of:

1. What is meaningful to the person or persons who will actually execute the work.
2. The depth of analysis that is required to determine the valid critical path or paths.

It is perhaps more appropriate to view the implementation of PERT as costing *initially* something in the order of twice that of a conventional planning system. This figure will vary significantly with such factors as:

- The degree of planning capability already available.
- The present effectiveness and homogeneity of the organization.
- The amount and quality of PERT indoctrination given.

The advocates of PERT are quick to point out that the savings achieved through better utilization of resources far outweigh the system's initial implementation costs. This better utilization of resources is achieved through concentration on critical path activities—for example, limiting overtime effort to these key activities as opposed to across-the-board use of overtime. Even more important are the "downstream" savings which are achieved by earlier and more positive action on the part of management to resolve critical problems.

USE OF STANDARD NETWORKS

Because of the considerable impact of PERT on many organizations where detailed planning has not had major emphasis, a trend has recently developed which can be characterized as "model or standard networking." This has to do with efforts to use the typical or established pattern of carrying out a new program in a particular industry. Model networking has many advantages (particularly in handling the large amounts of data involved in PERT), but it may also compromise one of the real objectives of PERT—i.e., *obtaining a valid network which is meaningful to the person or persons who will actually execute the work.* In the area in which PERT is used most effectively, no two programs are ever exactly the same, and no two individuals will have exactly the same approach to the development of a network. Therefore, model networks should be introduced with this caution: management should always allow for the possibility of modifications which will match the realities of the program.

In addition, the introduction of so-called "master plan networks" and the top-down structuring of networks for large programs involving many different firms, while very necessary from the point of view of long-range planning and the ultimate management of such programs, should be handled with a philosophy of flexibility. The cardinal principle is that a management control structure is no better than the adequacy and accuracy of the data at its base. In the future, the top-down structuring approach—which is already evident on some major defense and space programs—will probably increase; but internal objectives, at least, will be subject to reconfirmation or realignment at the level of industry, depending upon the development of actual operating networks. The top-down structuring approach is necessary, however, in order to preserve the mechanics of *network integration;* it is important that the data from lower level networks be properly and meaningfully summarized into higher level management data.

APPLICATION TO PRODUCTION

A final problem, and one that is often viewed as a disadvantage of the PERT technique, is the system's lack of applicability to all of the manufacturing effort. As has been stated, PERT deals in the time domain only and does not contain the quantity information required by most manufacturing operations. Nevertheless, PERT can be, and has been, used very effectively through the preliminary manufacturing phases of production prototype or pilot model construction, and in the assembly and test of final production equipments which are still "high on the learning curve." After these phases, established production control techniques which bring in the quantity factor are generally more applicable.

Note, however, that many programs of the Space Age never leave the preliminary manufacturing stage, or at least never enter into mass production. Therefore, a considerable effort is going forward at this time to integrate the techniques of PERT within some of the established methods of production control, such as line-of-balance or similar techniques that bring in the quantity factor.

COMPUTER OR NO COMPUTER

As a result of the Navy's successful application of PERT on the Polaris program, and other similar applications, there is a common impression that the technique is only applicable when large-scale data-processing equipment is available. This is certainly true for large networks, or aggregations of networks, where critical path and slack computations are involved for several hundred or more events. It is as desirable to have a computer handle a PERT problem when a large volume of data is involved as it is to use a computer in any extensive data-processing assignment.

Probably equally significant is the fact that several ingenious manual methods have been developed in industry by those organizations which have become convinced of PERT's usefulness. These manual methods range from simple inspection on small networks to more organized but clerically oriented routines for determination of critical path, subcritical path, and slack times on networks ranging from fifty to several hundred events.

This is sufficient proof that PERT can be applied successfully to smaller programs wherever the degree of interconnection and problems of uncertainty warrant it. For those organizations practiced in the technique, both the creation of small networks and the formation of time estimates and their reduction to critical path and slack analyses can be done in a matter of hours. Exhibit I shows the network for a relatively small electronics program. Developed in less than a day, the whole network required only two hours for manual computation.

It seems clear that the small business organization which wishes to participate in national defense and space programs, or to improve its own internal schedule planning and control, should not hesitate to adopt PERT merely because it does not possess large-scale data-processing equipment.

PERT EXTENSIONS

Variations of PERT to accommodate multiproject and manufacturing situations have already been mentioned, and these are merely representative of a basic movement to *extend* the approach into the areas of manpower, cost, and the equipment performance variable. The ultimate objective of these efforts is to quantify the trade-off relationships which constantly come up in development programs but are rarely acted on with explicit data in hand.

Though none of these extensions have as yet attained as much maturity and acceptance as PERT, anyone familiar with the current scene will be impressed by the amount of effort being given to them throughout the country in both the military and industry. One healthy offset to this particular trend is the fact that the U.S. Air Force has withdrawn its code name PEP (Program Evaluation Procedure), which was an equivalent for PERT. There remains, however, a great need for government agencies to standardize input and output requirements of basic PERT time before uniformly effective extensions can be made into the area of PERT cost.

Cost of PERT

Much of the research effort on the new management controls which has taken place throughout the country is concentrated on the problem of manpower and cost. This is probably a reflection of certain facts well known to most managers of complex development programs:

> The job-costing structures generally found in industry on such programs need a great deal of interpretation to relate *actual costs* to *actual progress*. They are rarely, if ever, related in any explicit manner to the details of the scheduling plan.
>
> Cost constraints, either in the form of manpower shortages or funding restrictions, have a great deal to do with the success with which a program of this type can be managed.

It seems clear that both of these problems must be solved in any valid PERT cost approach.

SOLUTIONS REQUIRED

The first problem means that an explicit relationship must be established between the time network and the job-cost structure, either on a one-to-one basis for each network activity, or for a designated chain of activities. As a minimum, it seems clear that more detailed job-cost structures are required than are currently in general use, although this requirement should present no serious limitation for organizations which possess modern data-processing methods and equipment.

With regard to the development of actual cost figures *from the time network,* an estimate of manpower requirements, segregated by classification, is usually considered the easiest place to start, since these requirements were presumably known at the time the network was established. In fact, however, the actual summation of such data often reveals a manpower or funding restriction problem, and forces a replanning cycle if no alternatives are available. (The summation may also reveal inefficiencies in personnel loading which can be removed by proper use of slack activities.)

Two other problems that should be mentioned are:

- *Handling of nonlabor items*—The costs for these items are often aggregated in a manner quite different from that which would result from analysis of a time network. For example, there is a tendency to buy common materials on one purchase order for a number of different prototypes, each one of which represents a distinct phase of progress in the program. A refined allocation procedure may be needed to handle this problem.
- *Coordination and control efforts* (e.g., those carried out by project or systems engineering[2])—These are often not indicated on time networks unless they result in specific outputs. For PERT costing, the network in all cases must be complete, i.e., it must include all effort which is charged to the program. This is one of the areas of deficiency in many present-day networks, and one which must be overcome before an effective PERT cost application can be made.

Each of the foregoing problems can be handled if the underlying network analysis is sound and subject to a minimum of change. As a result, a number of different approaches are being attempted in the development of costed networks which have as their objective the association of at least one cost estimate with a known activity or chain of activities on the network.

The ultimate objective of all this is not only improvement in planning and control, but also the opportunity to assess possibilities for "trading off" time and cost, i.e., adding or subtracting from one at the expense of the other. It is generally assumed that the fundamental relationships between time and cost are as portrayed in Exhibit III. Curve A represents *total direct costs* versus time, and the "U" shape of the curve results from the assumption that there is an "optimum" time-cost point for any activity or job. It is assumed that total costs will increase with any effort to accelerate or delay the job away from this point.

Exhibit III. Assumed Time-Cost Relationships for a Job

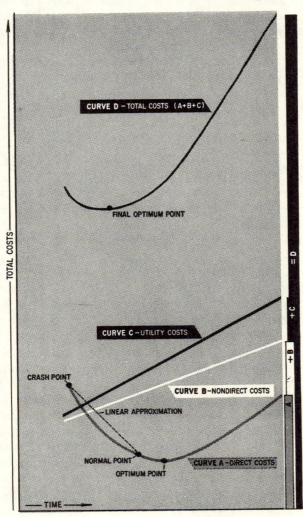

Some companies in the construction industry are already using such a time-cost relationship, although in a rather specialized manner:

> In one application, an assumption is made that there is a *normal* job time (which might or might not coincide with the theoretical optimum), and that from this normal time, costs increase linearly to a *crash* time, as indicated in Exhibit III. This crash time represents the maximum acceleration the job can stand. On the basis of these assumptions, a complete mathematical approach and computer program have been developed which show how to accelerate progress on a job as much as possible for the lowest possible cost. The process involves shortening the critical path or paths by operating on those activities which have the lowest time-cost slopes.

CHALLENGE OF COST DATA

Making time-cost data available for each activity in usable form is one of the fundamental problems in using PERT in development programs. At the planning stage, in particular, it is often difficult to determine time-cost relationships in an explicit manner, either for individual activities or for aggregates of activities. (There are often good arguments for characterizing time-cost relationships at this stage as nonlinear, flat, decreasing, or, more likely, as a range of cost possibilities.) If alternative equipment or program objectives are added as a variable, the problem is further compounded. While posing the problem, it should be pointed out that solutions for the technical handling of such data, in whatever form they are obtained, have recently been developed.

Curve B of Exhibit III indicates *total nondirect costs,* which are assumed to increase linearly with time. Clearly, accounting practices will have to be reviewed to provide careful (and probably new) segregations of direct from nondirect costs for use in making valid time-cost trade-off evaluations.

Curve C is a representation of a *utility cost curve,* which is needed to complete the picture for *total time-cost* optimization (indicated as the final optimum point on Curve D). The utility cost curve represents a quantification of the penalty for *not accomplishing the job at the earliest possible time,* and is also shown as a linear function increasing with time.

The difficulties of determining such a curve for many programs, ether in terms of its shape or dollar value, should be obvious. But it is significant to note that in certain industrial applications such utility cost data have already been developed, typically in the form of "outage" costs or loss-of-profit opportunities, and used as the basis for improved decision making. Further, in the military area, utility cost is the converse of the *benefit* concept in the *benefit-cost* ratio of a weapon system; this factor varies with the time of availability of a weapon system, even though judgments of benefit are made difficult by rapidly changing circumstances in the external world.

Conclusion

It is clear that there are difficulties yet to be overcome in advancing the new management controls—particularly in the new areas into which PERT is being extended. Yet it is equally clear that significant progress has been made during the last few years. Assuming that developments continue at the rate at which they have taken place up to this time, what position should top management adopt *today* with regard to its own internal policies on the new management controls? Here are the most important steps:

1. Management should review its present planning and scheduling methods and compare their effectiveness with that of the PERT system. (I refer here to time networks only—not time-and-cost networks.) If the company has no direct experience with PERT, it will certainly want to consider training and experimentation programs to acquaint the organization with the technique. Management may even decide to install PERT on all of its development programs (as some companies have done), even though it has no contractual requirement to do so.

2. Management may wish to enter directly into research efforts on the new management controls or, if such efforts are already underway in the organization, place them on a higher priority basis. As a minimum, it will probably want to assign someone in the organization to follow the numerous developments that are taking place in the field.

3. Executives should consider carefully the problem of organization to make the most effective use of the new management controls. They should consider the responsibilities of the level of management that actually uses PERT data in its working form, and the responsibilities

of the levels of management that review PERT in its various summary forms. Clearly, the usefulness of the new management controls is no greater than the ability of management actually to act on the information revealed. It should be realized that problems of "recentralization" will probably accompany the advent of the new tools, particularly when applied to the planning and control of large projects throughout an entire organization.

4. Finally, management may wish to assess the longer-range implications of the new management controls, both for itself and for the entire industrial community, since the forces calling for centralization of planning and control within the firm can apply equally well outside it. In the Age of Massive Engineering, the new controls will be utilized to an increasing extent in the nation's defense and space programs, which are in turn increasing in size and complexity. It seems clear that the inevitably closer relationships between government and industry will require the establishment of new guidelines for procurement and incentive contracting where these management control techniques are used.

Appendix

Readers interested in applying PERT may find it helpful to have a more precise formulation of certain calculations mentioned earlier in this article. The mathematics involved is basically simple, as the following material demonstrates.

EXPECTED TIME ESTIMATE

In analyzing the three time estimates, it is clear that the optimistic and the pessimistic time should occur least often, and that the most likely time should occur most often. Thus, it is assumed that the most likely time represents the peak or modal value of a probability distribution; however, it can move between the two extremes. These characteristics are best described by the Beta distribution, which is shown in two different conditions in the figures that follow.

Exhibit A. *Two Beta Distributions*

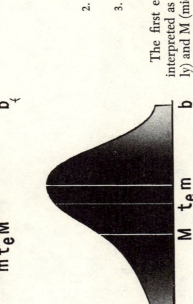

where:

a = optimistic time
m = most likely time
b = pessimistic time

$$M = \text{mid-range} \left(\frac{a+b}{2} \right)$$

$$t_e = \text{expected time}$$

As a result of analyzing the characteristics of the Beta distribution, the final approximations to expected time (t_e), variance (σ^2), and standard deviation (σ) were written as follows for a given activity:

$$1. \ t_e = \frac{1}{3}(2m + M)$$

$$= \frac{1}{3}\left(2m + \frac{a+b}{2} \right)$$

$$= \frac{a + 4m + b}{6}$$

$$2. \ \sigma^2 = \left(\frac{b-a}{6} \right)^2$$

$$3. \ \sigma = \frac{b-a}{6}$$

The first equation indicates that t_e should be interpreted as the weighted mean of m (most likely) and M (mid-range) estimates, with weights of 2 and 1, respectively. In other words, t_e is located one third of the way from the modal to the mid-range values, and represents the 50% probability point of the distribution, i.e., it divides the area under the curve into two equal portions.

NOTE: The Beta distribution is analyzed in the PERT Summary Report, Phase I (Special Projects Office, Department of the Navy, Washington, D.C., July 1958).

Exhibit B.   *Probability of Meeting Schedule Times*

On the basis of the Central Limit Theorem, one can conclude that the probability distribution of times for accomplishing a job consisting of a number of activities may be approximated by the normal distribution, and that this approximation approaches exactness as the number of activities becomes great (for example, more than 10 activities along a given path). Thus, we may define a curve which represents the probability of a meeting on established schedule-end date, T_S:

where:

$$T_E = \Sigma t_{e_1} + t_{e_2} + \cdots t_{e_n}$$

$$\sigma^2(T_E) = \Sigma \sigma^2(t_{e_1}) + \sigma^2(t_{e_2}) + \cdots \sigma^2(t_{e_n})$$

T_{S_1} = Scheduled Time (earlier than T_E)

T_{S_2} = Scheduled Time (later than T_E)

The probability of meeting the T_S date when given T_E and σ^2 for a chain of activities is defined as the ratio of (1) the area under the curve to the left of T_S to (2) the area under the entire curve. The difference between T_S and T_E, expressed in units of σ, is:

$$\frac{T_S - T_E}{\sigma}$$

This will yield a value for the probability of accomplishing T_S by use of the normal probability distribution table. Thus:

$$\frac{T_{S_1} - T_E}{\sigma} = -1.2\sigma, \quad P_r \text{ (accomplishment of } T_{S_1}) = .12$$

$$\frac{T_{S_2} - T_E}{\sigma} = +1.2\sigma, \quad P_r \text{ (accomplishment of } T_{S_2}) = .88$$

DETERMINING CRITICAL PATH AND SLACK TIMES

The computation steps required to determine the critical path and slack times for the network shown in Exhibit I are as follows:

Step 1. Determine t_e for every activity on the network in accordance with the equation:

$$t_e = \frac{a + 4m + b}{6}$$

Step 2. Starting with Event No. 001, determine T_E (or cumulative T_E) for all succeeding events by summing small t_e's for each activity leading up to the event, *but choosing the largest value for the final T_E figure in those cases where there is more than one activity leading into an event.* For example, Exhibit I indicates three activities leading into Event No. 013 (EM design complete). The three preceding events are No. 007 (test on mock-up complete), No. 009 (breadboard tests complete), and No. 012 (EM design started). The cumulative T_E figures for these three preceding events, as can be seen from Exhibit II, are 18.2 weeks for Event No. 007, 19.5 weeks for Event No. 009, and 14.4 weeks for Event No. 012. Now, add the respective activity times between these three events and Event No. 013 and examine the results:

Event No.	T_E	Activity Time t_e to Event No. 013	Total Weeks
007	18.2	1.2	19.4
009	19.5	2.0	21.5
012	14.4	6.2	20.6

The largest figure, which represents the longest path or earliest time at which Event No. 013 can be completed, is 21.5 weeks, and this path leads through Event No. 009. As will be noted from Exhibit I, Event Nos. 009 and 013 are on the critical path, since the T_E values of all other paths leading into final Event No. 014 are smaller.

Step 3. Having determined the critical path through the network of Exhibit I to be 23.5 weeks, we can now set the final date of Event No. 014 at 23.5 weeks, or we can use some arbitrary scheduled time. The process covered in Step 2 is now reversed. Starting with the final event, we determine the *latest allowable time,* T_L, for each event so as not to affect critical path event times. For example, Event No. 007, with a T_E

of 18.2 weeks, can be delayed up to a T_L of 20.3 weeks, before it will affect critical path Event No. 013.

Step 4. The difference between T_L and T_E, known as slack, is next computed for each event. These computations are shown in Exhibit II in the form of a slack order report, i.e., in order of lowest to highest values of *positive* slack. Note that along the critical path there is zero slack at every event, since by definition there is no possibility of slippage along the critical path without affecting the final event date. In this example, if the end schedule date of Event No. 014 were set at 23.0 weeks rather than at 23.5 weeks, there would be 0.5 weeks of *negative* slack indicated for every event along the critical path.

Step 5. The computation of variance and of standard deviation for this network is optional and involves adding the variances for each activity along the critical path, which are obtained from the formula:

$$\sigma^2 = \left(\frac{b - a}{6}\right)^2$$

The interested reader may verify that the variance for final Event No. 014, with a T_E of 23.5 weeks, is 1.46 weeks.

Notes

[1] See "Thinking Ahead: The Age of Massive Engineering," HBR January–February 1961, p. 138.

[2] See Clinton J. Chamberlain, "Coming Era in Engineering Management," HBR September–October 1961, p. 87.

5
Post-Project Appraisals Pay

Frank R. Gulliver

If your company is like most, you spend thousands of hours planning an investment, millions of dollars implementing it—and nothing evaluating and learning from it. As a result, you may not have answers for the most basic questions: Was the investment successful? What made it go according to plan? Did it go according to plan at all? As easy as these questions seem, the answers aren't always obvious.

British Petroleum (BP) built a plant in Australia to convert gas into a component of high-octane gasoline. It came in under budget and ahead of schedule. A similar facility in Rotterdam went over budget and was a year late. BP's managers first drew the obvious conclusion: the Australian plant was a success and the Dutch one a failure. But a second look challenged that first impression.

At the time the Australian project was proposed, that country was suffering from a balance of payments deficit, and the product was expected to help the country reduce its gasoline imports. The plant was completed earlier than expected. But by that time, Australia's economic situation had changed, and gasoline demand turned out to be lower than predicted.

Although the Rotterdam project had obvious problems, the market for the product remained strong in Europe. Thus that project's return on investment was in line with predictions, while that of its Australian counterpart was much lower. The Rotterdam project's success taught top managers at BP a valuable lesson: the planners needed to improve their market forecasting techniques.

279

There is an independent unit at British Petroleum's London head-quarters responsible for identifying these kinds of issues—the post-project appraisal unit (PPA). It examines the thinking behind selected investments as well as their management and their results. PPA's sole mission is to help British Petroleum worldwide learn from its mistakes and repeat its successes.

Since its inception at the end of 1977, PPA has appraised more than 80 of BP's worldwide investments, including onshore and off-shore construction projects, acquisitions, divestments, project cancellations, research projects, diversification plans, and shipping activities. The appraisals are not academic exercises; the unit seeks to improve company performance.

Through PPA, BP managers have learned how to formulate investment proposals more accurately, approve them more objectively, and execute them more efficiently than ever before. As a result, most projects now generate returns on investment at least as high as those forecast. These improvements have naturally boosted the company's overall financial performance: in 1985, BP's profits reached an all-time high of £1,598 million after taxes. While PPA isn't the only reason for this performance, managers at BP believe the appraisal unit has yielded dramatic results.

Wide-Angle Inquiry

In talking with business-people from large British and multinational corporations, I have found that few companies examine their completed projects in any depth. Most audits are narrowly focused attempts to check that proper controls are in place while a project is in operation. When our managers audit an oil refinery, for example, they gather detailed information about how the oil and gas is collected, measured, shipped, and accounted for.

A post-project appraisal, however, takes a much larger view. It first looks at the big questions: Why was the project started in the first place? Is it producing as much oil as the proposal predicted? Is the demand for oil at the forecasted level? Did the contractors deliver what they promised? Does the project fit well into BP's overall corporate strategy?

In "post-completion reviews," some U.S. corporations attempt a similar sort of wide-angle evaluation of past projects. But these differ from BP's post-project appraisals in two ways: objectivity and applicability. Because project members usually conduct post-completion reviews, they are more likely to have preconceived ideas or even a vested interest in the reviews' outcomes. The members of BP's PPA unit have no affiliation with the projects they appraise and so can evaluate investments more objectively.

Moreover, post-completion reviews usually don't guarantee that the lessons will reach the people who need them most, because the information spreads by word of mouth. PPA, in contrast, is a centralized department that can inspect any type of investment in any part of the far-flung BP group and transmit information from one site to another. It can learn lessons from an oil refinery project in France and teach them to planners working on a similar plant in Australia.

PPA is also part of BP's investment proposal procedure. The unit reviews all new investment proposals to make sure that no one repeats mistakes. When they have time, unit members will even work with project planners to formulate proposals.

Appraisal Operations

The PPA unit consists of a manager and four assistants, reporting directly to BP's board of directors. In the unit's nine-year history, the composition of the staff has, of course, changed a few times. PPA managers, however, have to meet the same criteria: they must be acceptable to the most senior echelons of management and must have at least 15 years of broad-based experience at BP. The company chooses the other staff members for their specific expertise. They might be engineers, chemists, physicists, economists, or accountants. A team of two or three unit members investigates each project.

An appraisal of a large investment generally takes about six months to complete. Because the company can absorb only so much information at a time, the unit limits its major appraisals to six per year. The most valuable lessons come from the largest projects, where BP stands to lose or gain the most money. PPA selects its projects carefully, looking for those that will yield the most valuable results.

The unit does not therefore investigate a project if its lessons will duplicate those drawn from a previous appraisal. Nor does it evaluate a project that BP is unlikely to do again. The unit once considered appraising a large crude-oil sale contract that BP had made with another big oil company. Because the Middle Eastern nations had nationalized their oil fields, however, BP no longer made such sales. The unit consequently decided not to study the project.

GETTING STARTED

BP is divided into 11 businesses, each with its own board of directors and chief executive. These businesses report to BP's central management, which is headed by the main board of directors. A corporate review committee of BP's main board must approve each PPA appraisal. This committee both oversees the unit's activities and examines all proposed capital investments for compatibility with BP's corporate strategy. PPA submits proposals for projects it could appraise in 18 months to two years, and the committee generally accepts them, though it occasionally adds or deletes one or two.

The unit staff then determines the order in which to carry out the appraisals and, with the chief executive of the project's business, sets a broad timetable for each investigation.

A PPA team examines a project from its conception—before the proposal is even written—usually until two years after it has become operational. The team tries to determine systematically how a project was handled: at the proposal stage; during the project's construction (or, in the case of an acquisition, during the target company's purchase); during the project's operation (or the acquired company's integration into BP); and during the post-operation (or post-integration) stage. PPA always tries to determine the important factors that contribute to a project's problems or success.

Although it usually learns more by seeing how problems developed, the unit also finds it useful to pinpoint the causes of success. The purchase of a Dutch nutrition company called Hendrix, top management agreed, was one of the smoothest acquisitions ever. PPA ascribed its success largely to the precision with which the planners had determined the extent of Hendrix's integration into BP.

FILES AND INTERVIEWS

At an appraisal's outset, the team relies on the files to become familiar with the project. This avoids wasting people's time. The team learns about the economic climate at the time, the identity of the contractors, or the chemical process used. Team members might spend the first two months of a six-month investigation just looking at files—both at project files and at material in related corporate files, in such departments as accounting, legal, or planning.

While the PPA manager will probably already know the senior managers who should be interviewed, the files provide a complete list. The team generally tries to interview everyone involved in the project. Since most projects have been completed for at least two years before the unit begins its work, however, the project members are working all over the world on other things. In one investigation, the PPA team talked to 80 individuals; the average is usually around 40.

In their interviews, the PPA team members make an effort to understand the psychology of the project members and managers. They interview in pairs so that one team member can ask questions while the other watches the interviewee. A furtive look often tells as much as a direct answer.

After the interview, the two team members compare notes and reconcile differences in their perceptions. The full story usually emerges in separate pieces: senior managers in London will give up one piece of information; engineers on an oil rig in the middle of the North Sea will give up another. By melding project members' different perspectives, the PPA people can come up with the whole picture.

PPA team members realize that project employees shed light on issues that may seem unrelated to their areas of expertise. Those working out in the field often live together, eat together, and go out drinking together. Not surprisingly, an accountant may offer a cogent insight about the head engineer, even though they did not actually work closely with each other.

Sending PPA teams into the field to conduct investigations is far more expensive than sending out questionnaires—and far more effective. Because a questionnaire is a set collection of questions, it can elicit only a limited view of the project. In an interview, people offer unexpected information; also, the PPA team can lead an interviewee away from digressions.

CONCLUSIONS AND REACTIONS

The post-project appraisal unit has had very little trouble getting cooperation from BP's staff. In the unit's nine-year life, the PPA teams have found that people genuinely want to help the company grow more profitable by joining in an examination of performance.

Even individuals who have been singled out for blame continue to see the unit's value. In one case, an appraisal concluded that a senior manager had not done his job well. The corporate review committee called him in and raked him over the coals. For some time, relations between the manager and the PPA unit were cool. But a few months later, he telephoned the PPA manager to ask if the unit had appraised any projects similar to one he was beginning. He wanted advice.

The staff cooperates with the unit partly because it gives them a chance to take issue with conclusions before they appear in PPA's report. It is a testament to the fairness and accuracy of the unit's work that no one has ever taken advantage of this opportunity.

After the team has exhausted the files, interviewed everyone involved, and digested and assembled the information in a preliminary draft to circulate to key managers, it submits a final draft to the business board and then to the corporate review committee. The committee carefully considers PPA's work and almost always supports the conclusions: it has received many hundreds of recommendations and has rejected only one. This suggestion—that BP maintain a staff of experts in different metallurgical technologies to supplement contractors—was simply too expensive.

BP does not circulate throughout the corporation the full reports on each appraisal, although these do go to relevant managers, but collates them into three booklets—one on acquisitions, another on joint ventures, and the last on project development and control. PPA regularly updates these booklets—adding lessons learned from later appraisals and occasionally deleting a lesson that no longer applies. One was a recommendation to build refinery plants on the Continent rather than in Britain because of poor labor relations in the United Kingdom. But labor relations have improved greatly since then.

BP's upper management expects project planners to use the information in the booklets as guidelines when writing proposals. A proposal that does not meet all the guidelines should not necessarily be abandoned. But if planners cannot comply with the guidelines, the corporate review committee will want to see that the proposal accounts for the possible risks.

PPA sends the booklets to the London headquarters of each of BP's 11 businesses and to each of the approximately 30 major BP associate companies worldwide. If any section of the corporation needs more copies, the unit willingly sends them along. The PPA philosophy is that the company's investment performance will only improve as more BP people learn what went wrong and what went right in the past.

From its experimental and tentative beginnings a decade ago, PPA has grown into an integral part of BP's planning and control process. It succeeds because of its consistent reputation for digging out the truth. The unit enjoys the full confidence of BP's senior managers and directors because they believe that both the facts and the conclusions in the reports are accurate. This accuracy is based on the investigating team's thoroughness, its understanding of the technical issues, its fairness in evaluating the evidence, and its sensitivity to the psychological forces motivating the staff. In that accuracy lies the usefulness of the lessons to the corporation and the success of the post-project appraisal unit.

Appraisal Lessons

There is a big difference between classroom lessons about business and lessons drawn from experience. What might seem self-evident or unlikely in theory may be the most important factor in an actual event. To illustrate, let me describe a project from a time before BP implemented many of the procedures PPA recommended.

In 1967, a director at BP responsible for engineering and refining wanted to explore a technology that Exxon and others were using but that was new to BP. The man was well respected within the company and had a great deal of influence. By the force of his personality, he pushed through a proposal for the construction of the biggest plant of its kind that BP had ever built. Exxon had a plant that turned out 30,000 barrels of oil per day on three production lines; the BP installation would produce that volume on a single line. This line required the largest compressors and pumps that BP had ever used and completely new technology in the reactor vessels.

During construction and testing, the company had difficulty with all three. It had particular trouble with the reactor vessels, which, because of their size, had to be thinner than conventional vessels and thus needed lining with stainless steel. Despite assurances to management that the job was easy, BP's contractor ran into one problem after another. Finally, BP's own engineers solved the problems at great expense.

BP learned much from PPA's investigation of this experience. It learned that it must assess proposals more carefully. It learned to assess a new technology's risks more thoroughly and more objectively. It learned that it had to improve its method of selecting contractors. Perhaps the company should have learned these lessons already. But obviously it had not—and the post-project appraisal process brought them to light, formalized them, and collected them in one place.

Managers in every company are making mistakes no one thinks could be made. Time after time, the post-project appraisal unit has uncovered these kinds of mistakes and helped British Petroleum avoid repeating them.

Appendix

Four Lessons

Over the past ten years, PPA has taught BP management four main lessons. These are:

Determine costs accurately. Before PPA existed, BP's management approved unrealistically low budgets because planners inaccurately predicted the scope of the project when they submitted the budget. Now BP approves budgets in phases, and each phase becomes more accurate as planners work out the project's details.

In the first phase, the engineers offer an approximate figure for the project's budget that could be off by as much as 50%. The board then approves about 1% of this sum to pay outside engineers and consultants to develop the case more fully. The engineers then submit a more accurate budget. Eventually, at the time the board approves the entire project, it adopts a final budget, which should be off by no more than 10%.

BP now pays more attention to the technical requirements of local health, safety, and environmental legislation. Company managers look beyond simply what the legislation requires; to estimate costs accurately, BP planners solve any design problems created by such regulations in the proposal stage.

Managers now are careful not to rush a project's approval so it can qualify for a government grant or other bonus. A rushed project is often inadequately defined and therefore out of control from the start, runs very late, and comes in over budget—so much over budget that costs substantially exceed the incentive.

The corporation no longer automatically awards a contract to the lowest bidder. Many low bids come in because contractors don't fully understand what BP needs. PPA has found a correlation between low bids and poor contractor performance.

Anticipate and minimize risk. Fearing that a competitor would snatch the opportunity, BP businesses wishing to acquire another company would often try to speed up the examination and the decision-making process. According to the PPA unit, such self-imposed deadlines are usually illusory. Moreover, the unit has found that if the company is not satisfied about the soundness of an acquisition proposal, BP will probably not regret the missed opportunity.

BP used to expand plant capacity without knowing whether it could sell all of the product the new plant could then produce. Now before adding capacity or introducing a product, the company requires planners to submit a full market survey to verify that a market will exist and be profitable.

Evaluate contractors. BP now has a contractor evaluation unit that monitors potential contractors' performance. When it solicits bids, the corporation already knows which contractor would be most likely to perform to its satisfaction. Formerly, BP used an unsophisticated method to select contractors. It was ignorant of contractors' deficiencies and performance for other companies in different parts of the world.

To make certain that a contractor has expertise in a project's process technology, BP now pays careful attention to the caliber of the contractor's key staff members and insists that they remain with the project to the end.

Improve project management. Engineers do not automatically make good managers. The company frequently used to send an engineer from a project in one part of the world to one halfway around the world. No one asked whether the engineer was familiar with the project, the country, or even the main contractor. At the recommendation of PPA, BP set up a projects department that helps engineers develop appropriate control techniques and procedures and ensures that the right person manages the right project.

To make project progress reports more constructive, the projects department has set up a projects control division. This division uses software programs, linked to each project, to help the project manager issue reports that identify likely problems and give reasons for missed milestones. These reports can be fed through the project control division's computer center for evaluation on a day-by-day, or even a minute-by-minute, basis.

The projects department ensures that project managers are appointed early enough to involve them with the design considerations, project strategies, and control mechanisms. With the projects department's guidance, project managers can make more independent decisions.

Capital investment analysts have usually swamped managers with advice based on well-meaning academic research, but it has been limited to questions about acquisition. Now, through post-project appraisal, managers can get sound advice on questions about many kinds of projects from the experience of their own companies.

About the Contributors

Jasper Arnold III is senior vice-president—Credit, Farm Credit Corporation of America, Inglewood, Colorado. His most recent article is "Three Keys to Effective Loan Negotiations" in *RMA Commercial Lending Newsletter.*

Norman R. Augustine is chairman and chief executive officer, Martin Marietta Corporation, Bethesda, Maryland. He began his career as a chief engineer and program manager. He has had extensive government service, including appointment in 1973 as assistant secretary of the Army and in 1975 as under secretary. He has received many awards and honors, including—four times—the Distinguished Service Medal, the Department of Defense's highest civilian decoration. The author of *Augustine's Laws* (Viking, 1986, hardcover; Penguin, 1987, paperback), he is also the inventor of a calculator for baseball managers.

David Davis is a director of Tate & Lyle, an English sugar and trading company. He has written articles for British and North American publications on such topics as politics, industrial relations, general management, and computers.

Paul O. Gaddis is professor of management and former dean of the Graduate School of Management, University of Texas at Dallas. He consults and lectures on multinational corporate strategy and has served on numerous boards in the United States and Europe. He is the author of *Corporate Accountability* (Harper & Row, 1964) and many articles, several of them in the *Harvard Business Review.*

Frank R. Gulliver is group internal auditor with the British Petroleum Company, where he has worked since 1949. He was a founding member of its post-project appraisal unit and it remains part of his management responsibilities.

Maurice Hardaker is senior consultant, IBM International Education Centre, in La Hulpe, Belgium. He has worked with senior management in IBM's Program for Business Process Quality Management. He has also advised the boards of directors of many IBM customers.

James E. Hodder is associate professor of industrial engineering and engineering management, Stanford University. He is the author of "Corporate Capital Structure in the United States and Japan" in *Government Policy Towards Industry in the United States and Japan* (Cambridge University Press, 1988).

W. Carl Kester is associate professor of finance, Harvard Business School. He recently contributed "An Options Approach to Corporate Finance" to *The Handbook of Corporate Finance,* sixth edition (Wiley, 1987).

Robert J. Lambrix is senior vice president and chief financial officer, Baxter International, Deerfield, Illinois.

Ferdinand K. Levy is professor of economics at the Georgia Institute of Technology, where he served as dean of the College of Management from 1972 to 1977. He has also been a consultant to corporations.

John D. Macomber is vice president for strategic planning and a director at George B.H. Macomber Company, a Boston-based construction company. He is a former director of the Winter Construction Company in Atlanta, Georgia, and has been a guest lecturer at the Center for Real Estate Development and Graduate School for Civil Engineering, Massachusetts Institute of Technology.

C. J. Middleton is a human resources specialist, General Dynamics Corporation, Fort Worth, Texas. He is past president of the Fort Worth chapter of the National Management Association.

At the time his article was published in the *Harvard Business Review*, **Robert W. Miller** was manager of administration for the Equipment Division of the Raytheon Company.

Ikujiro Nonaka is a professor at Hitotsubashi University in Japan. He is also director of the university's Institute of Business Research. Among his books and articles is "Managing the New Product Development Process: How Japanese Companies Learn and Unlearn," coauthored with Ken-ichi Imai and Hirotaka Takeuchi, in *The Uneasy Alliance* (Harvard Business School Press, 1985).

Henry E. Riggs is professor of industrial engineering and engineering management and president of Harvey Mudd College, Claremont, California. Previously, he taught and was vice president for development at Stanford University. Prior to that, he worked in industry in various financial positions for fifteen years. He is the author of *Managing High-Technology Companies* (Wadsworth, 1983).

Jerry Ross is an organizational psychologist at the Graduate School of Industrial Administration, Carnegie-Mellon University.

Surendra S. Singhvi is vice president and treasurer, Edison Brothers Stores, St. Louis, Missouri. He has written numerous articles, most recently "A Quantitative Approach to Site Selection" in *Management Review*.

Kathy A. Spiegelman, author of the appendix to John D. Macomber's article, "You *Can* Manage Construction Risks," is director of Physical Planning at Harvard University. She guides and oversees architect selection for all Harvard construction projects.

Barry M. Staw is a psychologist and the Mitchell Professor of Leadership and Communication at the School of Business Administration, University of California, Berkeley.

At the time his article was published in the *Harvard Business Review*, **Hirotaka Takeuchi** was associate professor at Hitotsubashi University in Japan. His research has focused on marketing and global competition.

Gerald L. Thompson is IBM Professor of Systems and Operations Research, Carnegie-Mellon University, where he has taught since 1959. He has served as a consultant to corporations and has published numerous books and articles.

Bryan K. Ward is senior consultant, Systems Management Consultancy Group, IBM United Kingdom. He has advised senior management of IBM customers about business planning and information technology strategy.

James P. Ware is a principal of Nolan, Norton Research Group, Lexington, Massachusetts. His responsibilities include directing systems planning studies and organizational restructuring projects for several large organizations. Prior to joining Nolan, Norton, he taught at the Harvard Business School.

Daniel E. Whitney is section chief, Robotics and Assembly Systems Division, Charles Stark Draper Laboratory, Cambridge, Massachusets. He and his colleagues are engaged in research and industrial consulting with emphasis in the design and assembly of products. He previously published "Real Robots Do Need Jigs" in the *Harvard Business Review.*

Jerome D. Wiest is professor of management, University of Utah. He has published numerous articles; his current research concerns project scheduling with limited resources.

Larry Wynant is associate professor and chairman of the M.B.A. program, School of Business Administration, University of Western Ontario. He is the author of *Handbook of Commercial Lending* (Warren, Gorham, and Lamont, forthcoming).

Index

DUE DATE